NORTH AFRICA

COUNCIL ON FOREIGN RELATIONS BOOKS

NORTH AFRICA

REGIONAL TENSIONS AND STRATEGIC CONCERNS

by Richard B. Parker

PRAEGER SPECIAL STUDIES • PRAEGER SCIENTIFIC

New York • Philadelphia • Eastbourne, UK
Toronto • Hong Kong • Tokyo • Sydney

Library of Congress Cataloging in Publication Data

Parker, Richard Bordeaux, 1923-

    North Africa : regional tensions and strategic
concerns.

    Bibliography:
    1. Africa, North—Politics and government. 2. Africa,
North—Strategic aspects. I. Title.
DT204.P34   1984   961   84-8298
ISBN 0-03-071846-5 (alk. paper)

Published in 1984 by Praeger Publishers
CBS Educational and Professional Publishing,
a Division of CBS Inc.
521 Fifth Avenue, New York, NY 10175 USA

©1984 by the Council on Foreign Relations

456789 052 9876545321

Printed in the United States of America
on acid-free paper

Contents

Preface

This book is the outgrowth of the meetings of a study group held at the Council on Foreign Relations in the spring of 1982. Devoted to discussion of current problems in North Africa, the meetings were chaired by Stephen Stamas, vice-president of the Exxon Corporation. A list of participants is in the Annex.

While the book reflects ideas and questions raised in those meetings, it is not the work of a committee or a collection of articles by different contributors, and the views and judgments expressed are the sole responsibility of the author. Acknowledgment is due, however, to the contributions of Jean Claude Vatin and Lisa Anderson, who submitted papers on Islam and on Libya to the meetings, and many of whose ideas have been incorporated in the text.

Special thanks also go to Jennifer Whitaker, associate editor of *Foreign Affairs*, Paul Kreisberg, Director of Studies for the Council, who proposed the project, and to Ellen Laipson of the Library of Congress and Keith Morton of the University of Virginia, who served as recording secretaries and helped with the research.

In search of material and observations for this book I traveled to Rome, Tunis, Algiers, Rabat, Madrid, and Paris in September of 1982, meeting and discussing current problems with private citizens and officials of the countries in question as well as with American and other diplomats. Many of the figures in the text were obtained either from these sources or from official publications of local governments and of the U.S. Department of State, notably the periodic Economic Trends Reports of our various embassies in the area and the Department's Background Notes on the countries of the region published in Washington. Particular thanks are due to the officers of the American Embassies concerned, who were very helpful in providing their own estimates.

diately impressed by the divergencies between data from different sources, even (or perhaps particularly) of the same government. Even when the data are reasonably accurate, their true meaning is often obscured by changes in exchange rates and inflation. In particular, the rise in the value of the dollar over the past two years has seriously affected Gross National Product and export-import figures. The figures provided herein have in general not been converted to a common base year and should be taken as indicating relative orders of magnitude, not as absolute and precise.

Much of the information about U.S., Moroccan and Algerian attitudes and actions, particularly regarding the Sahara problem, is based on my recollections from my service in North Africa, first as deputy chief of mission in Rabat (1970–74), then as ambassador to Algeria (1974–77) and finally as ambassador to Morocco (1978–79). My view of events in those two capitals does not always coincide with those of the Department of State or my colleagues at those posts, now or then. In that respect, this is a personal statement.

Introduction

An area of critical interest once in American history, North Africa does not bear heavily on the consciousness of the average American today. U.S. policy makers are usually too preoccupied with the Middle East, Europe, or Asia to devote sufficient time to it, and one looks in vain for meaningful coverage of North African events in the U.S. press.

This lack of attention should not lull us into a false sense of security; the stability of North Africa is perennially open to question, and it has a strategic and economic importance that can make it an urgent concern on short notice. It is considerably closer to the United States' vital European interests than Iran, Afghanistan, or the Levant, and while its petroleum resources are less important than those of the Near East, they are much more accessible to Europe.

Politically, the states of North Africa are senior members of the Third World community and have played a leading role in its affairs. Algeria in particular has had an influence in the nonaligned movement and on such matters as the North-South dialogue out of all proportion to its real wealth and the size of its population. Morocco, as one of the leading conservative powers of Africa, has played a major role in supporting like-minded political movements and regimes on that continent, and was instrumental in establishing the direct contacts between Israel and Egypt that led to Sadat's visit to Jerusalem. Tunisia is now the home of the Arab League and the Palestinian Liberation Organization, and has long furnished some of the most refreshing and pragmatic political views to be found in the Arab world. Libya has displayed an impressive capacity for making trouble and is one of America's principal *bêtes noires* today.

Both Libya and Algeria have substantial reserves of oil and gas, both are leading members of the Organization of Petroleum Exporting Countries, and both have been the scene of major activities by private U.S. companies in the field of petroleum and in economic development projects financed by petroleum revenues. Until recently the United States was the principal customer of both countries. The ease with which the United States dispensed with the purchase of oil from them in 1982 says something about the variable nature of such interests, but it was done in a time of petroleum surplus, and attitudes will be different when and if supply and demand get back into balance.

More constant, more abiding, and more important than energy resources in the long run is the strategic position these countries occupy along the southern shore of the great Mediterranean corridor, a corridor that is vital to the defense of Europe, and that impinges directly on Soviet ability to project naval power into the Atlantic.

The southern Mediterranean littoral has been a battleground since classical times. If some of the battles have been of secondary importance on a world scale, others have been crucial to the survival of one empire or another. Power has been projected both ways across the Mediterranean. Although over the past five centuries it has largely been a question of Europe's intruding into Africa, Hannibal, the Arabs, the Berbers, the Barbary Corsairs, and the Allies in World War II have all demonstrated the practicability of projecting power northward. There seems to be little likelihood of such projection today, but the littoral has assumed new importance because of U.S.-Soviet naval rivalry in the Mediterranean and because of the United States' perceived need to use Moroccan base facilities in order to deploy its military forces in the Persian Gulf region.

The United States and its European allies would be seriously concerned, for instance, if Morocco were to give the Soviets the same broad access to Moroccan naval and military facilities they once enjoyed in Egypt. Lying as it does on both the Atlantic and Mediterranean coasts, Morocco has permanent strategic importance. As Thomas Jefferson once said, "Our Atlantic as well as Mediterranean trade is open to his (the sultan of Morocco's) annoyance."[1]

Alternatively, such Soviet access to military facilities in Algeria, Tunisia, or Libya would greatly increase Soviet operational flexibility in the western Mediterranean, and would have serious implications for the Sixth Fleet and NATO. In fact, the Soviets already enjoy limited access to harbor facilities at Annaba in Algeria and to the French-built repair facilities at Bizerte in Tunisia. They do not have actual base facilities, however, that is, they do not control military enclaves as the United States once did in Libya and Morocco. Nor are they likely to as long as the states of this coast remain independent. It would be unwise, nevertheless, to exclude totally the possibility of the Soviets' eventually increasing substantially the access they now enjoy, particularly if the United States escalates its conflict with Qadhdhafi, becomes seriously engaged in strategic cooperation with Israel, or becomes too deeply involved in the wars in the Western Sahara or Chad.

The strategic importance of the North African states is not confined to their Mediterranean role. Their position astride the air routes from Europe to black Africa permits them a control over access to the latter that becomes crucial at times. The Soviet airlift to Angola in 1975, for instance, was staged through Algerian airfields (a matter of considerable embarrassment to the Algerians) and the inability of the plotters to cross Libyan airspace was the initial element in the failure of the coup against Sudan's President Numayri in 1971. On the other hand, Qadhdhafi's dispatch of troops to Chad in 1980 and 1983 shows that the Sahara is no longer an effective barrier to the penetration of black Africa from the north, even by local powers.

It has been argued that the region is actually more important to Europe than it is to the United States and that the latter should encourage its European friends and allies to take more responsibility for it. Propinquity, historic ties, and trade patterns all support this contention. Nevertheless, as long as a naval presence in the Mediterranean is a vital aspect of the American defense posture, or as long as we perceive the defense of the Persian Gulf to be a vital U.S. interest which requires access to Moroccan base facilities, the United States will have a continuing interest in the stability and independence of the states of North Africa. Its inability to rely on others to promote and protect its interests means that it must be actively engaged there. The United States is in fact already deeply involved in the region, more deeply than most Americans realize.

The purpose of this book is to acquaint the reader with the more prominent issues of the region and to give him or her a better grasp of the policy choices confronting the United States. To that end it will discuss certain common features and individual differences of the four North African states, explaining briefly in Chapter 1 the racial, historical, economic, and geographic factors that make them distinct from each other, and examining in the next four chapters the political, economic, and social situations in each state. One chapter will explore the background and dimensions of the Islamic fundamentalist movement in this part of the Arab world. Another will be devoted to the vexing guerrilla war in the Western Sahara. One chapter will be devoted to examining the interests of various foreign powers and their relations with the states of the area. The final chapter will discuss the policy issues and possible courses of action.

Each of these countries is worth a full book, and the treatment that can be given in the space allocated is necessarily brief. The author has tried, however, to make this a practical and interesting introductory study for the reader who does not have the time to explore deeply this fascinating area.

Note

[1]Report to the Secretary of State relative to the Mediterranean Trade. Communicated to the House of Representatives, December 20, 1790, and to the Senate, January 3, 1791.

1

The Maghrib: An Overview

That part of North Africa which lies west of Egypt and north of the Sahara
is called in Arabic *al-Maghrib*, or the Occident, where the sun sets, as opposed to *al-Mashriq*, or the Levant, where it rises. Views differ as to where
the Mashriq ends and the Maghrib begins, with many writers excluding
Libya from the latter and using that term to refer exclusively to Tunisia,
Algeria and Morocco, but it makes no sense to discuss U.S. policy in the
area without including Libya, and we will be guided by President Bourgiba's
purported dictum that the boundary between Mashriq and Maghrib is
where the people stop eating rice and start eating couscous, the staple starch
of North Africa. That line runs through Derna, in eastern Libya, where
people eat both, and which is the "Tripoli" of the Marine Hymn.

The phenomenon of exclusion is due to Libya's character as a transitional
country. It is clearly not of the Mashriq, but it is the least "Maghribi" of the
four North African states. To the traveler coming from the east there are
striking physical and cultural differences between the people of the Maghrib and those of the Mashriq, but they are markedly weaker in Libya.

These differences are due to a number of factors, among them the under-
current of Berber subculture that gets stronger as one goes west. The origin
of the Berbers, who gave their name to Barbary, who speak a language quite
remote from Arabic and who have inhabited the area from Egypt to the
Atlantic since before the dawn of history, is uncertain. They are of a different ethnic stock, and have a culture and a social organization quite distinct
from those of the Arabs. They do not call themselves Berbers. That term
presumably was derived originally from the Greek *barbarizein*, to speak like
a foreigner, and its Latin derivatives, meaning crude or uncivilized. Most
dictionaries cite the ultimate source as the Arabic *barbar*, or *barabir*, but
those words are probably borrowings from the Latin. In any event, Berbers
identify themselves as belonging to tribal confederations that speak different dialects, such as the Tashilhit-speaking Shleuh of southern Morocco, or

1

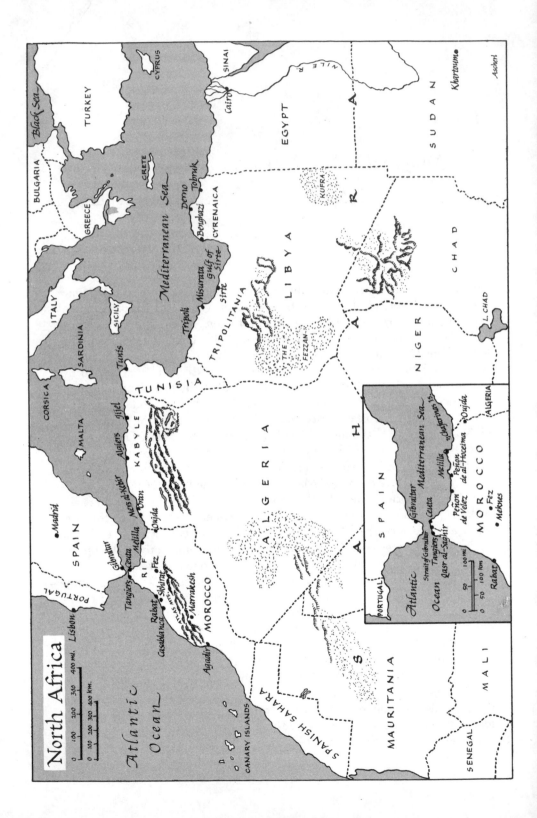

North Africa

the Taqbilt-speaking Kabyles of Algeria. The Berber dialects are spoken by about 30 percent of Moroccans and 20 percent of Algerians, but have almost disappeared from Tunisia and Libya, although elements of the populations in both those countries are still identified as Berbers. The Berber language has many Arabic loan words, particularly for abstract concepts and terms, but its structure and grammar are very different, and in that respect the two languages, although very distantly related, are as different as, say, Pashtu and Spanish. Many Berbers speak Arabic, but although Berber has strongly influenced North African Arabic, few North African Arabs speak Berber, even though most of them have a good deal of Berber blood in them. Indeed, intermarriage has been so common that there are few purely Arab or purely Berber people left in Morocco and Algeria.

The French sought to capitalize on Berber-Arab differences by setting up a separate legal and administrative system for the Moroccan Berbers in 1930. This was widely denounced by nationalist circles in Morocco and throughout the Arab world, but Berber particularism, not to say separatism, is very much alive today and manifests itself, particularly in the Kabyle region, in resistance to those activities of the central authorities that are thought to threaten the survival of Berber culture. The Berber factor thus remains important in Moroccan and Algerian politics. It also explains many aspects of the Maghrib that seem exotic to the eastern Arab, and most of the folklore that is appealing to the Western visitor.

Some intra-Maghrib differences can be explained by history. Although the ancient Egyptians had commercial and military contact with Libyan tribes over the centuries, the inhabitants of North Africa, some of whom were settled agriculturalists while others were nomadic pastoralists, were largely left to themselves until the coming of the Phoenicians of Tyre. The latter established colonies at Utica, in northern Tunisia, and Cadiz, in southern Spain, in about 1100 b.c., and conducted a more or less systematic exploration and settlement of coastal areas extending from Tripolitania to at least as far as the Atlantic coast of the Western Sahara. Their settlements were trading and fishing ports, and except in what is now Tunisia and eastern Algeria, which constituted the hinterland of Carthage (founded about 700 b.c.), they made little penetration of the interior.

Herodotus describes their silent trade with the natives of the Atlantic coast:

The Carthaginians recount the following: there is in Libya[1], beyond the Pillars of Hercules, a country inhabited by man. When the Carthaginians arrive at one of their settlements, they discharge their merchandise and lay it out on the shore, then return to their vessel and light a fire to give a smoke signal. When the inhabitants see the smoke, they come to the seaside, place gold beside the merchandise and then withdraw. The Carthaginians debark and count the gold. If it seems equal to the price of the merchandise, they take it and go away. If not, they remount their ships and wait. Then the natives return and add gold until the two sides are in agreement. Neither side is dishonest; the Carthaginians do not touch the gold until it pays for their merchandise, and the natives do not touch the goods until the Carthaginians take the gold.[2]

In about 631 b.c., the Greeks founded a colony at Cyrene, and subsequently others at Barca and elsewhere in what came to be known as Cyrenaica, the eastern province of Libya. Cyrene, whose lovely ruins still exist, was noted for its schools of medicine and philosophy, for its large Jewish colony, and for the beauty of its setting. (Geologically and climatically, northern Cyrenaica is different from the rest of Libya, being more mountainous and relatively well-watered, and it has always been distinct from Tripolitania in the West.)

The Romans, who first appeared with the conquest of Carthage in 202 b.c. in the Second Punic War, had occupied all the area from Cyrenaica to Morocco by a.d. 40, when Caligula had Ptolemy, the last of the kings of Mauritania, assassinated at Rome. The Romans divided the area from Tunisia to Morocco into four provinces: Africa (Tunisia), Numidia (the eastern third of Algeria), Mauritania Caesariensis (the western two-thirds of Algeria), and Mauritania Tingintana (roughly, modern-day Morocco north of Casablanca). Mauritania was the land of the Mauri, from which comes the term *Moro*, or *Moor*, applied somewhat indiscriminately to the Muslim inhabitants of North Africa in the past and now used to designate the ruling ethnic group in the present Mauritania.[3]

For the Romans, as for the Arabs, Morocco was the far west (its name in Arabic, al-Maghrib al-Aqsa, means just that), and the westernmost city of the Empire was Sala Colonia, near Rabat, a few miles south of which ran the *Limes Romanorum*, which marked the outer limits of Roman control. Morocco lay beyond the Pillars of Hercules, and its mountains still bear the name of Atlas, who, while Hercules held up the sky for him, went off to steal the golden apples from the Garden of the Hesperides, located by Pliny near the modern Larache, between Tangier and Rabat.

In both Mauritania and Numidia the Romans penetrated the interior more thoroughly than did the Carthaginians. Their imposing ruins are to be found well inland, at places like Volubilis in Morocco, 45 miles from the coast, and Timgad, 120 miles south of the Mediterranean in Algeria. Algeria was more important to Rome than Morocco and was more heavily settled, with Italian immigrants and legionnaires being encouraged to occupy sites throughout the country. The town Berbers of the northern agricultural region seem to have been integrated to a considerable extent into Roman provincial society, judging by the Latinized Berber names on tombstones, but rural Berbers seem to have resigned themselves to, rather than accepting, Roman rule, while the nomadic tribes of the south were never subdued, but only fended off. Nevertheless, the region controlled by the Romans was prosperous and was one of the granaries of the Empire.

To the east, the Roman conquest of Carthage did not mean the end of the Carthaginians or the disappearance of their city as a power center. Its proximity to Europe and its strategic position close to the Sicilian Strait assured it a continuing role as a target of military expeditions, as a resort of merchants, and as an intellectual and religious center. The *Confessions* of St. Augustine, who was from Tagaste (Suq al-Ahras) in Numidia and later became Bishop of Hippo (Annaba), lamented the dissolute life he led as a student in Carthage in the fourth century, and we know from his account that the city was fairly cosmopolitan.

Roman control of North Africa was broken by the Vandal invasion, which began in 429 with the crossing of the Strait of Gibraltar. The Vandals reached as far as Tripoli, but their principal area of settlement was the eastern half of Algeria. St. Augustine died during their siege of Hippo in 430. The Byzantines under Belisarius reconquered part of the area from the Vandals in 533, and Tunisia and the area around Tangier and Ceuta were in Byzantine hands when the Arabs arrived in 688. At that point, the urban population of Algeria and Tunisia was largely Christian. Although Latinized, some of these Christians still spoke Punic, or Phoenician, and Berber. They were called *Afariq*, or Africans, by the Arabs, and did not disappear from view entirely until the twelfth century. (Unlike in the Near East, where substantial communities of Christians descended from pre-Muslim comunities still exist, there are no native Christians in North Africa today.) Many of the Berbers who had become Christians apparently did so as an act of resistance against Rome rather than from deep conviction, and although the Berbers in general put up a prolonged and bloody resistance to the Arabs, they converted to Islam with remarkable speed. So quickly, in fact, that Berbers supplied most of the troops that accompanied Tariq Ibn Ziyad, himself a Berber, when he led the expedition which began the Muslim conquest of Spain in 711.

The Arabs did not succeed in consolidating their hold on North Africa until the eighth century, and that hold was tenuous, as their empire proved too large to manage and the great Berber tribal confederations began contesting the area, paradoxically becoming Arabicized themselves in the process. The history of the next twelve hundred years is a complex and confusing one of Berber and Arab dynasties and tribes warring with each other and seeking to establish control over the entire area from Morocco to Tunisia. This was accomplished only once, by the Almohads, a dynasty of settled Berbers from Morocco, who controlled the great arc from Saragossa to Tunisia in the twelfth century. Meanwhile, a series of independent Muslim states emerged in Spain, providing brilliant artistic and intellectual centers that maintained an ongoing cultural, intellectual, and military exchange with North Africa in general, and Morocco in particular, until the expulsion of the Moors in 1492.

What strikes the observer in reading about this period is the different courses of sovereignty in the regions of the Maghrib. In Morocco there was a succession of dynasties, Arab and Berber, which often did not control all of the country (the Berbers of the Atlas Mountains being dissident and disaffected much of the time) but which maintained a tradition of central authority throughout the more fertile regions of the plain on both sides of the Atlas. Although their control even of the plains was contested at times by the Portuguese and the Spaniards, and their maritime capabilities were all but eliminated by those powers for many years, the country did not break up into a collection of city states. At times the Moroccans had a powerful empire, and in those periods their courts were the resort of Western ambassadors and merchants seeking favors. At others they were less powerful, but they always maintained their independence. Even the French, who came in 1912 and established a protectorate, governed in the name of the sultan, as the king was then called.

Tunisia had a somewhat similar experience. When the Arabs arrived in 688 they made their capital at Kairouan (Qayrawan), 80 miles south of Carthage, where their mounted troops could maneuver easily in the open country, and from where they set out to conquer the rest of North Africa and Spain. Kairouan was enriched by booty and slaves from these campaigns, and became a major town and a center of learning and culture. Meanwhile, the ancient town of Tunis, on the southern shore of the bay near Carthage, was reviving and becoming the second city of Ifriqya, or Africa.

In the tenth century, control of Kairouan and of Tunisia was wrested from the Sunni Arabs by a faction of Berber reformers who were Shia, or partisans of 'Ali. Called Fatimids because their leader (like the Alaouites of Morocco) claimed descent from Fatima, the Prophet's daughter, they established a new capital at Mahdiya, on the coast. From there they launched expeditions against Egypt, which they eventually conquered and to which their leader, the Mahdi, or Divinely Guided One, transferred his seat. Thus began what is known as the Fatimid Caliphate of Egypt.

The Fatimids left control over Africa in the hands of a Berber family known as the Zirids, or descendants of Ziri, who in 1048 made themselves independent of the Fatimids, in retaliation for which the latter unleashed two troublesome bedouin tribes, the Banu Hilal and the Banu Sulaym, on the region. Although traditional accounts of their locust-like advance across the continent may be exaggerated, the Hilalian invasion seems to have given all but the *coup de grace* to the remnants of Roman-Christian civilization in North Africa, which had survived the original Arab conquest, and which has left scattered monuments from Cyrenaica to Rabat. The invasion coincided with the eruption of the Almoravids (or Murabitun), Berber nomads from the Sahara, who established a dynasty in Morocco and eventually swept into Spain and across North Africa as far as Algiers. Meanwhile, the Zirids were engulfed by the Banu Hilal and finally destroyed by the Normans of Sicily, who took Mahdiya in 1148.

The Almohads of Morocco arrived in Tunisia ten years later, and the last of the Christians in North Africa disappeared with their coming. In Tunisia a local dynasty, the Hafsid, which was descended from an Almohad governor, Abu Hafs, was established and lasted until the coming of the Turks in 1574. Even though much attenuated in its later years, its authority gave Tunisia considerably more stability and tradition of central rule than Algeria had.

In Algeria there were dynasties that ruled much or part of the country from time to time, notably at Qalaa al Banu Hammad and Bougie (Bajaya) in the center, and Tiaret (Tahert) and Tlemcen in the west, but the country was rarely united except under external rule, as under the Almohads. Not only were there perpetual problems of dissidence with the Berbers of the Kabyle and Aures region, but there were problems of tension between settled and nomadic tribes, complicated by interference from both Tunisia and Morocco. Although centers such as Bougie, Constantine, and Tlemcen were important, one does not read of great Algerian dynasties dominating the region, and there was little tradition of central rule before the coming of the Ottoman Turks in the sixteenth century. Under them the kingdom of Algiers, as Algeria was then called, extended from Morocco to Tunisia in the north, as it does today, but stopped at the northern edge of the Sahara.

Libya was a geographic expression, but not a great deal more. Under the Arabs, neither Tripolitania nor Cyrenaica was the center of much authority, although Tripoli became an important center of corsair activity after the Christian reconquest of Spain. Looking at the impressive ruins of Leptis Magna, east of Tripoli, one realizes that this was an important colony to the Romans, and the traces of Roman and Greek cisterns and irrigation structures testify to a degree of settlement and cultivation considerably above that which the country can support today. Not only does it seem that the climate has gotten drier, but Libya has never fully recovered from the invasion of the Banu Hilal, who made it their first stop on their route westward, and whose occupation led to the decay of the agricultural infrastructure.

The Arab conquest, the conversion of the population to Islam, the Muslim invasions of Spain and Sicily, and the continuing conflict with the infidels of Europe led to the almost complete severance of trade links between North Africa and Europe until the eleventh century, when Christian merchants began reappearing in North African ports. Stimulated by the Crusades, the Europeans began a quest for commercial advantage and territorial conquest that was to continue intermittently until the twentieth century. The Pisans and Genoese attacked Tunis in the late eleventh century, and the Normans of Sicily, who had taken that island from the Muslims, seized Mahdiya in 1148, as mentioned earlier. The medieval phase ended with the death of St. Louis, of the plague, while leading the last crusade against Tunis in 1270.

Serious, and quasi-permanent, incursions began with the Portuguese seizure of Ceuta, across from Gibraltar, in 1415. The Portuguese lost it in 1437, but returned to occupy Qasr al-Saghir, a small port between Tangier and Ceuta, in 1458, and in 1471 began methodically occupying the major ports between Ceuta and Agadir, controlling almost all of them by 1510, and completely dominating Moroccan maritime trade via the Atlantic. The Spaniards had meanwhile begun a similar process along the Mediterranean coast following the expulsion of the Moors from Granada in 1492. They took Melilla in 1497, Mersa el-Kebir in Algeria in 1505, Penon de Velez, which lay off Badis (now disappeared), the onetime port of Fez, in 1508, and Oran in 1509. Neither the Spanish nor the Portuguese attempted to colonize the hinterland, although the Portuguese at one time controlled a considerable area of the plain between Marrakesh and the Atlantic as well as a sizable area around Agadir. Instead, they kept small garrisons in fortified *presidios*, which harassed the surrounding inhabitants from time to time, suppressed local shipping, and provided sheltered harbor for shipping from the home country. By contemporary accounts, life in these presidios was grim and isolated, contact with the natives was limited and uncertain, and the garrisons were often dependent on ships for food. Furthermore, Portuguese and Spanish involvement elsewhere, notably in the New World, Asia, and Europe, reduced the resources available to support these installations, and they were often poorly defended.

The Moroccans began their own reconquest in 1541, with the recapture of Agadir, and had retaken most of the Atlantic ports, including Tangier, by 1561. The Spanish, however, are still in occupation of five of their Mediterranean presidios: Ceuta, Penon de Velez, Penon de al-Hucemas, Melilla, and the Chafarinas Islands. While not subject to armed attack today, they are still without significant local hinterland, still dependent on Spain, and still a net drain on the Spanish treasury. They are a point of contention, which is discussed in more detail in Chapter 8.

In 1511 the Spanish occupied a very small island in the bay of Algiers, from which they could bombard the town. In response, the Algerians eventually invoked the aid of an Ottoman corsair, Aruj, who took possession of Jijel, a small port further east along the coast, in 1514. He made a triumphal entry into Algiers in 1516, subsequently had himself made sultan of the town, and proceeded to occupy other towns and districts in an effort to create a strong Muslim state that could resist Christian attack. He and his successor (and brother), the great corsair captain Khayr al-Din Barbarossa, did not succeed in ousting the Spaniards from their island in the harbor until 1525. In the meantime, finding himself in some difficulty with the local population, which had begun to regret its loss of independence, Barbarossa had sworn homage to the Ottoman sultan and in effect made that part of North Africa which he controlled an Ottoman province. He was immediately rewarded with the title of pasha and commander of the province, and given the invaluable support of 6,000 men with artillery. Ottoman rule of North Africa had begun.

In 1534, Barbarossa took Tunis. This so alarmed the Christian powers that Charles V of Spain mounted a major expedition and seized the town in

1535, but instead of occupying it, contented himself with fortifying and garrisoning the islet of La Goulette, which commanded the entrance to the harbor. The Ottoman governor of Algiers retook Tunis in 1569; it was retaken briefly by Don Juan of Austria in 1573, after the Ottoman defeat at Lepanto in 1571, but was retaken again by the Ottomans in 1574, and North Africa between Egypt and Oran remained a nominal Ottoman province until the coming of the French in the nineteenth century.

The Ottomans did not occupy Morocco, and Algeria marked the western limit of their conquests. Their principal contribution was to bring a certain amount of order to what had been a very chaotic situation. As Charles-André Julien notes in his *History of North Africa* (see bibliography), "by substituting the concept of the defined frontier for that of border regions, which had been found sufficient until they arrived, they were chiefly responsible for the distinction which came into force in the sixteenth century between Algeria and Tunisia (the very names date only from the July Monarchy [Louis Phillipe 1830-48]) and Morocco."

Under the Ottomans, Algiers gradually assumed a good deal of autonomy from Constantinople and was ruled by a permanent floating junta of janissaries and corsairs. The former installed and deposed governors with remarkable dispatch, the unfortunate deposee often being executed. For much of the period, the principal revenues of the state were gained from piracy, which became very profitable in the eighteenth century, and the first official U.S. contact with the country came from the capture of an American vessel (the brig *Maria*, out of Boston) off the Portuguese coast in 1785, and the enslavement of its crew. (The Americans eventually paid $80,000 for the release of the vessel's crew as well as those of 12 other vessels captured subsequently.) While this practice was labeled as criminal and vicious by Westerners, to the Algerians, Moroccans, Tunisians, and Tripolitanians it was part of their struggle against the infidel and had the character of a holy war or crusade, as well as being profitable. Furthermore, it was not all that different from the privateering, or officially sanctioned piracy, carried on by the European powers, and the United States.

In 1830, as the outcome of a dispute arising from French failure to repay a loan from two Algerian money lenders who helped finance Napoleon's Italian campaign, the French landed an expeditionary force near Algiers. They had intended this as a punitive action rather than a colonial conquest, and proceeded to "pacify" the country without having decided what to do with it. They eventually opted for colonization, and made the area between Tunisia and Morocco into three *departments* of metropolitan France. Europeans were encouraged to settle there, while the natives became second-class inhabitants who did not even enjoy French citizenship until 1944, and who had no prospect for social or economic advancement except as surrogate Frenchmen, divorced from their traditional Islamic-Berber-Arab-Turkish heritage. Their lands were seized, entire villages were uprooted and transported elsewhere (the French pioneered here the creation of the first concentration camps), mosques were converted to churches, Islamic (and Roman) monuments were destroyed, and institutions were suppressed. The unenlightened treatment of the Muslim population was a scandal even in nineteenth century France.

By the end of World War II Algeria was ready for an eruption, which finally came in 1954, when the Algerian revolution officially began with the formation of the Front de Libération Nationale (FLN) which remains the sole political party of Algeria today. The struggle began with a series of terrorist acts by a handful of men. It lasted for seven-and-a-half years, with enormous casualties and suffering, and caused severe political dislocation in France. Although the French won the military contest, the political cost of keeping the country pacified was too high and they eventually agreed, under de Gaulle's guidance, to withdraw. The country became independent in 1962.

The Hafsid dynasty in Tunisia, installed so long ago by the Almohads, expired after unsuccessfully attempting to oppose the Turkish reconquest in 1574. The Ottomans ruled Tunisia as they did Algiers, through appointed governors who were supported by janissaries and who gradually acquired a good deal of autonomy. Unlike Algeria, however, Tunisia produced a local dynasty, which ruled as vassals of Turkey from 1702 until the imposition of a French protectorate in 1881. Under the latter the bey, or prince, of Tunis and his descendants continued in nominal authority while the French ran the country. The spread of 51 years between the occupation of Algeria and that of Tunisia, plus the stronger tradition of central control in Tunisia, gave rise to important differences between the governmental situations in these two countries at independence. Tunisia, some of whose leaders shared the nineteenth century interest in governmental reforms so popular in Turkey and Egypt, had already developed its own cadre of government officials and had progressed some distance along the road of modernization during this period. When the French came they found a functioning government considerably advanced over that which they had found in Algiers. Although the French had no evident intention ever to relinquish their protectorate, they did not incorporate Tunisia into France as they had done with Algeria, and the fact that the Bey was allowed to remain in office, even if he had no power, meant that the possibilities open to Tunisians in the economy and the government were considerably above those available to their Algerian counterparts. The Tunisians were therefore relatively well-prepared for self-government when independence came, and their approach to nation building has been more moderate than that of the Algerians as a result.

To return to the question of what makes Libya different: first of all, the French did not come there. It was colonized instead by the Italians, who declared war on Turkey in 1911 in order to seize that province. Libya therefore lacks the heavy overlay of French culture and social infrastructure that characterizes the rest of North Africa, and this makes it seem less Maghribi.

Perhaps more important are the climatic differences between Libya and the rest of North Africa. The region from Morocco to Tunisia, because it projects northward from the continent (Bizerte is on the same latitude as Granada and Syracuse), benefits from the moisture-laden westerlies coming across the Atlantic, whereas Libya is on their southern fringe and gets very little rain. Morocco, Algeria and Tunisia have important areas of rainfed cultivation and have population/cultivable land ratios that are favorable by Arab world standards (about 700 inhabitants per square mile of arable land in Morocco and Algeria and 300 in Tunisia, compared to something about 2,000 in Egypt and 440 in Syria.)

The economies of Morocco and Tunisia, but not that of Algeria, are still based largely on agriculture, and rural population constitutes about 50 percent of the total population in all three. Agriculture occupies an estimated 51 percent of the workforce in Morocco and 34 percent in Tunisia, but only 22 percent in Algeria. (The latter has witnessed a dramatic decline in its farm work force from 1.5 million fifteen years ago to some 600,000 in 1981, according to Algerian government figures.[4] Apparently, a large portion of the rural population is not counted as being in the work force.) Agriculture contributed 30 percent of the Moroccan Gross Domestic Product in 1981 and 16 percent of Tunisia's, but only 6 percent of Algeria's.

Libya, on the other hand, has a very small population (3.4 million), a very small agricultural area that produces only about 15 percent of its food requirements (although 48 percent of the population lives there), and very large revenues of oil. Although agriculture is the second largest sector of the economy, it produces less than 5 percent of the GNP. While Algeria and Tunisia are classified as "upper middle income" ($2,100 and $1,400 respectively per capita GNP estimated for 1981) and Morocco as "lower middle" ($869 +), Libya has been considered high income, with a per capita GNP in 1981 of almost $8,560 (down steeply in 1983, but no reliable figures are available). Its social and economic problems are accordingly somewhat different from the other states of the Maghrib, and so is its approach to solving them.

The economies of the other three also differ from each other, as well as from Libya's. Of the three, only Algeria has a wide-ranging and ambitious industrial development program, financed by revenues from oil and gas, and it aspires to something called industrial independence, that is, to being able to compete with European producers of industrial goods. Prognoses vary as to whether these expectations are realistic, but because of its ambition and organization, Algeria is already in a different economic category from the other two.

Morocco, with roughly the same population as Algeria (20–22 million) and a similar pre-independence industrial base, but without significant discoveries of oil and gas, has made a reverse allocation of its efforts, with industrialization taking second place to agriculture. While a number of foreign observers over the years have concluded that Morocco's economy is sounder than Algeria's, being less dependent on a wasting asset and foreign technology and being more prudent in its expenditures, Morocco is in serious financial trouble today for a number of reasons, including the continuing drought, the high costs of oil and the dollar, and the drain of the Saharan war.

Tunisia, which has the most modest resource base of the four, has also had the best organized and most effective political structure and the most Westernized leadership. It has managed a degree of development, based on agriculture, tourism, and exports of oil and phosphates, that gives it perhaps the best balanced economy of the four. Its population of 6.5 million enjoyed a Physical Quality of Life Index of 59 in 1980, compared to Morocco's 45, Algeria's 48, and Libya's 52.[5] (For comparison, Mexico's was 78; Poland's, 93; and Haiti's, 39.) It too is having financial troubles, however, because of disastrous floods, low phosphate and oil prices, and reduced French tourism.

In addition to significant economic differences, the four countries have different governmental systems and philosophies, and project national personalities that seem quite distinct to outsiders. Morocco is perhaps the most traditional of the world's surviving monarchies. The ruling Alaouite family, whose name means that they claim descent from the Prophet through his daughter Fatima and her husband Ali, has been in power since the mid-seventeenth century, and deeply ingrained rituals of dress and behavior characterize the royal court, often bemusing more republican-minded Arabs from the East. Algeria, on the other hand, has the archetypical revolutionary regime, and is one of the standard bearers of revolutionary ideology in the Third World. The product of quite a different history, it opposes most of what Morocco stands for: tradition and the status quo.

Tunisia has been governed by one man since independence, and he has marked it with his own personality and outlook. Of all the North African countries, it is the most open and has what looks like the most firmly based political institutions in the area. It would not do to over-emphasize the strength of those institutions or expect them to bear too much weight, but it is remarkable that in Tunisia one can discuss internal affairs with government ministers and get frank answers to questions on such matters as the prospects for the succession to the presidency that would never be answered in Algeria and be answered only with polite evasions in Morocco. This is a sign of political self-confidence and security which persist in spite of the sometimes Byzantine internal workings of the elite.

Libya, one of the original basket cases when it became independent in 1951, is led by an eccentric who has had massive sums available for foreign adventures. His tether is somewhat shorter today, thanks to the oil glut, but Qadhdhafi still has considerable resources for pursuing his aberrant and unpredictable policies. Of the four states, Libya alone has acute political problems with the United States, and it alone has followed a course which is essentially irresponsible in the eyes of the rest of the world, including the Arabs.

Thus, while there is a superficial unity of language and culture among these states, they are in fact quite diverse. That all four have racially similar populations (although the Berber/Arab ratio is different in each), are non-aligned, recently independent, Arabic-speaking, Muslim, Mediterranean states with similar living standards and common problems, and that all profess devotion to the same Arab and Third World causes weighs very little against their parochial interests and rivalries, which may have been aggravated by colonial rule but did not originate with it.

In the 1950s and 1960s there was much talk of a unity scheme called the Greater Maghrib, and a permanent consultative committee was set up with headquarters in Tunis and charged with implementing concrete measures leading toward greater regional cooperation. The committee still exists, and has some modest accomplishments in the fields of transport and communications to its credit, but these have been overshadowed by political differences and by the fact that the noncomplementarity of Maghrib economies makes substantial economic cooperation unlikely. Algerian concentration on industrial development and the inefficiency of Algerian agriculture may create markets for Tunisian and Moroccan produce, but given the fact that none of the states of the area is self-sufficient in food, and that all want to export the same agricultural products to Europe when they have them, the possibilities for intra-Maghrib trade seem limited, even were vested interests not a problem. In any event, Libya has withdrawn from the committee; ironically enough, it is the only one of the four states seriously interested in unification. None of the other three is prepared to surrender meaningful power to a regional grouping (although in 1983 there was much talk of Maghrib unity in statements being made in Algiers, Rabat, and Tunis and although at one point the Moroccans saw it as a way of getting at the Western Saharan problem).

Indeed, each of these states is profoundly suspicious of its immediate neighbors. Relations usually swing from correct to strained. While there may be periods of cordiality, as when Hassan and Boumediene were exchanging visits in the early 1970s, or when Bourguiba and Qadhdhafi made their abortive unity agreement in 1975, or when Qadhdhafi visited Morocco in 1983, they are fleeting. Relations between Morocco and Tunisia are usually good because both states consider themselves moderates threatened by their radical neighbors, and because they are geographically separated and have no bilateral problems to speak of. The Algerians and Libyans, on the other hand, who are both members of the Steadfastness and Confrontation Front (which rejects the Camp David accords), who theoretically share similar revolutionary goals and support movements of national liberation, who support radical causes at the United Nations, who arm the Polisario guerrillas fighting against Morocco in the Sahara, and who are generally lumped together in the anti-Western category by Western commentators, are not particularly friendly. The Algerians are wary of Libyan activities in the Sahara, and Libyan support for the Polisario is a matter of concern to Algerian leaders. They would rather not have the Libyans encroaching on their preserve, but so far have been unable or unwilling to prevent it, apparently because they feel it would be impolitic to block aid to a liberation movement. The Algerians, furthermore, have a border dispute with Libya, are uneasy over Qadhdhafi's erratic behavior and diplomatic improvisations, and disapprove of his involvement in Chad.

Since independence, the external problems of the Maghrib countries have largely been with each other. Even were there no Sahara dispute, Algeria and Morocco would be at odds much of the time. Not only is there a half-solved border dispute between them, a result of French annexation to Algeria of enormous areas of Morocco and Tunisia, but each is vying with the other for pre-eminence in North Africa. Each sees the other as a threat, and their national stereotypes of each other are much like those shared by the Poles and Russians, with the Moroccans being the Poles. There is a deep current of mistrust between them that goes back to tribal and dynastic rivalries long antedating the coming of the Turks and French. They were thought to be entering a period of relatively good feelings following a meeting between King Hassan and President Benjedid at Oujda on February 26, 1983. During the meeting they reportedly agreed to a phased restoration of relations, which had been broken in 1976, and to discussion of a compromise settlement of the Sahara problem. This was followed by a series of visits by Moroccan and Algerian officials to each other's capitals, but further progress has been blocked by inability to solve the Sahara problem, and the historic rivalry between the two countries remains a cause of suspicion and tension. Benjedid is understood to be anxious to resolve the Sarhara problem, but to be constrained by ideological hard-liners.

For its part, Tunisia has long feared Algeria and sees itself threatened by Libya today. Concern about Algerian intentions was heightened in January 1980, when Algerian officials allowed a Libyan-sponsored commando of some 300 Tunisian dissidents to transit Algeria in order to attack Gafsa, in southern Tunisia. The Libyans apparently hoped to spark a revolt by this action, but badly miscalculated, and the raiders were quickly overcome by the Tunisians. The authorities in Algiers maintained that local officials had acted without their permission. They purged their security services and opened a telephone hotline with Tunis as evidence of their sincerity and good intentions. The Tunisians feigned acceptance of Algerian assurances in this regard but did not in fact believe them. As with Morocco and Algeria, there is a residue of mistrust that is centuries old and is unlikely to be eradicated completely any time soon. Continuing efforts by President Benjedid to improve relations with Tunisia have ameliorated this mustrust, but it will remain a recurring obstacle to friendly commerce.[6]

Tunisians argue that the socialist regime in Algeria cannot tolerate on its borders a successful, nonsocialist Tunisia that serves as a constant reminder of the failures of the Algerian economy. They point out gleefully that in 1981 the Algerians allowed their nationals to travel freely to Tunisia, and 800,000 took advantage of the opportunity to come breathe the free air and buy consumer goods, including, somewhat comically, a Maghrib hot sauce called *harissa*, which was in short supply in Algeria. They note that the experiment was not repeated in 1982, and claim it was because the Algerian regime did not want its people to see how successful the Tunisians had been.[7]

In point of fact, the Algerians do not appear to be spending a great deal of time worrying about whether the Tunisian economic formula succeeds or fails, although they are concerned with the forthcoming presidential succession and the outlook for stability. The fact that the head of their security services was transferred over the Gafsa incident indicates that their protestations of innocence were probably genuine, and the primary reason they did not repeat the 1981 tourism experiment seems to have been the number of Algerians who crossed the border without funds or other means of support and became consular and police problems.

This is an instance, however, where the perception is more important than the reality. Whatever the latter, it is the former that determines actions, and the Tunisians, who have gone to considerable lengths to propitiate both the Algerians and Libyans, remain deeply suspicious of both. They have asked for more arms with which to defend themselves, and the United States is obliging.

Thus, while North Africa may look like a discrete cultural and geographic unit, politically it is a mixture of immiscible elements, each posing different problems and demanding different answers. Each state has its own interests, and they almost invariably conflict in some way with those of its neighbors; each state is suspicious of the others; and each wants more arms than it has today in order to defend itself against neighbors, no other threats being credible. The local Arab nationalist will maintain that these differences are an artificial creation of colonialism, and that the Maghribis are a band of brothers. The historical record shows something different, however. The differences long antedate the French, and will be with us far into the future.

Outside the immediate region, Maghribi relations with Europe are closer than those with either black Africa or the eastern Arab world. The North Africans are separated from the rest of Africa by the wide belt of the Sahara, and while they are concerned about what goes on below the Sahara, and have often been active in intra-African politics, their concern is more likely to find verbal than physical expression. Qadhdhafi's involvement in Uganda and Chad, and Moroccan involvement in Zaire and Angola (in support of Mobutu and Savimbi, respectively) are exceptions, and there undoubtedly will be others. Indeed, Moroccan occupation of the Spanish Sahara in 1975, was in a sense a North African push toward black Africa, although it can be argued that both the Spanish Sahara and Mauritania are part of the Maghrib, since their peoples speak Arabic and there is no clearly defined line of separation between blacks and Arabs north of the Senegal River. In general, however, the Maghribis feel their Mediterranean vocation more strongly than their African, they feel closer to the white Europeans than the black Africans (who complain of North African racial discrimination), and their trade and commerce are oriented toward the north, not the south. This does not prevent their following events in the Sahel, on the southern edge of the Sahara, with concern and interest, but this interest is born more of geopolitics than of any feeling of identity with the Sahelians.

The Maghrib is similarly separated from the Mashriq by the western desert of Egypt and the great Bight of Sirte (Sidra), where the Libyan desert comes down to the sea. These obstacles are not particularly formidable today, but the cultural patterns that dominate the regions in question were established long before the airplane and the automobile made desert travel relatively easy. For most of its history the Maghrib has been an island, surrounded by a sea of sand on the south and the Mediterranean on the north. It has developed separately from the eastern Arab world, and while travelers have maintained connections between the two over the centuries, the Maghrib and Mashriq are two distinct and separate regions, with different cultures and climates. The eastern Arabs in general know very little about the Maghribis and vice versa. Maghribi spoken Arabic is quite different, and while the educated Maghribi and Mashriqi can both converse in modern standard Arabic of the sort used in the media, Mashriqis who can understand the colloquial dialects of North Africa, particularly in Morocco and Algeria, are very rare. It is somewhat easier for the Maghribis to understand the colloquial dialects of the Mashriq, because they are slower and more distinct, but there is a communication problem in both directions. The Maghribis are, furthermore, oriented more toward French culture and thought, at least in Morocco, Algeria, and Tunisia, than they are toward the East, and their outlook on questions of the day is likely to be quite different from that of the eastern Arab, who spends his vacation in London rather than Paris. As King Hassan is fond of saying, the Maghribis are Arabs, but with a difference.

The Maghribis, who are rather taciturn, tend to look down on the eastern Arabs as people who talk a big game but are not worth much when it comes to a real fight. The Maghribis, and the Berbers in particular, have a long tradition of combat against outsiders, and against each other if need be, and a reputation in the Arab world for being tough. Their fighting qualities have been amply demonstrated on many occasions, as by the performance of the North Africans who fought for the French in the two world wars, and as by the heroic fight put up by the Moroccan detachment on the slopes of Mt. Hermon in the Ramadan War of 1973. The apotheosis of the Maghribi spirit was the Algerian Abd al-Qadr, who led the resistance to the French in western Algeria in the 1830s. Eventually exiled to Damascus, he earned the gratitude of the Western world by holding a Muslim mob at bay and pro-

Table A. Selected Data

COUNTRY	MOROCCO	ALGERIA	TUNISIA	LIBYA
Population (1982 estimate— millions)	22.5	20.2	6.7	3.4
Percent rural (1980)[1]	59	56	48	48
Percent urban	41	44	52	52
Arable land exploited ('000 ha)—1980[1]	7,497	7,719	4,970	2,000
Population/arable land	2.9/ha	2.6/ha	1.3/ha	1.7/ha
Irrigated land ('000 ha)	340	750	185	na
Pasture, forest & scrub land per rural person—1980[1]	3.4 ha	1.4 ha	1.6 ha	5 ha
Percent of work force in Agriculture (1981 estimate)	52	22[3]	34	19
Percent of work force in Industry	21	28[4]	33	28
Percent of work force in Services	27	50	33	53
Percent unemployment (est 1982)	20+	20–25	20–25	na
GNP/capita (1981)[2]	$869	$2,129	$1,417	$8,560
GDP 1982 (Economic Trends Reports estimates)	$15 billion	$40 billion	$6.4 billion	$13 billion
GNP/capita growth rate (1981–82)	1.7	4.0	1.5*	−55
Physical Quality of Life Index[2]	47	49	62	55
Birth rate per 1,000[2]	45	46	35	47
Death rate per 1,000[2]	14	14	11	13
Life expectancy at birth[2]	55	56	58	55
Infant mortality per 1,000 live births[2]	107	118	100	100
Literacy[7]	28	35	62	50
Per capita public education— 1979[2]	$49	$131	$67	$358
Per capita military expenditures—1979[2]	$44	$33	$9	$171
Total exports for 1981[2]— ($ millions)	2,160	14,056	2,209	16,391
Total imports cif 1981[2]— ($ millions)	4,487	11,505	3,923	15,414
Debt service ratio (1982 est)	36%	18–25%	12%	na

* based on dinar, not dollar, values

[1] From the World Bank's World Development Report for 1982 and conversations with World Bank officials.

[2] From *U.S. Foreign Policy and the Third World, Agenda for 1983,* The Overseas Development Council: Washington, D.C. (New York: Praeger 1983).

[3] U.S. Agricultural Attache Rabat, Report AG-2001 (May 3, 1982), Agricultural Situation.

[4] Revised to reflect decrease in agricultural percentage of work force in 1981.

Note: 1980 is the last "normal" year for Morocco for which data are available.

tecting the Christians and Jews of that city from massacre in 1860. Abraham Lincoln sent him a pair of horse pistols as a token of appreciation.

The North Africans reiterate their support for the Palestine cause when called upon, but except for Libya they have few resident Palestinians to reckon with, and their attachment to the cause is attenuated by distance and concentration on local concerns. Both the Algerians and Moroccans have shown their willingness to fight against Israel, and the Libyans have demonstrated considerable bellicosity in recent years, but they are not confrontation states and their interest is not as acute as, say, Syria's or Jordan's. A perhaps surprising exception is their interest in the Jerusalem question. A military campaign to liberate it from the Israelis would attract great support in North Africa.

There is today little trade between the Mashriq and the Maghrib, and while Libya and Algeria are both members of OPEC and the Arab subgroup OAPEC (Organization of Arab Petroleum Exporting Countries), each has its own national interests to pursue and their solidarity with each other, or with the other Arabs, has not been such as to negate those interests. While the North Africans will continue to give ritual support to Arab causes, they will remain apart from the eastern Arabs and we are unlikely ever to see meaningful steps toward Arab unity that involve them.

The Maghrib then, is different. It is in the Arab world and in Africa, but not of them. Nor is it European. It has its own personality and its own flavor, and it should be approached without preconceptions about Arab or African behavior.

The four chapters that follow discuss each of the states in turn and reflect the differences between them. In the Moroccan chapter the focus is on the monarchy; in the Algerian, it is on the revolutionary power structure and the prospects for economic development; in the Tunisian, it is on the succession to Bourguiba; and in the Libyan, it is on the nature of the revolution.

Notes

[1] To the Greeks, Libya was Africa.

[2] The Histories, Book IV.

[3] And applied to the Muslims of Mindanao by Magellan.

[4] Algerian Agricultural Situation, U.S. Agricultural Attache Report AG-2001, (U.S. Embassy, Rabat, May 3, 1982).

[5] U.S. Foreign Policy and the Third World, Agenda 1982, Overseas Development Council (New York: Praeger, 1982). The PQLI is derived from life expectancy at one year, infant mortality, and literacy.

[6] Benjedid paid an official visit to Tunis in March 1983, during which he and Bourguiba signed a treaty of "brotherhood and concord" and a special agreement on border demarcation. Coming on the heels of the Oujda meeting, this was taken as a sign that Benjedid was

anxious to break out of Algeria's isolation in the Maghrib. Algeria subsequently concluded border agreements with Niger and Mali, and Mauritania adhered to the Tunisian-Algerian treaty, which is open to all the states of the Maghrib, in December 1983. Reports that the agreement with Niger contains security guarentees have reinforced speculation that, Algerian assertions to the contrary notwithstanding, Algeria's purpose is to strengthen regional resistance to Libyan encroachment.

[7]For a discussion of the relative performances of the two economies, see John Nellis, "Comparative Assessment of Development Performances of Algeria and Tunisia," in *The Middle East Journal* (Summer 1983).

2

Morocco

Morocco, by its vegetation, its soil and its climate, reminds one of California. Exposure to movies like *Casablanca* and *Beau Geste* and popular impressions of the Arab world as being largely desert do not prepare the traveler for its fertile plains and lush orchards, often stretching far beyond the horizon. Hot summers and mild winters permit cultivation of a wide range of plants, and the markets are filled with vegetables of a variety, freshness, and taste rarely to be found in the United States.

Its 22-plus million people, of Berber and Arab stock, have traditionally depended on agriculture and grazing for their livelihood, and the majority of the population is still rural today. Centuries of instability and relative isolation from the East as well as the West delayed modernization, and there were no highways or public wheeled vehicles until the coming of the French in 1912, transport being by pack animal or horse, and the economy being based on agriculture and traditional trade and crafts. Except for the trade goods brought in by merchants, the industrial revolution had had little effect on Morocco, and it was a wild and exciting place in the eyes of foreign visitors, a place of armed horsemen and feudal rulers, of glorious vistas and remarkable folklore, and all of it untamed.

Today the vistas and the folklore remain, but the country has largely been tamed. It is an autocracy ruled by a hereditary monarch, Hassan II, who more than anything else symbolizes Morocco for the West, a modern monarch who maintains the most traditional of courts, and who has his feet in the present as well as the past.

Morocco has what John Waterbury and other students of the area have called a segmented society, one which is held together by the tensions between the competing individuals and groups who compose it—tribal group against tribal group, Arab versus Berber, family versus family. They are balanced off against each other through the play of interests and the native caution that characterizes societies where retribution is an ever present risk for the man who sticks his head too far above the crowd. Sometimes the process is manipulated from above, but it also works as an independent social mechanism. The man who gains too brilliant a victory over his rival knows that he is asking for trouble, and discretion is preferred above ostentatious success. Consensus in such a society is often difficult to achieve.

The country is run by an impressive elite, largely but not exclusively drawn from urban families, particularly from Fez, Casablanca, and Rabat. Well educated, urbane, and polished, the members of this elite move quietly through the corridors of power as cabinet ministers, directors general, and heads of companies, national and private. As with Louis XIV's courtiers, however, their future is entirely in the king's hands. They do not vie with him for power. He promotes and fires, chooses this one or that for a turn at the public trough, and banishes to outer darkness the man who displeases. Such power as there is in other hands flows from closeness of contact with the king. There are people in the country who have some political following based on family or tribe, or ascribed sanctity, or labor unions, or party activity, but they do not challenge the king. The latter rules as Commander of the Faithful and his word is law. Indeed, a famous decision of the Moroccan supreme court in 1970 found that he was beyond its jurisdiction and the legality of his acts could not be questioned.[1]

The king is both spiritual and temporal leader of his country, that is, he is the supreme religious authority in the state as well as being the supreme constitutional authority. (The spiritual role is not common to other Arab rulers today and is a distinctive feature of the Moroccan monarchy.) He speaks of his people as though they were his children and he the *pater familias*, referring to them as "my dear people." He is subject to the usual economic and political constraints that any rational ruler must face, but political opposition is closely monitored, not to say suppressed, and while the king must sometimes take other views into consideration, it is he who calls the tune. Opposition parties are allowed to operate but are restricted by ground rules that are understood rather than written. The most important of these is that they may not publicly criticize the king, or his family, or the institution of the monarchy. Since the king is the state, both in theory and practice, this means their choice of targets is severely limited.

Thus, although the parties are allowed to publish newspapers, they are subject to close surveillance and may not criticize royal institutions or behavior. In the early 1970s, for instance, an opposition editor was imprisoned for months without trial because his paper had printed a photograph of one of the young princes with his foreign nurse. Why the king took offense at this was never made public, but it was quickly understood that this sort of photograph should be cleared by the palace before being printed.

The traditional opposition, the Istiqlal, or Independence Party, is essentially conservative, old-line nationalist, and largely coopted and corrupted by the king through the award of cabinet posts to its senior members. The only meaningful, functioning opposition party today, the Socialist Union of

Popular Forces (USFP), a radical offshoot of the Istiqlal, is practically impotent following a series of misadventures. First the radical wing of the party was blamed for the Casablanca riots discussed below, and then its more moderate leadership was imprisoned for criticizing the king's decision to accept a referendum on the Sahara. The moderate leaders have since been released, but the party remains under threat of suppression, most of the radicals remain in prison, and its leadership is in disarray. So is its associated labor union, the Confederation Democratique du Travail (CDT). In November 1983, Hassan induced the USFP to participate in a new government of national union, which will have to bear responsibility for unpopular austerity measures, and the party's chief, Abderrahim Bouabid, joined the government as minister of state without portfolio, as did the leaders of the five other parties (excluding the Communists). This is a classic example of Hassan's cooptation tactics at work.

There is also a parliament[2] that includes members of the opposition, but it has no meaningful power and serves principally to ratify what has already been decided by the king and his advisers. In short, the opposition must be loyal and is allowed to exist primarily to confer legitimacy on the king, who suspended parliament for a number of years and would rather rule without it. He agreed to its restitution largely to refurbish his image as a moderate, not because hesincerely expects it to function along Western parliamentary lines.

At the time the French imposed their protectorate in 1912, Morocco had been divided for centuries into Bilad al-Makhzan and Bilad al-Siba, the Country of Government and the Country of Dissidence. The boundaries of Bilad al-Siba were variable, as was the degree of dissidence, depending on the state of the central government, but in the Berber tribal areas of the Atlas Mountains, the sultan's writ often did not run, even though tribal leaders might swear allegiance to him. The sultan's army was a collection of tribal levies around a small nucleus of regular forces, while the government establishment was rudimentary, consisting of the sultan and his numerous court, and the administration proper, composed of a handful of ministers, local governors and clerks. Government services were largely confined to security and collecting taxes to support the establishment, and the principal tool of governance was the royal procession, a large encampment that moved slowly about the countryside from time to time dispensing punishment and reward. Movement in the mountains for such a body was difficult, so those regions remained beyond the sultan's reach.

The French left the sultan's court more or less intact,[3] but imposed a modern administrative structure on the country and set about militarily pacifying the Bilad al-Siba, finally accomplishing the task in 1936 after some very difficult fighting during which they took high casualties (estimated by one source at 27,000 dead and 15,000 wounded). The present government, exercising its authority throughout the country and with no serious rivals for power, is the heir to this pacification.

The king's authority today rests ultimately on the security forces. As is the case in many former French colonies, and in present-day France, these are divided into sometimes competing elements. Most important are the Royal Armed Forces (the army, navy, and air force), with a total strength of about 140,000 officers and men. These are supplemented by a 11,000-man National Police force, and the 10,000-man Royal Gendarmerie, which is largely responsible for security in rural areas. There is a third police body, the 9,000-man Auxiliary Forces, a national guard-type organization controlled by the Ministry of the Interior. (The Gendarmerie comes under the army, while the police are controlled by the Sûreté Nationale, an autonomous body that reports directly to the king.)

The armed forces are well trained and effective. As noted earlier, Moroccan troops fought with distinction in the two world wars, and there is a strong fighting tradition among the Berbers in particular, although the pacification of their areas and the prohibition on rifled firearms instituted by the French has sharply diminished the feuding that was a way of life in nineteenth-century Morocco. Their equipment is modern, if modest by current Middle Eastern standards, and discipline is good. Accepted wisdom says they are loyal to the king, but this has not always been the case, and may not be tomorrow. He has had miraculous escapes from two very serious military coup attempts. The first, in July 1971, on the occasion of his birthday party at his summer palace at Skhirat, south of Rabat, led to the massacre of a number of guests, but the king himself emerged unharmed. The coup had been led by some of his most trusted officers. It failed because of poor planning and organization, not because of any effective response by those elements of the armed forces that had not been involved. Had the king been killed, as he would have had his hiding place in a guest suite been discovered, the rest of the armed forces probably would have gone along with the coup.

The second attempt occured in August 1972, when the air force, using U.S.-supplied F-5 aircraft, tried to shoot down the Royal Air Maroc Boeing 727 on which the king was returning from a trip to France. The inability of the air force to destroy an unarmed civilian aircraft said something about the quality of the instruction the pilots had received, the utility of the Northrup F-5, and the durability of Boeing aircraft. This plot had been masterminded by General Muhammed Oufkir, the minister of defense and chief of staff of the armed forces, who had been considered second only to the king and his most trusted lieutenant. Oufkir was executed and the armed forces drastically reorganized, with the king taking over direct command and all decisions of any importance being submitted to him first. Ammunition stocks were separated from the aircraft and units that could use them, no officers were allowed to have a rank higher than colonel for a number of years, all officer movements and transfers were screened by the king, and very little authority was left in the hands of the military. These measures led to an excess of centralization that interfered with military operations in the

Sahara, but they have been effective in keeping the armed forces under control. Hassan's tenure is, however, dependent on these forces remaining loyal. The wave of rumor and speculation that washed over the country after the death in January 1983 in a car accident of General Ahmed Dlimi, Oufkir's successor as the king's right-hand man, to the effect that Dlimi was assassinated because he was plotting a coup, indicates the depth of Moroccan skepticism regarding that loyalty.[4]

Hassan has some impressive assets. As the leading religious authority in the country, and as a man who has luck (as evidenced by his escapes in 1971 and 1972), which is an essential ingredient in Arab leadership, he clearly has *baraka*, or charisma. This was dramatically illustrated by the overwhelming popular response, particularly among poorer people, to his call for the Green March into the Sahara in 1975 (see Chapter 6), although how much of that response was spontaneous and how much was organized is moot. The response was to his quasi-religious appeal as much as it was to the fact that this *terra irredenta* had become a popular cause. His appeal was increased by the fact that he got away with it. He has also shown great skill and determination in coopting and supressing potential opposition, both within the armed forces and in the civilian elite, and in dealing with a series of crises. Barring accidents he may be able to continue this balancing act indefinitely, but his position is threatened by forces over which neither he nor anyone else has control. Foremost of these is the demographic factor and the increasing gap between production and population which it generates.

On June 20, 1981, the discontent generated by unemployment and inflation broke through the surface briefly at Casablanca, when a demonstration to protest price increases in bread and other basic commodities got out of hand and turned violent. A government communique three days later reported 66 persons had been killed, but diplomats in Morocco reported that 450 was a more accurate figure. The demonstration was organized by the Confederation Democratique du Travail (CDT), the union associated with the Union of Progressive Socialist Forces, the principal opposition party. According to a union official speaking a year after the event, neither the union nor the party had realized the depth and strength of the forces they were unleashing, but others claim the party's radical wing was deliberately trying to provoke a confrontation. The security forces may have overreacted in killing so many people, but less drastic action would perhaps not have sufficed to quell the riot, which had spread to the modern section of downtown Casablanca, and which could have led to a popular revolution if not promptly suppressed. CDT leaders were arrested following the incident, and some are still under arrest at this writing.

That this happened in Casablanca was not surprising. That city has long been the prime target of the rural-urban drift in Morocco. For years visitors have been taken to see its extensive and ever growing *bidonvilles*, or shantytowns, and have shaken their heads over the social problems they pose. The proportion of the population which is urban in the country as a whole has been growing at a rate of about 1 percent per year over the past 15 years. In 1960, 71.6 percent of the population was rural and only 28.4 percent urban. Today the respective figures are 52–55 and 45–48 percent, depending on your source. Casablanca, the largest city and the principal commercial and industrial center, has been growing at a rate of something close to 5 percent, and its population is approaching 4 million. Assuming that 3 percent of that growth is due to natural increase, 2 percent is made up of migrants. For the most part they are poor rural people who are looking for work. Unemployment, however, is close to 20–25 percent, and if we count underemployment, it approaches 40–50 percent. The absorptive capacity of Casablanca and other cities is limited and they cannot begin to meet the demand for jobs.

The debate over how to stem the tide has been going on for years, and the Moroccans have been no more effective in this regard than other countries that face the same problem. Population growth and limited rural employment create surplus rural population, and people drift into towns and cities looking for jobs and services. While the bidonvilles they live in are depressing to look at, they actually offer a somewhat higher level of living than is available to the rural poor. They provide electricity, potable water, and access to government schools and clinics as well as to the superior employment and entertainment facilities of the city. A great many of their inhabitants, however, are unemployed or underemployed young men, who make prime riot fodder.

These youths are by and large disaffected with the monarchy and do not share their parent's perception that the king has baraka. This disaffection seems to be more prevalent among urban than rural youth, the latter being less politicized and more conservative than the former. To a certain extent disaffection is obviously a function of education. The activists in the streets are often students, and university students traditionally have been more active than secondary, although the latter have been involved in bloody clashes in Casablanca in the past. As in other societies, family and job responsibilities that accrue after leaving school rapidly eat into the willingness and time for such activities. The high unemployment rate, on the other hand, tends to prolong the political activity period. Active ranks are also swollen by the nature of education in Morocco, which produces large numbers of half-educated youths who feel too educated to work as farm laborers but who have no skills to offer in the job market. They want to be clerks or messengers and to avoid getting their hands dirty. Unfortunately, there are not enough white-collar positions to go around, and these youths end up in a limbo between the manual and the office job.

The biggest single factor in producing disaffected youth is, of course, the population growth rate, traditionally described as one of the highest in the world, at 3.2 percent per year. In September 1982 Morocco underwent a new census, which may eventually tell us a good deal more about the birth and death rates used to calculate population growth (although there is a good deal of skepticism about the 20.5 million total figure given by the census, which may have been rigged, according to critics, because of the government's desire to appear less improvident than it actually is in its population policies).[5] Current estimates by U.S. population specialists indicate that the growth rate may be as low as 3 percent, which represents some improvement, but is still well beyond Moroccan abilities to feed. The problem is illustrated by the grain production and population figures.

At independence Morocco had been for some years an exporter of grain, largely to European markets, and as recently as 1956 cereals made up 18.5 percent of exports, but 1959–60 was the last harvest year in which Morocco was a net exporter of grain. There has been a substantial increase in *average* production since then, in spite of wide variations from year to year due to climatic differences, but it has not kept pace with the population. Whereas there was an exportable surplus in "normal" years before independence, today a "normal" crop only meets 65 percent of domestic requirements, because the population has roughly doubled.

Production of grain in 1980, for instance, was 40.3 million quintals (a *quintal* is a *hundredweight*, or 100 kilograms), an increase of 24 percent over 1958, which was described as a "very good" year in which 32.4 million were harvested. This increase is a remarkable achievement and reflects decades of patient development effort, but during the same period population increased 90–100 percent and it will continue to outstrip increased production without pause for at least the rest of this century. (U.S. experts estimate that Moroccan agriculture is producing at only 40 percent of capacity, but they do not expect the other 60 percent to be made up under present circumstances and policies.)

Agriculture in Morocco is divided into two sectors, the modern and the traditional. The former, developed by the French, uses modern machinery on large acreages of the better land, while the traditional sector uses primitive methods and very little if any machinery on small holdings that are often of marginal quality. The modern sector is efficient and profitable. It employs 3 percent of farm labor, farms 34 percent of the land and produces 85 percent of the commercial crops grown in the country. It produces most of the agricultural exports, but does not produce enough grain to feed the urban population. The other 97 percent of farm labor produces enough to feed the rural population (80 percent of all wheat produced is consumed on the farm) but does not actively market the surplus when it has any because much of the traditional sector is still subsistence and barter oriented. This discourages interest in newer farming methods, even where the marginal quality of the land is not already a serious obstacle.

The government, rightly or wrongly, has placed most of its emphasis on expanding the modern sector through large scale irrigation and development projects and has given low priority to the traditional, largely dry land sector. Steps are now being taken to correct this imbalance, but they are unlikely to have any dramatic impact, and thanks to the quality of rural life, the traditional sector will continue to provide recruits for the bidonvilles for years to come.

Unfortunately, there is not enough industry to absorb these recruits. On becoming independent, Morocco had a small industrial base, largely French-financed and concentrating on light industry, phosphates, and cement. This has undergone some expansion but not much. Contrary to popular impressions, mineral resources are limited. Morocco has 70–75 percent of the world's phosphate reserves and is the world's largest exporter of that mineral. This is the only mineral being exploited on a large scale today. Morocco also has large reserves of oil shale, but plans to exploit them that looked promising four years ago have not come to fruition because the price of oil has been too low to make them economic. Three U.S. companies are now prospecting for oil. A substantial gas field, enough to supply 25 percent of the country's energy requirements according to initial estimates, has been found in the area west of Marrakesh, but the petroleum age has not yet arrived in Morocco, occasional royal statements to the contrary notwithstanding.

Phosphate mining and a related chemical complex at Safi, on the Atlantic coast 100 miles south of Casablanca, have been the principal industrial successes of the country, successes that in the recent past have been augmented by the high price of phosphates, although demand and price have fluctuated in ways the Moroccans have been unable to control. There are, for instance, plans for extraction of uranium from phosphoric acid at the Safi plant, and negotiations with French and American companies over the contract have been in course for over five years, but they are in abeyance today because the price of uranium has dropped and the project is no longer economic. Morocco also has some of the richest fishing grounds in the world, but in spite of much discussion and planning, its fishing industry has yet to get started in a serious fashion. There has been limited development of iron ore deposits in the Rif area of northern Morocco, and there has been some expansion of light industry, notably textiles, handicrafts and a television assembly plant, but neither industry nor agriculture is keeping pace with the growth of population and labor supply. Fortunately, remittances from workers in Europe, which amounted to about $852 million in 1982 (down from $1 billion in 1981) and tourism, which brought 1.3 million foreigners to Morocco in 1982 (down from 1.65 million the year before), contributing about $300 million (half the 1981 figure) to foreign exchange earnings, have been important sources of income. Tourism, at least, can certainly be expanded, but both it and remittances have inherent limits and are subject to many variables, such as recession in Europe, which are not under Moroccan control, and which caused a net reduction of 350,000 in the number of tourists in 1982 as compared with 1981, a reduction that probably continued into 1983, judging from what what happened in Tunisia.

Worker remittances are now the largest single source of foreign exchange, but they are threatened by European efforts to reduce the numbers of foreign workers.

The government has long had a family planning program, under the Ministry of Health, but heretofore it has not been an area of high priority, and the attitude of Moroccan nationalists has been essentially natalist. The Istiqlal Party, for instance, maintains that Morocco can and should support a much larger population if it is to play its proper role in world affairs. Recent research in Marrakesh and elsewhere, however, indicates an unanticipated receptivity to family planning on the part of women belonging to modest, traditional families, and contraception appears to be practiced more commonly than had been thought. The king, who has by his private remarks indicated that he appreciates the need to bring down the birthrate, has been hesitant to do anything about it publicly for fear of eroding his support among the traditionalist elite. He seems finally to have moved, however, and the Moroccan government is undertaking a modest but imaginative campaign to bring family planning to rural women. This has had to be packaged as a mother and child health improvement scheme, rather than a population control operation, in order to avoid offending sensibilities of the traditionalists.

Meanwhile, and more ominously in the short term at least, Morocco has been living well beyond its means. In spite of massive input of foreign aid (by Moroccan government figures, foreign aid in 1981 totaled roughly $1.75 billion, to which should be added perhaps another $1 billion for arms purchases funded by other Arab states and not going through the budget), the Moroccans were already having difficulty meeting their current obligations in 1982 and were in arrears on payments to a wide range of creditors. Their debt service ratio reached 36 percent in 1982, and there was no relief in sight (barring discovery of substantial quantities of oil). Thus, Morocco had already joined the procession of Third World countries facing a spiraling indebtedness due to a concatenation of circumstances when the Saudis and other Arabs had to cut back their subventions because of reduced revenues due to the oil glut. No precise figures are available, but there seems to have been a drastic curtailment of such aid during the last half of 1982 and the first three quarters of 1983. This, plus the continued rise in the value of the dollar, precipitated a credit crisis that led to an international effort to reschedule and refinance about $1.8 billion of Morocco's short-term debt. As of the end of the third quarter in 1983, Morocco had no foreign currency reserves and an annual balance of payments deficit on the order of $2 billion per year; its long-term indebtedness was about $12 billion by April 1984 and its debt service ratio, not counting invariables, was put at a staggering 41 percent. As indicated earlier, much of the problem is due to circumstances beyond Morocco's control.

The 1980–81 drought, for instance, perhaps the worst of the century, entailed losses estimated at about 18 percent of the value of the GNP. It reduced grain production by over 50 percent and forced the importation of an added $350 million worth of grain. The three subsequent years have also been drier than "normal," and the country still considers itself to be in a drought. (Algeria and Tunisia have also been affected, but not as severely.) Other factors increasing indebtedness were the increased value of the dollar (which rose 35 percent against the dirham in the first half of 1981 and as of September 1983 cost roughly twice as much as it did in 1979), the rise in interest rates, the 1981 increase in oil prices, which must be paid in more expensive dollars, and the soft market for phosphates due to the European recession. To this should be added the cost of the Sahara War, which is difficult to determine because few figures are public. Estimates by local observers, however, put military expenditures at something between 35 and 40 percent of the government budget as of the end of 1981 (compared with 20 percent in Algeria) and this does not include the expenditures for arms financed by other Arabs, nor the sizable amounts going into civilian infrastructure in the Sahara. It is argued that with the military situation in the Sahara stabilized, expenses there do not add all that much to the inevitable expense of maintaining a military establishment. This argument overlooks the fact that the military establishment has had to be expanded greatly over its pre-Saharan size (from 85,000 to 140,000), which would not have been necessary had there been no Saharan war. The added logistics burden of supporting the distant Sahara campaign is furthermore a serious addition to military expenses, not to mention the added expense of the fuel and munitions involved in maintaining the current military posture, even while sheltering behind a defensive wall. As a result of these demands, military expenditures per capita quadrupled in the period 1973–1978, according to Overseas Development Council figures.

In 1978 U.S. government specialists estimated that the war was costing Morocco $1 million a day. That figure should at least be doubled and probably trebled to make it current. (There are no reliable figures on the cost of the war to Algeria. Its principal expenses are the feeding of Saharan refugees and the supply of water, gas, and oil to the Polisario guerrillas.) The king's efforts to find a settlement based on a referendum reflect his realization that this leak must be plugged before it becomes fatal to his regime. Although universal Moroccan support for the Saharan annexation has mitigated the risk somewhat, the drain on resources limits his ability to deal with underlying social problems, which broke through the surface again in widespread disturbances in January 1984. They were apparently sparked by rises in food prices and unpopular policies regarding school fees and smuggling. It would be a mistake to conclude, however, as the CIA did in 1979, that the days of the Alaouite monarchy are necessarily numbered. That prediction was a hedging operation by an organization under fire for its poor performance in Iran, and foretelling disaster in the Arab world has always been a way to gain a reputation for prescience, because something bad usually happens sooner or later. The prediction was premature in 1979, and still is. Hassan is likely to be with us for some time.

His road will not be easy, however. There has been continuing, and sometimes violent, opposition to Hassan among urban intellectuals and youth almost from the day of his ascension to the throne. This is based as much on opposition to his person as it is on ideology or bread and butter issues. A young man with a reputation for dissoluteness and arrogance while crown prince (in sharp contrast to the rather saintly reputation of his father, Mohamed V), he was and is cordially disliked by many of the regime's intellectual have-nots—university students and professors, opposition party officials, labor leaders, and those other politically active individuals who have not yet been coopted by government favors (as many of them have).

The formal opposition was largely pre-empted by the Green March, however, and there has been something of a political truce in effect ever since. All of the parties have supported the king's Sahara policies, the only exceptions being when he has been accused of taking too soft a line, as by the USFP in the summer of 1981. That party withdrew from Parliament in protest following the arrest of its leaders for criticizing the king but returned to rally around the government when the Moroccans suffered a major defeat at Polisario hands at Guelta Zemmour in October of the same year, showing the unified support Hassan has for a hard-line Saharan policy. Opposition leaders have made it clear, however, that their unity in the face of external opposition does not mean they have accepted the king's domestic policies, the most controversial of which is his monopoly of power. His rigging of the June 10, 1983 municipal elections, for instance, was severely criticized by the Istiqlal Party's paper. Once the Sahara conflict is resolved the opposition will return to the fray over a host of internal issues, from denial of civil liberties and maldistribution of wealth to waste and corruption in the royal establishment, and it will contest Hassan's right to decide all issues.

Hassan thus faces a series of challenges, the most difficult of which is the socioeconomic one. Settlement of the Sahara dispute is also crucial, for reasons of army loyalty as well as economy, and so is the problem of political expression. His success in dealing with these problems will determine whether or not there is stability in Morocco and, ultimately, in the region.

The subject of stability, and how to maintain it in the Third World, is complex, and there is not space to examine it in any detail here, but a few words are perhaps appropriate. The various recipes for dealing with instability narrow down to two approaches: repression and close control, on the one hand, or institution building and socioeconomic development on the other. The difficulty with the second approach in the Third World is that for one reason or another the body politic is rarely able to develop and maintain enough loyalty to the state, as opposed to the family, tribe, sect, or other group, to permit the building of viable and permanent institutions. The rule of law is too abstract, and too unreliable, given the corruption of local officials and leaders, and government almost inevitably becomes the personal affair either of autocratic leaders or autocratic party elites. These leaders, when not motivated simply by a desire for power, face a common dilemma: how to share power without losing it. Power is finite; to share it is to lose some of it, and sometimes all of it. Autocrats are therefore required to rule autocratically if they want to survive, and they rarely have opportunities for creating democratic institutions, even when they want to. When they try, it rarely works, and when it does, there are exceptional circumstances. Whatever the autocrat does, change is inevitable, and often it will be rapid and violent. The problem for Third World leaders is not so much how to prevent it, which can be done to a certain extent by repression, as it is how to permit it and keep it within tolerable limits.

Fears of instability in North Africa and the Middle East have been increased since 1979 by the specter of Islamic reformism, commonly called fundamentalism, which is generally perceived as a threat to the established order from the right. Indeed, the fundamentalists call into question the legitimacy of all governments of the region, with the possible exception of Iran's. While it appears that the forces of order in the states of North Africa are strong enough to keep their activities under a reasonable degree of control, they are a pole of attraction for dissidence, and opposition forces strong enough to pose serious threats to local regimes may one day coalesce around them (a fuller discussion of this subject will be found in Chapter 5). They apparently played an active role in the Tunisian and Moroccan disturbances of December–January 1983–1984. An autocratic regime is generally better able to prevent this happening than a democratic one would be, but suppression does little to eliminate the basic causes of dissidence, which relate to the regime's disregard of Islamic principles in favor of Western ideas and techniques (in this respect, Marxism is considered by the neoreformists to be as much a Western ideology as is capitalism).

In the case of Morocco, the question is whether the risks of instability are manageable and, if not, what can be done about them. The sobering fact is that there is not much that outside powers can do about such problems in advance of local collapse. Nor is it at all clear that they should try. The responsibility is primarily that of the local government, and while outsiders can offer advice and help, their ideas are not necessarily the best. After the coup attempts of the early 1970s, for instance, various prominent Moroccans urged U.S. representatives to convince King Hassan of the need for land reform along the pattern of the shah's White Revolution. Given Hassan's intolerance of unsolicited advice, the Americans did not try a direct approach, but prevailed on the shah to speak to him as a brother monarch who had bitten the bullet. The shah tried and failed. Hassan was apparently unwilling to listen. There was no distribution of royal lands (which are extensive) and no breaking up of large Moroccan holdings, but remaining French holdings were eventually expropriated and distributed. At this point it is too early to tell whether Hassan erred or was correct. He probably would point to the shah's fall and ask where land reform got *him*. The point is that just because some remedy seems necessary and useful to reasonable outsiders does not mean it will work in practice, or that the outsider has the right to suggest it, much less impose it.

There is a considerable body of opinion supporting the thesis that economic and social development are the long-term keys to political stability, and yet the effects of education and economic advancement, two of the concomitants of development, are often destabilizing. We need somehow to promote both change and stability at the same time, or to ensure that change is evolutionary, but this requires a maturity of political systems and outlook that is rare in the Third World. Hassan has at least shown a consistent approach to this problem. He pursues policies of limited economic and social development that, while misguided, insufficient, and unsatisfactory to many, are at least rational. Meanwhile he controls the opposition, repressing it when it is fractious and rewarding it when it cooperates. He has thereby managed either to compromise or to buy off many of his critics. This demands agility, and the long-term outcome is uncertain, but it has worked in the sense that matters are no worse than they were in most respects, and are better in some: the country functions with relative efficiency; if there is not much money to spread around, there also are none of the grandiose sinkholes one finds in the oil-producing states; there is some upward social mobility; there is some room for the opposition to maneuver in and let off steam; and the army follows orders. While one can never be certain, the risk of violent change in Morocco is probably no greater than it is in other states of the region, which have neither Morocco's sense of national identity nor its long history of independent rule.

Hassan's reaction to the 1981 disturbances in Casablanca, for instance, was to revamp radically the city's government, breaking it up into five separate prefectures and putting eager young officials in charge of them, each competing with the others. They have made a determined effort to clean up the city and the bidonvilles, and to find employment, even if only leaf raking, for the unemployed. At the same time, the Confederation Democratique du Travail, which organized the demonstration that became a riot, has been reduced to a paper organization for the time being, its leaders in prison, its meetings banned, and its funds frozen. This is the classic Moroccan balancing act, punishment for the rebellious and rewards for the docile.

The cleanup of Casablanca costs money, however, and we return to the never-ending problem of where the funds will come from to provide the jobs and the food for the expanding population. While foreign aid and a good deal of hard work have helped the country make some impressive progress in urban infrastructure and amenities, they have also led to an unhealthy dependence on foreign generosity, which can be turned off at any time if circumstances change. As noted earlier, this has now happened, thanks to the oil glut, and Morocco is now in serious financial trouble. Various austerity measures are being taken, and this will severely limit expenditures for social welfare, development, and job creation. The January 1984 riots showed how unpopular austerity is, and this could eventually prove fatal to the regime.

So the speculation about Hassan goes on. It is remarkable how ready the outsider is to believe the worst, and Moroccans are weary of visitors asking when the explosion will come. Tunisian officials, for instance, seem to believe the situation in Morocco ready to blow up at any moment. Spanish officials in Madrid think Hassan's days are numbered because he is corrupt and extravagant. French officials are concerned that socioeconomic problems make the situation very dangerous, and the Algerians believe U.S. support is the key to Hassan's survival. These concerns and predictions seem much more pertinent in Madrid or Paris than they do in Rabat, but they reflect a common perception that the situation in Morocco is essentially unhealthy.

Hassan has shown himself to be aware of his country's problems. He has said that he has many contacts, that he has a stethoscope constantly connected to his people and knows when they are sick and when they are well. This is pretty fatuous, because he suffers from the isolation common to all leaders, made even worse in his case by a servile press and court, with none of his advisors being willing to contradict him, but he does have a very competent intelligence service, relying on a wide network of informers, and it is in a position to know what is going on. Such systems inevitably corrupt the messages they transmit, of course, and this one has failed twice to detect the most serious threats to his life, but it still seems to function better than, say, SAVAK. He at least knows what some people are saying about him, and his public remarks reflect this from time to time, as when he emphasized in a speech in 1982 that something must be done about the extremes of wealth and poverty in the country. These extremes are not as striking today as they were in the early 1970s, but there are many Moroccans to whom this is a vital issue, and it is to Hassan's credit that he realizes this. Whether he can or will do anything meaningful to level the differences is another question. Judging by past performance, he will not, and wealthy Moroccans continue to invite the revolution by engaging in conspicuous consumption.

Hassan must also be aware that corruption in and around the royal establishment, although modest by Third World standards, is another continuing problem. The proximate cause of the 1971 coup attempt (the assault on the king's birthday party at Skhirat) was corruption, then very widespread at the highest levels of the government, and involving cabinet ministers and the royal family. Today corruption is still pervasive at the lower levels, as it always has been, beginning with the unfortunate patient in a government hospital who must pay a bribe to insure that he gets the medicine prescribed for him. At the upper levels, it is less conspicuous than it once was, but there are a number of royal cronies who continue to profit from their positions, and the popular perception is that corruption is still the rule rather than the exception. If nothing else, the opposition will eventually make an issue of the money the king is spending on palaces and real estate in Morocco and abroad.

The regime is also periodically accused of denying human liberties. In spite of official denials that there are political prisoners in Morocco, there have always been a number of them, and Amnesty International anually gives Morocco (as well as most Third World countries) a poor report card. The arrest of USFP leaders for criticizing the king's position on the Sahara was an illustration of what occurs regularly. The Moroccan record is, however, not bad by Third World standards. Moroccan security authorities are fully as brutal as their colleagues elsewhere, but this is not as much of an issue it might be in a Western society, because it comes within a long tradition of brutal treatment, which if anything is milder today than it was 20 years ago.

Put these all together and what conclusions does one draw? To the Eastern Arab, Morocco seems particularly blessed, with productive soil and water, with a variety of resources that can be exploited, and with social, economic and political problems that seem moderate by Near Eastern standards. The Arab-Israel problem is remote, industry is not dependent on foreign workers, and the Moroccans are admirably independent and self-assured, without the neuralgic complexes that bedevil many eastern Arabs, or so it seems. If the Moroccan people are mobilized to exploit their resources—their fisheries, their soil, their minerals, their skills—more effectively than they have been, they should be able to cope with the population dynamic.

The reality, however, is that they are unlikely to be effectively mobilized under the present system, which is too much concerned with keeping the Alaouites in power and not sufficiently concerned with what is happening at the lower levels of society. While Hassan may be kept aware of his country's problems, his ability to deal with them is limited by a shortage of resources and ideas. The elite that surrounds him is not allowed to think for itself and is therefore incapable of coming forward with the leadership that the country needs. Thinking is the king's prerogative, and he thinks he is smarter than anyone else. This is a common disease of autocrats. Indeed, Hassan *is* smarter than most of the people around him, but they have been picked more for loyalty than brains. That loyalty may survive adversity, but it does not provide the intelligent support he needs.

It is unlikely, for these and other reasons, that Morocco's problems will be solved, but they never have been, and this need not mean Hassan will fall. Rather, I would expect him to last indefinitely if for no other reason than that the alternatives are worse. The risk for him is, as in the past, a military coup, the leaders of which will not have given much thought to what will come after, or assassination by some individual who feels wronged. Either of these could occur tomorrow, but there is nothing inevitable about them. Certainly, with any luck Hassan will outlast the present Republican administration in Washington.

The heir to the throne, Sidi Muhammad, is a young man in his early twenties. He is at present an unknown quantity, as are his chances of acceding to the throne in the event his father should be displaced (rather than die a natural death). Many observers of the local scene do not think his chances are very good, but he may surprise all of them. He is increasingly being used by the king as his personal representative, and this should be useful training for him. On the other hand, he projects a very undynamic and uninspiring image.

The most likely alternative to the Alaouites is rule by a military leader or junta. No organization other than the military has the power base with which to take over. General Dlimi was the obvious leader of such a junta, although his loyalty had not been questioned before his death. The most probable formula today would be a military coup led by a group of middle-grade officers (the ones at the top being too closely identified with the king), perhaps touched off by popular discontent with domestic policies, or by military discontent with Sahara policies, such as a compromise settlement that brought Moroccan sacrifices there to nought. What the orientation of the officers who came to power would be is hard to say. They could very well take a line like Qadhdhafi's, or they could be essentially moderate pragmatists. Dlimi, for instance, had close working contacts with American intelligence officers for years and was highly regarded by them. One would have expected him to be a moderate, not to say conservative, leader. On the other hand, the Ahmed Rami mentioned above, who said that Dlimi had been plotting a coup and was in touch with him, claimed to be a Nasserist and said Dlimi had asked him to get in touch with the Libyans. He also claimed that Dlimi had been in touch with other Moroccan opposition figures in exile. If this story is true, it would indicate that Dlimi might not have been all that moderate inside.

These allegations highlight the perennial problem of the political forecaster in this part of the world. In a climate of suppression, people dissemble and pretend to be something they are not. It is hard to know what they are like until they are free of constraints and can act themselves. For most of them, that never happens until it is too late to help the forecaster.

In sum, then, Morocco is a case of arguing whether the glass is half full or half empty. It has many assets, but it has problems that are insoluble in the short term, and perhaps in the long term as well. Inertia being what it is, the most probable course for Morocco to follow is a continuation of its present one. It may be diverted from it by some cataclysm, but otherwise it will continue to rock along in a way that satisfies no one, but that is at least tolerable.

Notes

[1]For a discussion of the legal implications of the king's position as Commander of the Faithful, see the article by Jean Deprez, "Perennite de l'Islam dans l'Ordre Juridique au Maghreb" in *Islam et Politique au Maghreb*, edited by Ernest Gellner and Jean-Claude Vatin (Paris: CNRS, 1981).

[2]Seven of the eight recognized political groups or parties were represented in the last parliament (whose mandate expired in 1983; a new one is to be elected in 1984): National Group of Independents (RNJ)—84 seats, a royalist bloc led by the king's brother-in-law, Ahmad Osman; created at royal direction in 1977, it is the officially designated opposition; Democratic Indepedents—57 seats; Socialist Union of Popular Forces (USFP)—13 seats; The Popular Movement (MP)—41 seats, a largely rural, Berber grouping loyal to the king and conservative in view; Party for Progress and Socialism (PPS)—1 seat, the Moroccan Communist party, now legal. The party is too small to have influence but has a following among youth and the disaffected.

In January 1983 the then prime minister, Maati Bouabid, himself a former USFP leader who relinquished his opposition role to accept the more tangible benefits of high government position, announced plans to form a new "centrist monarchical" party. This was an exercise in redundancy, and meant a pro forma reshuffling of alignments among the already docile. The party, called the Constitutional Union, elected Bouabid as its president on April 10, 1983.

The eighth group, the National Union of Popular Forces, the original radical opposition party, now much weakened by internal divisions and the loss of members to the USFP, did not participate in the last parliamentary elections (May 1981) and was not represented. It is associated with the largest labor federation, the Union Marocaine du Travail (UMT).

[3]Waterbury describes it as having been put in mothballs.

[4]See, for instance, the account in the February 24, 1983 *Le Monde* of the declaration by Ahmed Rami, a former junior officer of the Moroccan army, who maintained that Dlimi was the leader of a group of "free officers" called the August 16 Movement, in commemoration of the August 16, 1972 attack on the royal Boeing. There has been no confirmation of his allegations, which are discounted by officials in Washington. In Paris, on the other hand, "no one" believes Dlimi's death was accidental, according to North African observers there.

[5]The official figure was 20,419,000, of which 8,730,000, or 42 percent, were urban. This would give a population growth rate of 2.6 percent, which is probably too low. There are Moroccan observers who argue that the figure is closer to 28 million. The Department of State is using a compromise figure of 22.5 million.

3

Algeria

Algeria, like Morocco, surprises by its fertility. The traveler who lands at Algiers expecting to see date palm and sand finds himself in a semitropical garden on the edge of a rich agricultural region extending far inland. Its 20 million people, like those of Morocco, are mixed Arab and Berber, traditionally dependent on herding and agriculture, but having enjoyed considerably less isolation and immunity from external pressures than the Moroccans. The Ottoman Turks were in occupation here and, more importantly, so were the French, who brought Westernization 80 years before it came to Morocco, and who left a lasting imprint on the Algerian personality as well as on the industrial, administrative, and social infrastructure of the country.

If there is one single fact to be kept in mind about the Democratic and Popular Republic of Algeria, it is that this state came into being as a result of a particularly bitter and prolonged struggle for national liberation. The harshness of that struggle, and the odds against which the Algerians fought, have given them a sense of moral superiority not unlike that of the early Americans. Unlike most Third World peoples, they won their independence the hard way rather than as the result of political action by others. To them, their revolution ranks with those of China and Russia, and their credentials give them great confidence, not to say smugness, in arguing what policies other countries should follow.

The revolution lasted for eight years, from November 30, 1954 until July 5, 1962. Estimates of casualties vary widely, the number of Algerians killed being put at 250,000 by the French and at 1,500,000 by the Algerians. Perhaps one-third of the native population was displaced from its villages and hamlets, and as many as 8,000 of the latter were destroyed. The French committed an army of 500,000 men and 200,000 Algerian auxiliaries to fight the war, which more than any other single independence struggle set the seal on the colonial period in Africa. It also scarred and unified the Algerian people, and it has deeply affected the way in which the country is run today.

When the French finally left, they took most of the trained cadre with them, because it was 80 to 100 percent non-Algerian, depending on the sector. They had avoided educating the Algerians, who had been destined to remain second class, and only 10 to 20 percent of the latter were literate in any language. Even the blue collar jobs as blacksmiths, plumbers, mechanics, and carpenters had been held largely by immigrants from Spain, Italy, Corsica, and France, who had been encouraged to come and swell the European segment of the population. The most the poor Algerian could realistically aspire to was employment as a laborer or field hand or, if he was very lucky, as a clerk. While a small Algerian bourgeoisie survived it all, in part by adapting to colonial rule, the bulk of Algeria's 10 million people were ignorant, poor, and untrained.

With almost no experienced personnel left to run the apparatus of government, to manage the economy or to repair anything, there was a near collapse of both government and economy, and of agriculture in particular, a trauma that was made worse than it need have been by the erratic policies of the first independent government under President Ahmed Ben Bella. These difficulties did not prevent Ben Bella and his associates from playing a major role in Third World politics, however. Indeed, their devotion to cutting a wide swathe abroad was one factor that made the domestic situation so chaotic.

When Houari Boumediene came to power, through a military coup in 1965, he began a determined effort to establish a disciplined and effective government and to put the country on the road to economic development financed by oil and gas revenues. He also pulled in Algeria's international horns and shunned the flamboyant image that Ben Bella had projected. The ascetic and impersonal nature of his approach was indicated by his first television performance—the screen was blank and only his voice was heard.

Boumediene was a product of the revolution. The son of a poor farmer in eastern Algeria, he had received a traditional, that is, religious, education and then gone off to study first at the Zitouna University in Tunisia and then at its Egyptian counterpart, al-Azhar, both centers of traditional Islamic learning. In Egypt he began to work at the headquarters of the provisional Algerian government established there, and eventually became a military commander, emerging as a leading member of the Oujda Clan, a group of military commanders in the west who were rivals for influence with other clans in the central and eastern regions. Boumediene owed his rise to prominence to, among other things, the fact that he was one of the few Algerian leaders who was literate in Arabic and who could speak the language correctly, because he had had a traditional education.

Boumediene brought with him a conspiratorial outlook born of his revolutionary past. He had come to power by plotting against Ben Bella, and was always alert to the possibility of plots against himself, living a secretive private life, trusting few people, and keeping a tight hold on the reins of power. The revolution had been conducted under collegial leadership, however, and at least a semblance of collegiality was maintained through the single party, the same Front de Liberation Nationale (FLN) that had conducted the revolution and that had a highly structured political organization going down to the village level. The party served more as window dressing, however, than as an effective political instrument, and so did the National Assembly, or Parliament, which was largely a projection of the party. There was also the National Council of the Revolution, made up of the surviving leaders of the revolution, who were supposed to concur in major policy decisions. In actual practice, the decisions were made by Boumediene, and the Council of the Revolution was summoned rarely, usually in order to confer legitimacy on something Boumediene had already decided. He had to take its views into account, and he had to think about public opinion and attitudes within the party, but he was fully as autocratic as Hassan II.

During the Ben Bella period, and in the early years of Boumediene's tenure, service in the revolution was the principal qualification for government office. Education and technical competence were secondary, partly because there were not many educated people around. Boumediene gradually reversed this situation, bringing in a group of educated young technocrats, many of whom had been sent abroad to study during the revolution, and who were given significant parts of the government to run, particularly in the economic and foreign affairs sectors. Of a caliber equal to that found anywhere, it is this technocratic elite that largely runs the country today, sharing power with the army and with an administrative elite composed of senior officials and party leaders. The technocrats tend to be modernizers with Western ideas, while the administrative and party elite is more traditional, given its popular roots. The military are the moderating force between the two.

Algeria has thus developed a tripartite political system. While the public has a voice through local, provincial, and national assemblies, these, as well as the FLN, serve principally as transmission belts for guidance going downward rather than ideas coming up. An exception was the rather refreshing debates, conducted in public and on television, about the drafting of a national charter in 1976. Individual Algerians would stand up and over national television make complaints about governmental corruption and incompetence for all to see and hear. These complaints were reflected in the final document (152 pages in its English version) produced by the debate. A statement of principles on all aspects of domestic and foreign affairs, it describes itself as the "supreme source of the nation's policy" and was designed to guide the drafting of the new constitution as well as the actions of the government. It is used more to justify than to guide decisions, but at least it institutionalizes the national consensus on such matters as the meaning and nature of Algerian socialism.

Boumediene died of a rare malady in December 1978. There was no prime minister or vice president and there was no designated successor, but in spite of the lack of what Western commentators consider viable political institutions, the Algerians proceeded with remarkable calm to pick one—Chadli Benjedid, military commander of the Oran region. This was independent Algeria's first peaceful succession.

Benjedid was selected by a special congress of the FLN as the single candidate to be confirmed by a national election the following month.[1] The fact that this leftist party would pick a man considered to be a middle-of-the-road moderate rather than his more radical opponent, Col. Muhammad Salah Yahyawi, executive secretary of the party, was significant. It occurred because Ben Jedid had the support of the military faction, which had 640 of the 3,290 delegates in the party congress and which represented the 70,000-man Algerian People's Army. As John Entelis notes, "the military remains the most decisive elite group in Algerian politics today."[2] Broadly based in geographical and social terms, the Army is the most cohesive organization in Algeria and has consistently played a strategic role in internal political struggles. In spite of revolutionary rhetoric, it has acted as a stabilizing force, apparently motivated more by professional considerations than politics. Its support of Boumediene against Ben Bella, for instance, was at least partly designed to restore stability and discipline. Its support of Benjedid seems to have been motivated by a desire to moderate the policies followed by Boumediene, particularly in the economic and social fields, and to avoid the more radical policies Yahyawi's election would have implied. (Yahyawi was subsequently dismissed from his FLN party coordinator position and from the Central Committee as well as the Politburo.)

Benjedid's powers theoretically have been reduced from those held by Boumediene, who was head of state, chairman of the Council of the Revolution, minister of defense, and president of the FLN, and who functioned as his own prime minister. After his death a 160-man central committee of the FLN and a 17-member politburo were established, and a prime minister selected by the central committee. These reforms have not been totally effective, however. By the summer of 1980, Benjedid had reduced the politburo to seven members, later increased to ten, half of whom are military, taken the interior ministry away from the prime minister, Mohammed Abdul Ghani, and reestablished the army general staff, which had been dissolved 13 years earlier after an abortive coup attempt against Boumediene. The Fifth Party Congress subsequently elected a new central committee of 164 members and established the politburo's membership as 9 to 15.

Under Benjedid, there has been a substantial moderation of policies followed by Boumediene, particularly in the economic and social fields, but also in the field of foreign affairs. This trend was confirmed and strengthened by the Fifth Party Congress resolutions. While it is too early to start writing a balance sheet, he seems to be considerably more pragmatic and less ideological than Boumediene, and Algeria under his leadership is playing a perceptibly less dynamic role in Third World politics.[3] Compared to its revolutionary past, Algeria has become something of a status quo power.

If one is permitted a second fact to remember, it is that Algeria has an unusual dynamic potential compounded of its oil and gas resources (development of which began in the colonial period), and the determination of its leaders to play a world role. While Algerian expectations in both regards have sometimes been disappointed, it is remarkable what has been accomplished to date in terms of domestic nation-building and gaining international stature.

Boumediene maintained that there could be no political independence without industrial independence. States that had to rely on the industrialized powers of the West and East to supply finished products in return for their raw materials would never be able to resist the economic and political pressures those powers could exert. He was determined to make Algeria industrially independent, and with the dramatic increase in oil prices after the 1973 embargo, his potential for so doing appeared to increase proportionately. Although burdened by a serious shortage of trained manpower and handicapped by a perceived necessity to follow a centralized socialist path on which there was no room for significant private enterprise, the Algerians set out to achieve the dream of industrial self-sufficiency. They made a number of costly mistakes against the advice of most outsiders, whether private U.S. consultants or Soviet advisers, guided by a philosophy that said they could produce machine tools competitive with those made in Germany if they only put their will and money to the task. Admirable as this goal might have been, it was totally unrealistic given their desperate need for trained technicians and the absence of a tradition of craftmanship or mechanical skills in a very badly educated population.

In their search for the modernity, and their disdain for traditional colonial enterprises such as textiles, the Algerians opted for capital-intensive, high technology projects and industries instead of more modest, labor-intensive undertakings that would have been closer to their capabilities. As a result, the country is strewn with overly ambitious industrial plants that are functioning at only a fraction of their capacity, if at all.

Some of these mistakes have been, or will be corrected, and Algeria will eventually arrive at least part way to the goal set for it by Boumediene, but the errors have been costly not only in terms of overspending, but also in terms of social consequences. The austerity imposed on the country in order to save petroleum revenues for development, combined with the capital intensive approach, led to a serious unemployment problem (or rather, did not resolve the one that already existed)[4] and to considerable public discontent with the lack of goods and services.

While the technocrats concentrated on industrialization, the Algerians largely neglected agriculture. Here, as in Morocco, the French left behind a network of flourishing, modern farms, and these had made Algeria the richest agricultural region in North Africa. Because the French had run their farms to the exclusion of the Algerians, few of the latter had any management experience to speak of. This, plus the revolutionary outlook of the

Algerian government, made it inevitable that the farms would either be run by the government or turned over to workers' committees. The workers' ignorance of management was tragic enough, but their task was further complicated by the installation of a burdensome bureaucracy above them that served to stultify efforts at rational production and marketing.

For their part, the farm workers were paid whether they worked well or not, and many naturally lost interest in doing a good job. Their interest was further reduced by the practice of paying the collectives in chits redeemable only at pitifully stocked cooperative stores, with none of the desirable consumer goods that might have incited the workers to produce. Farm production and maintenance plummeted as the farm laborers and managers worked to supply their own needs and were little interested in creating a marketable surplus. Using the techniques of revolutionary socialism, the Algerians had succeeded in creating a situation remarkably similar to that which prevails in the traditional sector of Moroccan agriculture. Unfortunately, they did it in the modern sector, which employs half the farm labor force.

The result was an appalling shortage of agricultural produce and the expenditure of vital oil revenues to import potatoes from Scotland and eggs from Poland into what should have been a flourishing market garden with an exportable surplus. Meanwhile, the lack of consumer goods and distractions in the countryside, and the unexciting career prospects of socialist agriculture, drove large numbers of young men into urban centers, where capital intensive industry offered little change of employment but where the lights were brighter.

Although the Algerians have by and large avoided the bidonville plague, and although their people are generally better fed and receive better education and social services than the Moroccans, they too have a serious problem with hordes of half-educated young men who have nothing to do. A stroller in either downtown Rabat or Algiers on a sunny winter afternoon will encounter very similar concentrations of young male idlers, who often make walking on the sidewalk impossible and who provide a ready supply of potential dissidents. In spite, or perhaps because, of Algeria's oil wealth, unemployment in Algeria is, if anything, higher than it is in Morocco, because free social services and subsidies make it easier to live there without working.

It is not clear which of these populations has the greater capacity for violence, the Moroccan or the Algerian. There have, however, been many instances of civil disobedience in Algeria over the years since independence, particularly among university students and among the Berbers of the Kabyle region east of Algeria, and although the population is closely controlled it is far from docile. It would be a mistake to assume that because of its revolutionary rhetoric the Algerian regime is safe from further revolution. Indeed, the rivalries of different revolutionary factions and the discontent of many Algerians with the socialist policies of Boumediene, a discontent manifested at one point by widely circulated antiregime tracts, could eventually have led to serious unrest. This did not happen, however, because, for one thing, policies began to change with Boumediene's death. For another, there are limits as to how far any such unrest can go as long as the armed forces remain loyal.

After promising to continue the path staked out by Boumediene, Benjedid has gradually steered the country along a more pragmatic and less ideological course, cautiously liberalizing political life, reorganizing the FLN to make it more responsive to popular needs, encouraging private enterprise and loosening the regime of austerity imposed by his predecessor. One of his first acts on assuming office was to lift the requirement that Algerians have exit visas in order to leave the country. This, plus a general, if limited, lessening of political surveillance and pressure, has permitted a much needed letting off of steam and led to a perceptibly more relaxed atmosphere. The lifting of the exit visa requirement in particular lightened considerably the rather oppressive air of Algiers, and it has been taken advantage of widely. Thus, the American Embassy, which issued almost no tourist visas in the mid-1970s, issued close to 2,000 during 1982, mostly to parents visiting children studying in the United States.

Benjedid's encouragement of the private sector says something about the nature of Algerian socialism. While the National Charter of 1976 refers repeatedly to Algeria as a socialist state, and goes into great detail to explain the application of socialist principles to the various facets of society, it also makes clear that this is a pragmatic socialism, which " . . . does not proceed from any materialist metaphysics and has no connection with any dogmatic conceptions foreign to our national genius. The building of socialism in Algeria is identified with the full development of the Islamic values which are a basic constituent in the personality of the Algerian people." In other words, it is not scientific socialism as defined by Marx (who is not mentioned in the charter), but an eclectic mixture, the fundamental principles of which, as listed in the charter, are: (1) "Abolition of the exploitation of man by man," meanwhile recognizing "private ownership which does not exploit the workers," the continuance of which "is not governed by temporary convenience but by ideological choice" and the existence of which is "not inconsistent with the present historical stage in which the socialist sector occupies a predominant place." (2) "Integrated and harmonious development on a planned basis, scientific in conception, democratic in elaboration and imperative in application." (3) "Work: not only a right but also a duty and an honor." (4) "Priority to the satisfaction of the basic needs of the popular masses." (Accent is on the *basic*. Elsewhere the charter makes clear that for the time being, austerity will be the rule because of development needs.) (5) "Liberation of the individual and his promotion as a responsible citizen."

While it is made clear that the workers and the peasants are the political vanguard, and owners of businesses are disqualified from public office, there is no talk of class struggle, and while capitalism, feudalism, and the comprador class are all rejected, Algerian socialism "rejects the simple minded egalitarianism which takes no account of personal merit and individual talent and merely rewards mediocrity." Elsewhere the charter makes it clear that Algerian economic cooperation with capitalist states is necessary for purposes of development, although it warns that it must be done on Algerian terms and that the Algerians must guard against capitalist attempts to set up labor-intensive industry in Algeria because it is no longer profitable at home. This language may have been considered necessary to justify the very substantial cooperation with American, French, British, Italian, Brazilian, Belgian, Japanese, and other firms from capitalist states. At the time the charter was written, American companies held or were bidding on some $2 billion worth of construction contracts in Algeria, a figure that subsequently increased dramatically as additional liquefied natural gas facilities were planned, and then shrank back to $2 billion or less as the price problem and Algerian decisions to husband their gas reserves more carefully resulted in reduced contracts. (The liquefied gas problem is discussed further below.)

The charter is now eight years old, and although still described as a basic document, it is a product of the previous regime, many members of which have been put out to pasture, or even indicted, by Benjedid, and it is clear that he is even less dogmatic about socialist ideology than the drafters of the charter were. One of the most important areas of liberalization has been in the encouragement of "non-exploitive" private enterprise, officially announced in December 1981. Consumer goods have reappeared in local markets, which are visibly better stocked than they were five years earlier, and a surprising number—several thousand, by one estimate—of private enterprises had come to light or been started by mid-1982. A good deal more money had remained in private hands than had been suspected, and now that private enterprise is no longer considered disreputable much of it has come out of the closet to reveal that there had been some substantial light industrial operations, particularly in textiles, going on all these years behind blank facades. Many of the several thousand are only cottage enterprises, but at least 60 have work forces of more than 100. Although this represents only a small portion of the economy, the Algerians hope that private activity will create more employment as well as consumer goods, and that it will provide some of the infrastructure that public sector industrialization has failed to do, particularly in housing.

The government is also selling to Algerians some 145,000 residential and business properties abandoned by the French and administered by the government ever since. The process has come up against some basic economic realities, however. The urban dwellings in question have long been occupied by Algerians at nominal rents. They are now asked to buy the properties at prices that will greatly increase the expenses of the occupant, who will then be responsible for their upkeep. Since maintenance to date has been minimal or nonexistent, the structure the occupant is inheriting is often in very poor condition, and it does not look to him like a bargain. The significance of this operation, however, is that the individual Algerian is getting a chance to become an urban property owner. This will make a difference in his outlook and that of his children. Property owners tend not to be revolutionaries.

Perhaps more important than the encouragement of private enterprise is the government's decision to reduce the proportion of its investment in heavy industry, to rationalize and decentralize its development efforts (it has, for instance, split up 70 state enterprises into 404 smaller ones), and to make more investment in social infrastructure and services, and particularly housing. Urban housing has been critically short for years, and the squalor in the old Algiers Qasba, for instance, has been as great or greater than anything to be witnessed in the worst Moroccan bidonville. Fifteen percent of total government investment was to be devoted to housing during the period 1982–84, and 2 million dwelling units are to be built by 1990. At five persons per unit, this would house about 40 percent of the population, which would be a major achievement.

Less concentration on heavy industry also means a more realistic approach to Algeria's industrial potential and is an encouraging sign that in spite of the ideological content of their speeches, the Algerians are not always prisoners of their ideology and are capable of pragmatic flexibility when the occasion demands. They nevertheless have a good deal of repair work to do, given their past mistakes.

In contrast to Morocco, Algeria enjoys a substantial petroleum income, which provides about 60 percent of its total budget. Although the oil glut has reduced crude sales substantially,[3] this was compensated for by increased sales of refined products and condensate and by the fact that Algeria is paid for its hydrocarbons in dollars, which it spends mainly in nondollar areas, thus benefiting from the increased value of that currency.

Although it is crude oil that has largely financed the Algerian development effort, future prospects are dependent on the exploitation of natural gas reserves. While Algeria's oil reserves are modest by world standards (an estimated 1,023 million tons) it has the world's fourth largest gas reserves, after the Soviet Union, Iran, and the United States. Much of the development effort to date has been directed at building the infrastructure necessary to exploit these reserves—treatment plants, pipelines, and liquefaction plants. This investment is beginning to pay off, and by 1983 Algeria had a liquified natural gas export capacity of 30 billion cubic meters per year, compared with 15 billion at the end of 1981. Export plans, however, have been held up by disagreements over price; the Algerians are now asking substantially more for their gas than the price set in the agreements with American and French purchasers in the early 1970s, maintaining that the price should be tied to that of crude oil. The French came around and signed, on February 3, 1982, a contract for liquefied natural gas at a price of about $5.20 per million BTUs.[6] The Algerians reached a similar agreement with the Italian government in 1982 on a price of $4.41 per million BTUs for the gas to be put through their recently completed pipeline (which transits Tunisia and then crosses the Mediterranean and which was built at a cost of $3 billion, of which the Italians put up $2 billion), and the gas started flowing in the summer of 1983. Agreement with the United States is much more problematical. American importers have been prepared in the past to meet the Algerian price (which meant a price in the United States of approximately $7.57 CIF per million BTUs at Lake Charles, Louisiana, where Panhandle Eastern Corporation has its $567 million regasification terminal), but the American government and consumer groups have not. Today's Algerian gas price compares with a price of $4.94 per million BTUs for gas imported from Canada. The federal government has termed the difference too much and has sought modification of the contract. There has also been concern about the security of supply, some opponents of the transaction arguing that the Algerians could interfere with the flow of gas for political reasons, or raise the price arbitrarily on short notice. Some of this opposition is political rather than economic, reflecting a pervasive view that Algeria is essentially unfriendly and therefore unreliable. The Federal Energy Department had yet to approve the transaction when, on December 14, 1983, Panhandle announced that it was suspending its shipments under the contract because "Algerian gas made our gas the highest priced . . . in the market." Meanwhile, Distrigas in Boston has been importing 1.9 billion cubic meters of Algerian gas per year for some time, on terms similar to those accepted earlier by Panhandle, although its CIF price is appreciably lower, for complex reasons. The outcome of this saga, which is still being negotiated, is not clear yet, but the symbiosis between Algeria and consumers in the Northeastern United States, some 15 percent of whose domestic fuel requirements were to have come from this source according to U.S. projections in the mid-1970s, has not developed as anticipated, and it seems unlikely that it will any time soon.

The Algerians have also failed to reach agreement with the Spanish and British (although a limited quantity of gas is being sold to Spain) and a long-discussed pipeline from Algeria to Spain has yet to reach the implementation stage. The attitude of these prospective customers is, of course, affected by the availability and price of cheaper forms of energy, particularly at a time of reduced demand and softer prices for crude oil. If supply and demand come back into balance, however, as the International Energy Agency predicts, then Algerian gas will look more attractive and the Algerians are probably correct in counting on demand to absorb their production eventually. They appear to be headed for a difficult market in the short run, however.

Agriculture remains a disaster area. Even in good crop years, such as 1980, the country now produces only 45 percent of its grain needs (compared with Morocco's 65 percent) and the percentage is expected to decline rather than increase as population grows and farm labor declines. Algeria is still the world's largest importer of eggs,[7] shipping them in by air at times, and while there has been noticeable improvement over the last five years in the variety and quantity of fresh produce available in local markets, the latter still contrast unfavorably with the well-stocked markets one finds in Morocco. Here as elsewhere in the economy, production continues to be hampered by the dead hands of socialism and government monopoly. For instance, much of the commercial chicken population (chicken raising has become a popular field for private enterprise) died in the summer of 1982 when the government, which has a monopoly on imports, failed to import enough feed. No one who has had much experience with the Algerian bureaucracy[8] would expect an import program run by it to function well, and it is unlikely that private enterprises dependent on imports will reach anything like capacity production until and unless there is a relaxation of government attitudes towards imports and exports. While there has been some movement in that direction in the past four years, a senior government official told the author in 1982 that the government would have to continue to exercise a monopoly on imports because it was essential to the operation of the Algerian system that it do so. This principle is enshrined in the national charter, but it will need modification eventually.

There is some movement on the farm front, however. The government, like its counterpart in Morocco, is moving to reduce dependence on the vagaries of the weather by increasing irrigated areas some 30 percent. It is also taking steps to break up the 2,000 "self-managed" state farms into 6,000 smaller units and to put more trained agriculturalists into the operation of such farms. Credits to farmers are being liberalized and marketing restrictions have been relaxed somewhat. This has helped the surprisingly large number of private farmers, who own an estimated 53 percent of Algeria's farm land (4 out of 7.5 million hectares), much of it unfortunately being marginal. In Algeria, as in Morocco, French settlers were given or acquired the best land, which was organized into relatively large, commercial units. After independence it was these properties that were turned over either to so-called self-managed state farms (2 million hectares) or cooperatives (1.5 million). Between them, they control most of the good land in the country, just as the modern sector controls most of the good land in Morocco. It is these lands that receive most of the benefits of modern technology, but they support only a portion of the rural population. (The modern sector employs 50 percent of the agricultural labor force, as indicated earlier, versus 3 percent in Morocco. This implies a heavy rate of underutilization of labor in the Algerian modern sector, and a relative lack of labor in the traditional sector.)

In the agricultural sector, as elsewhere, a major problem is the inefficiency of state-run distribution and marketing systems, which buy farm products and distribute them to municipal markets. The government agencies involved have shown a distressing disregard for both consumer and producer and the system has worked very poorly. Whether the Algerians will ever surmount these self-imposed obstacles is not clear, but at least they realize they have a problem and are willing to try alternatives. They are at the moment reorganizing and rationalizing both distribution and marketing, and this could substantially increase the availability of Algerian produce.

Meanwhile, Algeria, like Morocco, continues to maintain a birth rate that gives it a population growth rate of somewhere between 3 and 3.2 percent per year. It will continue to outstrip the growth of agricultural production for the rest of this century,[9] but hydrocarbon revenues give the Algerians much more latitude in dealing with increased demand than the Moroccans have. Boumediene was fond of saying that the way to deal with the growth of population was to create more jobs and grow more food, not to limit births. His economists knew this would not suffice, but were bound by his policies. At the same time, the Algerian government was deliberately avoiding the labor-intensive industries that would have created the jobs he was talking about. Benjedid's program of economic liberalization should result in expanding the job market; nevertheless, there is a large reservoir of unemployed to be absorbed, as noted earlier. Agriculture as well as industry needs to be reformed to do this, and even then it is not clear that the resources available will be adequate for the job over the long term. Meanwhile, a national policy of support for family planning is badly needed.[10]

Algeria also has a number of social problems connected with education, religion, and race. Among these are recurring tensions, sometimes leading to violence, between students receiving their education in French and those following the Arabic curriculum. Those students who opt for the latter find themselves at a disadvantage in the job market, where Western languages are the key to preferment. On the other hand, there are deep nationalistic and religious sentiments generated by Arabic and this often makes rational approach to the question difficult. In particular, Arabic is the language of the traditional conservatives and the fundamentalists, for whom French symbolizes unwanted Western ideologies and cultural influence. This is true to a greater or lesser degree in all three countries of the western Maghrib, but feelings have run higher in Algeria, perhaps because the permeation of French at the expense of Arabic had been much deeper during the colonial period and the common Algerian's command of his national language was notably inferior to that of his peers in Tunisia and Morocco.

Running across this traditionalist-modernist linguistic disagreement is a racial-cultural one, between Arabs and Berbers. The latter, who do not mind education in French, and are even prepared to learn Arabic, have their own rich oral literature and traditions they wish to preserve in their own language. The Berber strain tends to be purer and attachment to Berber culture stronger in mountain areas, such as the Kabyle region east of Algiers. The Kabyles want Berber to be taught in the school system, even though it is not used as a written language, and they object to the imposition of Arabic as the sole language of instruction in the early grades. They also object to what they consider a lack of attention to their region and have been perennially dissident ever since independence (as well as before).[11]

In common with Morocco and Tunisia, Algiers has felt the tremors of the Islamic revival, which is discussed in more detail in Chapter 8. Indeed, the manifestations of dissent from the religious establishment are much more public in Algeria than they are in Morocco, and while no serious threat is posed to the regime, the fundamentalists have enough following to inhibit government policies on matters relating to social and religious issues, such as the status of women.

While none of these problems by itself is fatal, there is a synergistic effect from these ingredients coming together in a country whose revolutionary leaders are aging and who must eventually pass the baton to a younger generation which will not have their own, rather remarkable background. The younger generation, at least in the towns, obviously does not share many of the convictions and passions of the older, and this is often a signal for the effective delegitimization of a regime and its replacement by something different. The outlook, for the short term, however, is for a continuation of the present regime, with its ideological commitment perhaps being attenuated with the passage of time and with its increasing interest in Western respectability.

Benjedid has followed a somewhat more moderate course than Boumediene abroad as well as at home. Boumediene felt, or said he felt, great affinity for Castro and Kim il-Sung, and was inclined to take positions as a matter of ideology, whatever the consequences might be, when he felt this was required by Algeria's position as a leader of the radicals in the Third World. Benjedid has distanced Algeria somewhat from Castro, has followed a generally more moderate course in African politics, and is considered to be the moderate among the members of the Steadfastness and Confrontation Front. Algerian involvement in the early stages of the abortive Libyan and Iranian effort to have Israel expelled from the General Assembly in 1981 indicates that ideology is not foresworn completely, but, the Algerian performance in the matter of the Tehran hostages could not have been more helpful and was an indication of a growing Algerian desire to be accepted in the West as well as the East.

The full story of the hostage negotiations has yet to be told (although a serious effort will be made in a book the Council on Foreign Relations is planning to bring out in 1985 on U.S. management of the crisis). The Algerians were, however, a natural choice as mediators. They had been recipients of the United States' first circular request to appropriate governments after the seizure of the hostages, asking them to do whatever they could to facilitate their release. Their chargé in Tehran had visited the hostages, with three other chiefs of mission, in November 1979, and Algeria was named to represent Iran's interests in the United States when relations were broken in April 1980. But in the first half of 1980 even those who had the best relationships with Iran's leaders found it difficult to influence them while the struggle for control of the revolution continued.

That struggle came to rest momentarily in August 1980, when the Islamic Republican Party gained control of the newly elected Majlis and approved a prime minister, Muhammad 'Ali Rajai. When Rajai came to the United Nations in September 1980 to plead Iran's case in the face of the Iraqi attack on September 22, he was impressed with Iran's isolation as a result of the hostage crisis, an impression that was heightened by the lectures he was given on the subject by the Algerian ambassador to Washington and Algeria's permanent representative to the United Nations in New York. Rajai returned to Tehran via Algiers, at Khomeini's instruction, to express condolences to the families of the victims of the al-Asnam earthquake. He got more advice there about how the hostage problem was blocking Iran's efforts to build support for the revolution and tarnishing the image of revolutionaries everywhere. Meanwhile, in early September, Khomeini had stated four conditions for release of the hostages and a committee of the Majlis began elaborating on those conditions.

The debate was prolonged by the Iraqi attack, but the war may have spurred Iran to release the hostages. Just before the presidential election in the United States the Majlis decided that a settlement to the issue should be negotiated, passed a resolution to that effect, and instructed the government to carry it out. The government conveyed its terms to the Algerians, who in turn conveyed them to Washington in November 1980.

The negotiations which ensued were enormously complicated, with the Algerians playing the key role through their foreign minister, the late Muhammad Bin Yahya, their ambassadors in Washington and Tehran, Redha Malek and Muhammad Ghorayeb, and Director Mustafai of the Algerian National Bank. Eventually the American team, led by Deputy Secretary of State Warren Christopher, moved to Algiers to simplify and speed up the process as the days of the Carter administration waned. Agreement was finally reached on January 19, 1981, the day before President Reagan's inauguration. Last-minute complications then arose regarding banking aspects of the agreement, and they were not resolved until the early morning of January 20, Algiers time. The hostages were placed on an Algerian plane in Teheran but did not actually take off until 35 minutes after President Reagan had been sworn in. Whether the Iranians were being bloody-minded and trying to deny President Carter even a last-minute satisfaction, or whether it was incompetence, will probably never be known. To the public it looked like a mean-spirited gesture.

The Reagan administration refused to endorse the transaction pending review, although it welcomed the hostages at the White House. In a notably insensitive posture toward the Algerians, whose mediation was critical in achieving the hostages' release, the administration barely uttered a word of thanks, and appeared to be signalling its real feelings by announcing, as

Secretary Haig's first act the following day, the signing of a decision to sell 108 M-60 tanks to Morocco, Algeria's arch rival.

To say that the Algerians were nonplussed and disappointed would be an understatement, but they did not complain audibly. For one thing, it is considered bad form in Arab countries to ask for gratitude when you have done a favor. For another, the Algerian ambassador received enough expressions of gratitude from private Americans to compensate somewhat for the ingratitude of the new administration.

What moved the Algerians to undertake this role? According to people involved on the American side of the negotiations there were three motives that emerged from conversations with the Algerian team: (1) A sense of obligation to straighten out a human and moral situation that never should have arisen. (2) A sense that the Iranians were destroying their revolution—and tarnishing the image of revolutionaries everywhere—through factional maneuvering over the hostages. (3) A belief they could improve relations with the United States. They had some satisfaction on the first and second counts, but little on the third. The top officials of the Carter administration gave the Algerian team the highest marks for their professionalism, their perseverance and their diplomatic skill, but Secretary Haig came to office with an obsolete picture of the Algerians and never seemed to take the trouble to understand the new Algerian leadership.

Although Benjedid's pragmatic approach looks more likely to succeed than Boumediene's did, both internally and externally, there are serious problems confronting him, and there are obvious constraints on his freedom of movement. Algerian failure to find a way out of the Sahara dilemma, for instance, indicates that Benjedid must take into account the ideological commitments inherent in the national charter as well as in the positions Algeria has taken over the years on domestic and international problems. On the other hand, the reorientation of domestic priorities away from forced draft industrialization is an encouraging sign that the Algerians can take pragmatic decisions in spite of ideological rhetoric and commitments. The track record to date indicates that they will continue to seek rational solutions to their problems, but the apparent failure to effect a significant, long-term improvement in Algerian-Moroccan relations is a sign of the continuing difficulties of doing so.

Notes

[1] The process was repeated by the 5th party congress in December 1983, which reelected Benjedid as party secretary and sole candidate in the presidential election the following month.

[2] *Political Elites in North Africa*, Zartman, Tessler, Entelis, Stone, Hinnebusch, and Akhavi (New York: Longman, 1982), p 96.

[3]While this is generally ascribed to Benjedid's desire to follow more moderate policies, there is also a theory that it reflects his lack of interest in and knowledge of foreign affairs.

[4]Out of a work force of 4.2 million, 700,000 were unemployed in 1982. This does not include underemployment. In order to cope with the population increase, 200,000 new jobs should be created each year. The public sector expected to create 160,000 in 1983. IMF preliminary figures indicate there was an increase of 4.9 percent, or 171,5000, for the economy as a whole.

[5]The United States, which was Algeria's principal oil customer, buying 500,000 barrels a day or over half of its production in January 1981, has bought no crude since February 1982. It has bought substantial quantities of condensate, or natural gasoline, however.

[6]The decision to pay this price was made for political reasons, and the French government has had to subsidize the gas purchases in order to hold down the domestic price. The Italian government will have to do the same. The French are now pleading inability to take the full quantity for which they contracted.

[7]$50 million worth in 1982. Syria, the second largest importer, brought in only $5 million worth. In the same year Algeria also imported $450 million worth of milk, cheese and butter. The Algerians expected to be self-sufficient in eggs by 1984 (January 1983 Economic Trends Report, U.S. Embassy, Algiers); but the IMF expected them to reach only 70–75 percent of their target by the end of that year.

[8]Or any other, for that matter.

[9]The discussion of the production-population equation in the chapter on Morocco applies even more forcefully in Algeria, where the percentage of food needs covered by local production is well below what it is in Morocco.

[10]Algeria has a "birth spacing" program but it is unpublicized and ineffective. The average Algerian family in 1982 had nine living children (January 1983 Economic Trends Report, U.S. Embassy, Algiers). The Fifth Party Congress of the FLN passed a resolution calling for bringing the population growth rate under control and this is an indication of official awareness that something more effective must be done. As such it is a hopeful sign.

[11]Taking advantage of this fact, the Moroccans on one occasion dropped arms into the Kabyle region in the mid-1970s in retaliation for Algerian support of the Polisario guerillas. It is not clear whether they expected to spark a revolt, or merely to show Algerians that two could play at the same game. The arms were turned over to the authorities and there was no surface indication of trouble brewing at the time, but gun-running has long been a local pastime in the area, and the authorities in Algiers were understandably upset.

4

Tunisia

The atmosphere of Tunisia recalls that of pre-1975 Lebanon. It is farfetched to see this as the result of the ancient Tyrian connection; we really do not know all that much about the Tyrians, for one thing. On the other hand, both countries are the smallest in their respective regions, both have been modestly endowed with natural resources and their people have had to sharpen their talents to survive, both have catered to Mediterranean tourism with considerable success, and both are marked by a practical approach, being careful to avoid letting ideology get in the way of making a living, but not always succeeding. To carry the parallel further, today Tunisians speak of replacing Lebanon as the Switzerland of the Arab world.

Tunisia's people are a Berber-Arab mixture, as are those of Morocco and Algeria, but its mountains are less formidable, its refuge areas less inaccessible, and the Berber element less noticeable. Those who still speak Berber are reportedly less than 1 percent of the population. Although having less rainfall and arable land than Algeria and Morocco, Tunisia still has sizable fertile areas, and agriculture is a major component of the economy, occupying a third of the work force, as noted earlier, and contributing about 16 percent of the GNP.

Although the southern half of the country is largely desert, Tunisia's vocation is Mediterranean. It has a long coastline relative to its area and the most fertile and heavily populated areas of the country are close to the sea. The Tunisians have long been exposed to foreign influences and ideas and they seem more cosmopolitan, more Levantine, than the other North Africans as a result.

Tunisia today is largely the creation of one man, Habib Bourguiba, and of a compact elite who staff his Destourian (Constitutionalist) Socialist Party. Both have aged a good deal and have lost the refreshing *élan* they had in the early years. Bourguiba has been president ever since independence, which was granted in 1956 following several years of organized political opposition and disorder. He more than anyone else was the architect of the political structure that emerged from the independence movement, and his unique role has led him to think he is indispensable. He has accordingly refused to lessen his grip on the party in spite of advancing years (he is over 80) and diminishing physical and mental powers. While he has shown remarkable stamina, recent visitors report that even in his "periods of lucidity" his mental powers are failing.

Meanwhile, the aging junior leadership of the party, deprived of its proper role of increasing authority, has become either dissatisfied or sclerotic. More importantly, the party has lost touch with the youth of the country and membership in it has become a matter of self-interest for people looking for favors or advancement, not a matter of political conviction. The party hierachy, which was a dynamic young cadre 25 years ago, is now largely middle-aged and there are few young people within the party who are being groomed for eventual accession to power.[1] The party is still governing the country, but it is dying at its roots. Thus, speaking to the magazine *Jeune Afrique* in the summer of 1982, the prime minister, Muhammad Mzali, said the party had some "hundreds" of followers on the university campus but was outnumbered by the "Khomeinists," that is, the fundamentalists. This state of affairs in a country as cosmopolitan as Tunisia and in a sector once dominated by the Destourians is indicative of the party's irrelevance to the country's youth.

The party's condition is in part due to Bourguiba's unwillingness to tolerate opposition. Although there is remarkable openness of expression in Tunisia today, and Tunisians feel free to criticize the head of state and his government openly and in ways that would never be tolerated in Morocco or Algeria, much less Libya, Bourguiba can be ruthless in suppressing dissent, and he has prevented even the essentially loyal opposition from having a meaningful voice in national affairs.

The political climate has improved perceptibly since Mzali became prime minister in 1980. He has adopted, or been allowed by Bourguiba to adopt, a much more liberal position than his predecessor, Hedi Nouira, and has eased political restrictions in important respects, most notably in allowing opposition newspapers to be published and permitting the almost unrestricted import of foreign newspapers.[2] The result is that today one can actually find Tunisian newspapers with meaningful news in them, which was rarely the case during the 1970s.

Mzali and his colleagues even convinced Bourguiba he should permit free elections to Parliament (Bourguiba is president for life) in the fall of 1981 and let opposition parties put up candidates. Although the fundamentalist Mouvement de Tendance Islamique was suppressed well before the elections, other opposition organizations, notably the Communists and the Mouvement des Democrates Socialistes of Ahmed Mestiri, were presenting candidates and had been led to expect a reasonably open contest in which they would be likely to win a substantial number (perhaps 35 percent) of the seats. At the last minute, Bourguiba changed his mind and ordered the minister of the interior to see that only Destourian candidates won. The latter did his job so well, according to local observers, that even the government did not know how people had actually voted. (The Destourians ran in alliance with the Union Générale des Travailleurs Tunisiens (UGTT), the trade union federation. Of the 136 seats in Parliament, 27 were won by UGTT candidates running on a joint list with the Neo-Destour. This has since become a seriously divisive issue within the union, with those coelected being accused of undermining union autonomy by cooperating with the regime. As a result, a splinter group has set up a competing trade union, the Union Nationale de Travailleurs Tunisiens.)

In effect, then, Tunisia has a one-party system, with all the risks such arrangements usually imply, and Tunisians are quick to say that all bets will be off when Bourguiba eventually departs from the scene. The constitution provides that he be succeeded by the prime minister. Mzali, a former university professor, is not an exciting leader, but is universally respected for his honesty and intelligence. It is generally expected that he will succeed to the presidency, although some doubt was thrown on this by an interview with Bourguiba's wife, Wassila, that was published on July 28, 1982 in *Jeune Afrique*. She was quoted as saying she thought the succession should be determined by election rather than be automatic. Since she plays a major role as *éminence grise*, this immediately gave rise to questions as to whether Bourguiba intended to pull the rug out from under Mzali. There is no indication that this is in fact his intention, and his support of Mzali at the time of the December 1983 riots would argue against it, but it would not be inconsistent with the sometimes Machiavellian conduct of Tunisian politics, or with Bourguiba's own style. He could take such action at any time, and Wassila has continued to advance the idea that the succession should be determined by election and that Mzali, if he does succeed, should function only as a caretaker until elections can be held. She has significant support for that position.

Given the traditional moderation of the Tunisians, there is a reasonable chance that there will be a peaceful transition to a new regime, whether under Mzali or some other member of the elite. Indeed, as Bourguiba fails, the transition has already begun. The question is, What comes after it? The problem is not so much the succession as it is the need to make the Destourian Party relevant again and to let other parties operate normally. The Tunisian word for this is *pluralisme*, allowing political tendencies and ideologies other than those of the party in power to find free and public expression.[3] There is also a need to do something about regional and social inequalities and discontent. Even though Tunisia has the highest Physical Quality of Life Index in the Maghrib, many of its people perceive themselves as discriminated against, either because they live in the underdeveloped interior of the country, as opposed to the more prosperous coastal areas, or because they do not have access to the centers of power, and they complain that the rich are getting richer while the poor are getting poorer.

Measuring and comparing the extremes of wealth and poverty is difficult in the absence of statistics. While one reporter will find the inequalities represented by the villas and palaces of Carthage compared to the slums of Tunis shocking, another will find them less obvious than those encountered in Morocco. A third, coming from Egypt, will be impressed with the general prosperity of Tunisians and see no squalor at all. What is important in such cases is the perceptions of the people themselves, and whether they are ready to accept their lot in life. The measure of Tunisian discontent was displayed briefly in January 1978, when the UGTT called for a general strike and went into the streets of Tunis to protest the policies of the government and was savagely repressed by the army. (Official accounts admit that 47 people were killed. Unofficial claims put the total as high as 200.) In a sense, this was Tunisia's Casablanca. In both places there was a brief eruption that was quickly put down with serious loss of life, and little was done to remove the underlying discontents that led to the outbreak.

The UGTT blamed *agents provocateurs* for the violence in 1978, and claimed that the union leadership fell into a trap laid for it by hardliners within the regime. The army, which repressed the strike, was untrained for riot control operations and overreacted badly. Ever since it has resented the role it had to play. In short, the incident probably need not have happened, but it is symptomatic of societies in which the channels for dissent are limited and often closed that when discontent finally erupts it has built up a head of steam that cannot be controlled by the usual means. That is the danger in Tunisia today. Indeed, the relatively calm surface in Tunisia hides some deep political divisions which have antecedents going back to the colonial period and which have become more lively since late 1983. To begin with, there are the so-called Youssefists, after the former Destourian leader Salah Ben Youssef, who split with Bourguiba on the eve of independence and was assassinated in 1961, presumably on government orders. His personal following was in the conservative wing of the party and was related to his support for traditional nationalist themes—Islam and Arab solidarity—that Bourguiba rejected as obscurantist and negative. Tunisian belief in those themes did not die with Ben Youssef, however, and there is a strong strain of such sentiment waiting to be aroused. The 300 or so Tunisian dissidents who took part in the Gafsa raid, for instance, were led by a man described as a "Youssefist."

Another tendency, a radical socialist one (as opposed to the minimal socialism of the Destourians) is led by Ahmad Ben Salah, a former labor leader and cabinet minister whose efforts to socialize agriculture in the 1960s had disastrous economic, social, and political results, leading to his dismissal and subsequent imprisonment. Living in exile in Europe since 1973, he has his own opposition movement, the Movement of Popular

Unity (MUP), which seems to be more of a nuisance than a threat today but which represents those who believe in radical, leftist solutions to Tunisia's problems. Given the relative deprivation of many Tunisians, it is difficult to believe that there are not substantial numbers of them who think in such terms. (The MUP-II, authorized to function by Bourguiba in November 1983, is an offshoot of the Ben Salah MUP.)

There is also the 400,000-member UGTT. Although allied with the Destourian Party, and subject to government interference and intimidation, it has shown its ability to defy the government and it is a contestant for power. It has impressive leadership, now badly split over the issue of electoral cooperation with the Destourians mentioned earlier.

So do the fundamentalist youth, who are discussed in more detail in Chapter 6. Their ranks are swelled by the unemployed and by the disaffected university students, who tend to be either fundamentalists or leftists, with the Destourians among them confined to a narrow space in the middle. Paradoxically, but perhaps inevitably, the fundamentalists have been more conspicuous in this relatively open country than in the other states of North Africa. Their strength is due not just to unemployment, but also to discontent with the corruption and secular policies of the regime and to the lack of institutionalized means of dissent.

The inherent fragility of the Tunisian equilibrium was shown by the outbreak of serious street violence in the last week of 1983, leading to the imposition of a state of emergency by Bourguiba. The immediate cause of the violence, which began in the poorer regions of the south and spread to the rest of the country, was a rise in the cost of food, the basic cause of the Casablanca riots discussed in Chapter 2. The regime blamed outsiders for provoking the trouble, and it managed to impose order by using the army again, but there clearly is deep social discontent today as there was in 1978, and it cannot be dealt with routinely.

Bourguiba's problem, as it is Hassan's, is how to insure the continuation of the present political system. If he shares power with the loyal opposition, he may lose all of it. His reaction therefore is to share none of it, and to hope that the momentum of the past will keep things on their present course. This may endure as long as he does, but his successor will have difficulty keeping the same game going. For one thing, the Destourian Party itself may not hold together when he departs. For another, his successor will not have his reputation and charisma. Although recent visitors report that Mzali is growing with the job, his leadership undoubtedly will be contested within the party.

One of the factors to be reckoned with is Wassila, who has long been considered the power behind the throne, although Bourguiba often goes out of his way to show his independence of her. She guards him jealously and has used her position to promote the fortunes of her favorites, who tend to come from the bourgeoisie of Tunis. (Bourguiba leans toward his home town, Monastir.) When Bourguiba dies, Wassila's powers will be sharply curtailed and she will be open to attack. She obviously has an interest in assuring that people who are well disposed toward her come out on top in the transition struggle, and she can be expected to use her influence to affect the outcome. Particularly as time goes on and Mzali has more chance to make decisions that are unpopular, the likelihood that she will be able to promote the fortunes of some alternate candidate increases. The December 1983 riots may have been seen as offering such an opportunity; but if Wassila sought to exploit it, she was frustrated by Bourguiba's support of Mzali.

As noted earlier, Tunisia's economy is the best balanced in the Maghrib. In 1981, 16 percent of Gross Domestic Product came from agriculture, 29 percent from industry, construction and mining, 33 percent from commerce and transportation and 4 percent from tourism. The GDP has shown a steady and respectable growth rate, averaging 7 percent per year in the period 1971–1981, and the debt ratio was only 12–14 percent. 1982 was a difficult year, however, largely owing to factors outside Tunisian control, such as climate and the European recession, which affected agricultural production on one hand and the market for Tunisian phosphates on the other. As a result, the GDP growth rate dropped to 1.5 percent and the debt service ratio rose to 17.5 percent. There was marked improvement in the growth rate in 1983, when it went up to 4.5 percent, but a disatrous grain crop and a slump in tourism and other factors brought the debt service ratio up to 18.2 percent, and the trade deficit was $1.25 billion.

Government planners are part of the problem. Tunisia has a mixed economy. Private investment, foreign and domestic, is encouraged, and there are many private businesses, particularly in the service and agricultural sectors, but most of the larger enterprises are owned by the government, and as in Algeria, this makes for inefficiency.

Tunisia has social problems, too. Although its population growth rate of 2.3 – 2.6 percent (depending on your source) is somewhat lower than those of its Maghrib neighbors and is itself an indicator of greater modernization, it has also been experiencing an unemployment rate that is officially put at 10–15 percent but is probably closer to 25 percent. In common with their brothers in Algeria and Morocco, its young men are migrating to the cities in search of employment and entertainment and finding only the latter. There is considerable dissatisfaction among these youths, whose aspirations have not been met by the government or the economy, and they speak of Bourguiba and those around him in unflattering terms, much as their contemporaries in Morocco speak of Hassan and his court. While intensive development of tourism has provided a useful source of hard currency and employment, it has social features that many Tunisians (as well as Moroccans) see as corrupting, and there are limits as to how far it can be pushed, particularly in an era of rising Islamic reaction against seminude women, both Tunisian and European, cavorting on public beaches. It is furthermore very sensitive to the economic situation in Europe. Thus, the number of tourists dropped from 2.2 million in 1981 to 1.38 million in 1983.

Agriculture has been intensively developed, but is limited by croppable area, rainfall and restrictive government policies, which have slowed modernization. As a result, in 1981 Tunisia imported $180 million more in agricultural products than it exported, in spite of a production increase of 50 percent over the previous 20 years, and the volume of agricultural production actually declined by 8.7 percent from 1981 to 1982, and declined another 1 percent in 1983 (cereals were down 28 percent, olive oil by 31 percent and citrus by 16.5 percent). Nor do there appear to be important mineral possibilities other than relatively modest deposits of phosphates and petroleum. Production of the latter has increased, however, with discoveries of new oil in 1982 that have raised output from 100,000 to 114,000 barrels a day, and Tunisia's exports of petroleum products exceeded imports by $487 million in 1982. This may help finance industrial and agricultural development that could affect the unemployment problem, but the total impact is likely to be moderate. Hopes for major additional crude from an offshore area disputed with Libya were dashed by the International Court of Justice, which found for Libya in a decision announced in February 1982.

While Mzali and his government understand the need to make agriculture more productive and the countryside more attractive, they are unlikely to reverse the migration to the cities.[4] In the meantime, they are encouraging the exportation of their workers in a much more systematic way than their Moroccan and Algerian colleagues. Worker remittances in 1982 were estimated at $342 million, a substantial foreign exchange contribution to the economy. As of September 1982, out of a total work force of 1,810,000, there were an estimated 288,000 Tunisians working abroad, of whom 150–175,000 were in France, 60–80,000 in Libya, 20,000 in Algeria, and 12,000 in Germany, with the rest elsewhere in Europe and the Arab world. Unfortunately, many of these are skilled workers who could be used in Tunisia.

The relatively high educational standards of Tunisia and moderate wage rates give it certain theoretical advantages in terms of exporting to Europe, but the Tunisians, like the Moroccans, have come up against trade quotas raised by the Common Market against imports of textiles and other commodities produced by the light industries of North Africa. Tunisians also see themselves menaced by the eventual admission of Spain and Portugal into the Common Market, which will put Tunisian olive and citrus exports at a severe disadvantage. Fortunately for them, Spain poses its own problems for the other members of the market. Its admission did not occur as scheduled on January 1, 1984, and is not expected anytime soon.

While each of these economic problems is serious, they look manageable. Agricultural and social problems can be ameliorated substantially with resources now available, or likely to become available, plans are afoot to deal with them, and nowhere does one encounter the seemingly hopeless ratios that are so common in the Third World. The political problems, on the other hand, are more difficult and are probably insoluble. Or rather, they will not be solved by Bourguiba but will be left to his successor. Tunisia may be able to deal with them successfully provided it is spared interference from its neighbors.

Tunisia's relations with those neighbors are in part a function of their relations with each other. Thus, when Algerian-Libyan relations are on the upswing, relations with Tunisia tend to decline, and vice versa. In this atmosphere, the Tunisians display an understandable nervousness about which way Qadhdhafi is going to jump. Their relations with Libya may wax and wane, but they are always uneasy, because Qadhdhafi has considerable potential for causing trouble. While the employment of 60,000 to 80,000 Tunisians in Libya has been a useful escape valve to let off some of the unemployment pressure, Qadhdhafi could expel them at any moment, and that would be a serious blow. At the same time, Qadhdhafi is giving military training to an estimated 5,000 Tunisians, ostensibly being readied to liberate Palestine, but perhaps to liberate Tunisia instead. He could be planning to try another Gafsa raid on a larger scale. Indeed, there was a second incident on a much smaller scale, at Kasserine in April 1982, that indicated he was still trying.

Tunisia also lives in uneasy symbiosis with Algeria. It hopes to get the Algerians to invest in Tunisia, to collect substantial revenues from the Algerian-Italian gas pipeline, to increase the number of its workers in Algeria, and to export more agricultural produce (notably eggs) there. At the same time, as indicated earlier, the Tunisians harbor deep suspicions about Algerian intentions. Justified or not, these suspicions are a fact of life. They have been much lightened by the 1983 friendship treaty, but fundamental incompatibilities have not been removed, unless the Algerians have had a radical change of heart and are abandoning their ideology, which seems unlikely.

One reason for Tunisian feelings of insecurity is the weakness of the army. Although its 46,000 officers and men are competent enough, their equipment is skimpy and their ability to resist either the Libyans or Algerians is very limited. The United States increased its military aid to Tunisia from $95 million in sales credits in fiscal 1982 to $87 million in 1983 plus $15 million in grant assistance, and planned to supply with the credits a squadron (12) of F-5 fighter aircraft and a battalion (54) of M-60 tanks. The Tunisians have decided to buy this equipment more as a deterrent and to show they are prepared to make sacrifices in order to be taken seriously than in the expectation it will permit them to make more than token resistance to a determined attack by either of their neighbors. They are not interested in making the expenditures that would be necessary to give them that capability. Indeed, the decision to buy even these limited arms has been questioned seriously within the military and political establishments as a useless expense and as starting Tunisia on the road of ever-greater military expenditures and dependence on foreign suppliers. The argument of such critics is that Tunisia does not have the resources to finance the armed forces it would need to defend itself against either Libya or Algeria, and that it should concentrate on increasing domestic solidarity through paying more attention to political and economic complaints because it is internal dissidence that provides the justification and the vehicle for foreign intervention.

The conjuncture generally perceived as the most dangerous in terms of foreign intervention is the transition between Bourguiba and his successor. There are apprehensions that either the Libyans or Algerians will try to influence the succession in their favor. Libyan sponsorship of the Gafsa raid shows the lengths to which Qadhdhafi is prepared to go, and it is not to be excluded that he would attempt a more substantial interference if the transition is not made quickly and quietly, or that he might even attempt to field his own candidate early enough in the process to derail it. Libyan money could be an important factor in the contest.

Algeria also has a direct interest in the outcome, and it could not afford to stand by idly and see the Libyans intervene militarily. Benjedid reportedly warned Qadhdhafi in 1981 against any efforts at destabilizing Tunisia, and the Algerians would be seriously disturbed if large amounts of Libyan money began turning the heads of Tunisian politicians the wrong way. There is thus the obvious risk that both Algeria and Libya will become involved in the succession. The Tunisians are keenly aware of this danger, and this is one reason they are expected to keep the transition quick and peaceful, and to look for outside support against their neighbors. Their only politically reliable support in the immediate area comes from Morocco, and the Tunisians see that state as having such problems of its own that they cannot count on it in an emergency. They therefore tend to look outside the region, notably to the United States and France, for help in adversity.

While the United States and France have been traditional sources of economic and military help, Tunisia is also interested in integrating itself more fully into the Arab world, where it has often been a loner because of Bourguiba's pragmatic approach to its problems. He was, for instance, almost ostracized in 1965 for suggesting publicly, after a meeting with Nasser in which the latter had agreed with him privately, that the Arabs should accept the partition of Palestine as proposed by the United Nations in 1947. He has also been viewed with suspicion, not to say derision, for his modernist approach to Islam. Now that the rest of the Arab world has belatedly come around to Bourguiba's view on Palestine, and has almost found the courage to say so publicly, Tunisia is in a position to play a more active role in Arab politics. The Tunisians, for example, maintained that the plan for Middle East peace drafted and adopted by the Fez conference in September 1982 was inspired by Bourguiba as well as King Fahd, and the conference communiqué confirmed this.

There are other indications that Tunisia is moving into the mainstream of Arab politics, notably the move of the Arab League headquarters from Cairo to Tunis and the decision by Yasser Arafat to move PLO headquarters from Beirut to a location outside Tunis. He was apparently motivated by the belief he would have more freedom of action in Tunisia than in Syria. Wassila, who was in constant telephonic contact with Arafat during the siege of Beirut, is given much of the credit for persuading Arafat to come, but he undoubtedly had his own reasons.

The above is not to suggest that Tunisia is likely to become radical in its approach to Arab problems, although Tunisians were greatly upset by the Israeli invasion of Lebanon, for which they held the United States indirectly responsible. (They boycotted the U.S. embassy's Fourth of July reception in protest and organized street demonstrations against Israel and the United States.) In the future we are likely to see other occasions on which the Tunisians will wish to place some daylight between themselves and the United States on such issues, and it would be a mistake to take perpetual Tunisian moderation for granted. The Palestine question, which has never been a serious issue in U.S.-Tunisian relations in the past, has become perceptibly more important to Tunisians today, and they will not abandon the Arab caravan lightly. This was confirmed by the lectures Secretary of State Shultz received in Tunis in December 1983, when U.S. partisanship for Israel was being attacked with particular vigor throughout the Arab world.

Whether or not Tunisia takes a more radical stand on the Palestine question is unlikely to weigh greatly in the contest for the Middle East. What is going to affect that contest, and Western interests, is instability in Tunisia— an instability that will increase tensions in the area and will pose serious challenges to the interests of all concerned. The risk of such instability is directly proportional to the amount of time Bourguiba remains in office. The longer he stays, the more difficult it will be for his successor to assume the mantle, unless Bourguiba makes some effort to effect the transition before he dies. As of now, it does not look as though he can be brought to do so before it is too late, that is, before he either becomes completely senile or dies, or before he has delayed the process so long that his charisma no longer works and he cannot guarantee the transition. Indeed, we have already passed that point according to some Tunisians, and we must therefore expect a good deal of uncertainty about the succession.

Notes

[1] In 1978 the country's average age was below 25, but the average party member's was almost 40, and all of the senior political leadership was over 50.

[2] According to Paul Balta in *Le Monde* of February 19, 1982, over 800 foreign periodicals, including 400 in French and 200 in Arabic, are sold without censorship. These figures seem high, but even if halved this amount of free circulation would be significantly more than is permitted elsewhere in North Africa.

[3] There was a significant move in this direction on November 19, 1983, when Bourguiba authorized the Mouvement des Democrates Socialistes (Mestiri) and the Mouvement de l'Unite

Populaire II (MUP-II) to function as legal political parties. They joined the Communists, already permitted to function, in the legal opposition.

[4]The phenomenon appears to be irreversible. For a discussion of the increasing urbanization of the Maghrib, see the review *Maghreb-Machrek*, no. 96 (April/June 1982), entitled "l'Explosion Urbaine au Maghrib."

5

Libya

For most Americans the problem of Libya is the problem of Mu'ammar Qadhdhafi, Philosopher of the Revolution. If he would disappear, so would the problem, or so the argument goes. It is questionable whether this simplistic approach is realistic. For all his eccentricities, Qadhdhafi represents a strain of anti-imperialistic Arab nationalism that runs very deeply in Libya and elsewhere in the Arab world, and we are likely to have trouble with his successor too, until and unless our relations with the Arab world as a whole improve. It is difficult to imagine that any conceivable successor would not be an improvement, but Qadhdhafi is a product of his time and environment. He has gone too far in letting his fantasies determine Libyan policies, but the revolution he has led will not be entirely undone when he goes.

To understand why this is so one must understand something of Libya's history. For most of the last 5,000 years Libya has been a zone of transition rather than a power center, and its existence as an independent, unified state within its present borders began only in 1951. Although for centuries Libya was a backwater boasting a few scraggly towns on the coast and scattered oases in the interior, it benefited to some extent from the Ottoman reforms of the nineteenth century, and by the beginning of the twentieth century there had developed in Tripoli a small, educated elite that had some experience with government administration and the outside world.

Although a few families from this elite survived, most of it was eliminated by the Italians, who invaded the country in 1911, after declaring war on Turkey. They encountered stiff resistance from the Libyans, backed by the Turks, which did not end in Tripolitania, the western province, until 1918. Cyrenaica, the eastern province, was not completely pacified until the 1930s. An estimated 50 percent of the population perished in the process, and the story of the Italian occupation, particularly during the Fascist era, is painful. The degree of Mussolini's solicitude for the local population is shown by the fact that at independence the country had a total of seven university graduates.

Libya was, of course, the scene of some of the bitterest combats of the North African campaign in World War II. As the battles raged back and forth, much of the very limited urban infrastructure of Cyrenaica was destroyed, and Libya emerged from the war an impoverished backwater with three principal exports—cuttlefish bone, esparto grass (used for making paper currency) and scrap from the battlefields. There was little money in cuttlefish or esparto, but several members of the Sanusi family became moderately rich on scrap.

When the war ended the British were in occupation of the country, and an early debate at the United Nations revolved around the question of what to do with it. The Italians asked to have it back, while the Soviets asked for a trusteeship over it. But self-determination and independence were in the air, and, in any event, the British had promised Idris al-Sanusi that they would not let Cyrenaica go back to Italy if his men would fight against the Italians and Germans, which they did.

Idris was the leader, and grandson of the founder of the Sanusiya brotherhood, a North African religious order which was particularly active in Cyrenaica and the Sudan. Devoted to the cultivation of religious learning and a certain amount of practical enlightenment, the order had been active in opposing the Italians in 1911 and subsequently, and the head of the order, the so-called Grand Sanusi, was surrounded with a certain mystical aura, like that of Abdul Qadr in Algeria and Abdul Krim in Morocco, leaders of resistance to the French and Spanish, respectively. The contribution of his followers to Britain's North African campaign was perhaps modest, but they served loyally, took casualties, and kept their part of the bargain. Furthermore, the British had more interest in making Libya independent than in turning it back to the Italians.

What emerged from the United Nations was agreement on establishment of the United Kingdom of Libya under Idris as King. What was united were three separate provinces: Tripolitania, Cyrenaica, and the Fezzan (in the south). Each province had its own government under a federal system modeled on those of the United States, Canada, and Australia. A device of this nature was thought necessary because of the often bitter regional rivalries, which were particularly strong between Cyrenaica and Tripolitania. The federal system was abolished in 1963, but the rivalries it was set up to accommodate have persisted, and they are still a political factor today. The Tripolitianians look down on the rustic Cyrenaicans and Fezzanis and the compliment is returned.

Idris was a mild-mannered, rather ineffectual-looking ruler, with wire-rimmed, tinted spectacles, and always in traditional Libyan dress (which has its origins in the Roman toga). He was convinced that his fate, and Libya's, lay with the British and Americans, who had supported the creation of the Libyan state and who were its principal sources of funds through modest annual subventions. These were, in effect, rent for the military installations they were occupying. (The British had an airbase at al-Adham, near Tobruk, and several small detachments elsewhere in the country, while the U.S.

Wheelus Air Force Base was just outside Tripoli.) Although the British and American relationship to Libya was widely regarded in the Arab world as tutelary, and Idris often looked to the Americans and British for guidance on foreign policy and economic issues, he was quite independent-minded, particularly with regard to domestic matters, and was far from being a stooge of anyone. If he accepted British or American advice it was because he saw the course recommended as being in Libya's or his interest. British and American aid was not sufficient to justify ignoring the national interest, even if it had been suggested.

Idris's mild demeanor did not prevent him from ruling with severity. A cunning, traditional politician who had no use for the modern Westernized dissidents who surfaced immediately after independence, he took swift and ruthless action against some of them, and thanks to his external support was able to rule without being seriously questioned or challenged. Given his age (he was 61 in 1951)[1] and temperament, the day-to-day administration of the kingdom was inevitably turned over to a few trusted advisers, who just as inevitably became corrupted by the wealth that began pouring in after the discovery of oil in 1959. Indeed, Libya was notorious for the venality of its officials and for the fact that no contract could be signed unless payments were made under the table. Although the amounts involved seem insignificant compared to some of the commissions subsequently paid in Saudi Arabia, they were very substantial for the 1960s and were a cause of serious concern to the U. S. government, which feared that sooner or later such blatant corruption would lead to a coup d'état.

When a group of young officers staged a "revolution" in 1969, Idris was in Turkey on a visit and refused to try a return to power, perhaps because the British and Americans were not willing to support him militarily, but also because he was weary, and had been for some time. He went into exile in Egypt and died there in June 1983.

The revolution was no surprise, but it was surprising that the military establishment, which Idris had carefully nurtured and supervised, did not resist and that it crumbled so quickly. This apparently was due to initial confusion in Libya as to the identity of the rebels, who were widely assumed to be Idris's advisers working in concert with the Americans and British, a coup d'état having been rumored to be in the works for some time. The new leaders were unknown. Some had been to the United States for training, but the American officers who had supervised their training seem not to have been impressed by them.

Although there were early hopes that the United States might be able to maintain reasonable relations with the new leadership, it was inevitable that there would be difficulties. There was already a good deal of anti-Western, specifically anti-American, sentiment in Libya. Aside from the natural resentment engendered by the paternalistic relationship the Americans and the British were perceived to have had with Libya, and aside from the continuing irritations arising from the presence of Wheelus, there were deeper discontents arising from the maldistribution of oil wealth and the flagrant corruption, partly blamed on American companies, and from Idris's close identification with Israel's principal supporter.

Wheelus had long been a sore point with Tripolitanians. Not only were there the usual annoyances that accompany any active foreign military presence, particularly one as noisy as Wheelus, but it was also a symbol of Libya's continued alignment with and dependence on the United States. Resentment became stronger after the catastrophe of the Arab-Israel war in June 1967, during which there were serious anti-American incidents and the U.S. embassy staff in Benghazi was saved from death only by the timely intervention of a nearby British military detachment. Had it not been for Idris, the country would have embarked on a virulently anti-American course then, if not sooner. Libyan opinion was ripe for Qadhdhafi.

True to the usual pattern in such affairs, Qadhdhafi did not surface immediately as leader but emerged after two weeks as the first among equals in the council of the Revolution. The council was nominally a collegial body, as its precursor in Egypt had been, and there was a good deal of speculation initially about who was in control.[2] When Qadhdhafi was eventually identified, the world knew little more. He was a signal corps officer in his late twenties or early thirties who claimed to have been born in a Bedouin tent in the Sirte, or Sidra, region, lying between Tripolitania and Cyrenaica. Although his circumstances were humble, his tribe was of maraboutic, or saintly, origin, and this gave him a certain social and political standing. He had been to Britain briefly for a signals course and was a graduate of the Libyan military academy. He spoke reasonably good English. He proclaimed himself a supporter of Nasser and almost immediately began a series of rather naive attempts to establish an Egyptian-Libyan union, attempts which the Egyptians resisted with some embarrassment.

While Nasser and other Arab leaders at first found Qadhdhafi's youthful enthusiasm refreshing, even touching, they soon began to tire of his improvisations and his practice of making impromptu visits to his fellow rulers. The logistics and protocol problems alone that such visits posed were enough to cause severe irritation. They also began to perceive that his innovative approach to international and domestic problems, while it might please some Arab crowds, was dangerous and destructive to the established order, such as it was. They rejected the notion that he was psychotic, but put him down as eccentric and unreliable. The borderline between psychosis and eccentricity has often been hard to discern in his case, however.

The United States and Qadhdhafi

For the United States, how to deal with revolutionary governments in the Arab world has been a recurring conundrum over the past 30 years. More likely than not, the revolution is against an old order that is identified with the West or the United States in particular, and the United States is usually damned before it starts, whatever its motives or intentions. This is not always the case. Early relations with Nasser and his colleagues were friendly and cooperative and did not turn sour until it became clear the United States was not going to provide the arms Egypt needed on terms Nasser would accept. With Iraq, on the other hand, the United States has not been on what one could call friendly terms at any time since the 1958 revolution. The same could be said of Syria since the 1954 ouster of Adib Shishakly. Sometimes the revolution and its leaders mellow, as in Algeria, but this rarely happens with a leader who comes to power with a firm anti-American bias. Qadhdhafi apparently was such a person.

As noted earlier, when the revolution came in 1969 there were hopes that the United States might be able to maintain relations with the new regime, but they were not very strongly held and there was much skepticism that, given American identification with the old order, cooperation with the new one would be fruitful. Nevertheless, a decision was taken to make every reasonable effort in that direction, to be tolerant and flexible, and to meet reasonable demands without undue delay. One of the first of the latter was for the evacuation of Wheelus Air Base, which had been seen as inevitable from the first day and which was agreed to with little resistance, somewhat to Qadhdhafi's surprise.

In succeeding years, under both Republican and Democratic administrations, serious efforts were made to maintain normal diplomatic relations and to walk the extra mile in accommodating the unpredictable exigencies of the Libyans. Not only was there a large economic stake in Libya, but its strategic importance was well understood. A hostile Qadhdhafi was not in the U.S. interest. Unfortunately, although he occasionally made noises indicating that he wanted good relations, Qadhdhafi did not seem to place great value on them. While he was correct, if tough, in his dealings with U.S. companies working in Libya, he was soon deeply involved in actions far beyond his borders that were inimical to U.S. interests, much as Nasser was in the mid-1950s. (These are discussed briefly below.) As a result of continued frustration in attempts to deal with him, U.S. diplomatic representation in Tripoli was reduced to the chargé level with the departure of Ambassador Joseph Palmer in November 1972. One of the principal points of irritation as far as Qadhdhafi was concerned became American refusal to turn over eight Lockheed C-130 military transport aircraft that Libya had paid $48 million for in 1972. The United States initially held up delivery because it feared Qadhdhafi would use the aircraft for military adventures, as in Uganda. Later, at a time when Uganda was off the agenda and Chad not yet on it, the United States was dissuaded from supplying them by President Sadat, who was bitterly opposed to Qadhdhafi.

Every once in a while Qadhdhafi would send out feelers saying he wanted to improve relations, but attempts to follow up led nowhere, or to the dead end of the C-130 issue. The Libyan effort to use Billy Carter to spring these aircraft for them indicates the depth of their interest in the matter.

The final straw as far as the Americans were concerned was the attack on their embassy in Tripoli on December 2, 1979. U.S. diplomatic personnel were withdrawn and the embassy was closed. Diplomatic relations were not severed, however, and a Libyan diplomatic mission remained in Washington, finally being ordered to leave on May 6, 1981, because of "a general pattern of unacceptable conduct." On the following day, the Department of State warned U.S. companies operating in Libya to start an orderly withdrawal of their personnel from Libya. Initial response was very sluggish because Americans working in Libya did not feel in any particular danger.

These actions reflected a new, tougher policy by the Reagan administration, which came into office resolved that something should be done about Qadhdhafi, that his continued involvement in terrorism around the world and his flouting of the norms of international behavior could not be tolerated. Speeches by Secretary of State Haig and Assistant Secretary of State for African Affairs Crocker made it clear that the administration was going to oppose Qadhdhafi actively by giving aid to his intended victims and mobilizing opinion against him. The most dramatic manifestation of the new policy was the clash over the Gulf of Sirte on August 19, 1981, when aircraft from a U.S. carrier shot down two Libyan aircraft that had opened fire on them.

Libya had announced on October 11, 1973, that the Gulf of Sirte was Libyan territorial water, and that foreign vessels could not enter it without Libyan permission. The United States rejected this claim soon after, since most of the Gulf lies well outside Libya's 12-mile line, and the Sixth Fleet ignored the Libyan claim on a number of occasions, but under the Carter administration it was decided to avoid a confrontation over the issue and the Sixth Fleet quietly avoided the Gulf, or at least avoided talking about going there. Under the Reagan administration, however, the issue was pressed. It was announced that the fleet would be entering the Gulf during its routine maneuvers and its presence there was well advertised. Precautions were taken indicating that an armed confrontation was expected, and the shooting down of the Libyan aircraft was widely welcomed within the administration as a salutary lesson to a tinhorn dictator.

Reaction in the rest of the world was mixed. The Algerian man in the street, for instance, was reported to be delighted, but European governments were disturbed by what they saw as a reckless, even bullying action on the part of the United States, and many Arab governments privately expressed their dismay at the boost they saw the incident giving to Qadhdhafi's position in the Arab world. He had lost the engagement, but he had stood up to the Americans, and no disgrace attaches to losing an unequal contest of that sort. Ironically, Qadhdhafi himself was out of the country when the incident occurred and it is not clear whether he ordered the Libyan fighters up, or whether this was the decision of a subordinate.

Next, on December 3, 1981, came the revelation that a Libyan hit squad had been sent to assassinate President Reagan. The unprofessional comments of various senior officials at the time, who showed little appreciation of security considerations in talking about the affair, gave rise to doubts, perhaps unjustified, as to the seriousness of the allegations being made by the administration. Skepticism was inevitable, particularly when it became known that the CIA and the FBI differed on the seriousness of the threat. Nevertheless, given the record of various governments, including that of the United States, in supporting operations of this nature against foreign heads of state, together with the amorality Qadhdhafi has often displayed on other occasions, there is nothing inherently implausible about the allegation. It is quite possible that he was guilty as charged. In any event, the administration felt it had forced Qadhdhafi to give up the idea by letting him know that retribution would be swift and overwhelming.

The next step was President Reagan's call on December 10, 1981, for all Americans to leave Libya as soon as possible. The deputy secretary of state, William Clark, said the president was required to take legal measures to require Americans to leave because they were in "imminent danger," and it was announced that U.S. passports, except those of journalists, were no longer valid for travel to Libya. In point of fact, the Supreme Court had found earlier that the government cannot deny its citizens the right to travel where they wish; it therefore cannot ban travel to Libya.

U.S. businessmen and academics continue to travel to Libya, although they risk bureaucratic complications some day in the future. This has deterred some people, particularly those who are concerned about working for the government some day, but others have gone. As of the fall of 1983, there were an estimated 600 Americans living and working in Libya (compared to 2,000 in 1981) and company officials report that Libyan treatment of them was unexceptionable.

The justification for not permitting travel to Libya was that the lives of Americans who went there were in danger and the United States could not extend normal protection to them. The existence of any danger was denied by Americans on the spot, but many left anyway out of loyalty to their government or for personal reasons. U.S. companies that continued to operate there were forced to hire other nationalities to replace them. The lack of clear signs of danger or threat posed by the Libyans gave rise to speculation that the administration's undeclared purpose was to clear the decks for further retaliatory action against Libya, perhaps including military intervention. The latter seemed highly unlikely at the time, but the speculation itself may have been encouraged as a deterrent and there is no question that the measure was perceived in Washington as a way to increase the political-economic pressure a notch. This was alleged in Washington to be part of something referred to informally as the "Wolfowitz Plan" after its reputed author, the then director of policy planning in the Department of State.

What further steps the administration might have had in mind were not announced, but it was understood that they included a series of steps designed to increase the political and economic pressure on Qadhdhafi, and an unsuccessful effort was made to get the European allies to follow suit with regard to the oil embargo and travel restrictions. Other conceivable steps, short of military intervention, included seizing Libyan assets in the United States, deportation of Libyan nationals, a formal break in relations, banning of all exports to Libya, a boycott of other countries trading with Libya, and a blockade. The last two, which are probably too drastic to be taken in peacetime, would be the only ones on the list that would have much effect.

The *New York Times* reported on December 17, 1983 that President Reagan had asked the Department of State to urge other nations to join in a "curb on exports to Libya, particularly of items that might help the Soviet Union." The same report said he had also barred export licenses for a Libyan oil refining and petrochemical plant being built at Ras Lanuf. The administration had few illusions about the likelihood of other nations joining the curb on exports, but was responding to criticisms of its inconsistency in continuing to do business with Libya, and to suspicions that the Soviets were using Libya as a pass-through for acquiring banned high technology items from the United States. This action was significant as an indication of continuing administration concern, but was not expected to have much impact on Libya's economy. Similarly, The *New York Times* of April 30, 1984, reported that the administration was planning to consult with Britain and other allies about concerting pressure on Qadhdhafi.

Meanwhile, the United States presumably is giving some covert support to the Libyan opposition in exile. The nature and extent of that support can only be conjectured, but it would be surprising if it did not include such standard activities as paramilitary training and financial help. It would also be surprising if other governments, such as those of Egypt and Morocco, were not at some point engaged in similar pursuits.[3] This is in contrast to the Americans' actions in the early 1970s, when they passed warnings to Qadhdhafi on two occasions of plots against him, warnings that were transmitted with considerable reluctance and that gained no kudos from anyone, including Qadhdhafi.

Chad

For a while in July and August of 1983 it looked as though the Chad crisis would lead to another, much more serious, armed confrontation between Libya and the United States. Fortunately, the administration prevailed on the French to assume the principal burden of deterrence, while the United States confined itself to giving material aid to Chad and mounting Airborne Warning and Control Systems (AWACS) and carrier-based surveillance of Libyan military activities. The crisis has, however, removed what few doubts may have lingered in Washington minds about Qadhdhafi's designs on Saharan Africa. The common wisdom is that he is trying to build a Muslim empire there, exploiting the internal weaknesses of regimes such as those of Chad and Upper Volta and suborning local leaders through gifts of money and arms. Washington would have welcomed a more vigorous French response to the Chad invasion, including strikes at the Libyans, in order to stop Qadhdhafi in his tracks.

Although this particular crisis is now momentarily on the way to being forgotten, the likelihood that it will erupt again makes it useful to review the history of the problem.[4] A huge, poverty-stricken country, much of it desert and parched grazing land, Chad has been burdened since independence with crippling political, ethnic, and religious divisions too complex to describe here. The struggle today is between factions led by two Muslims from the wild Tibesti region near the Libyan border, Goukouni Oueddei and Hissene Habre. Between them they have dominated Chadian politics since 1979, when Oueddei overthrew the then president, General Felix Malloum, who himself had come to power as the result of the assassination of his predecessor, François Tombalbaye, first president of the republic, in 1975.

Oueddei and Habre were once friends and collaborators, although Oueddei claims noble origins while Habre is plebeian (if those terms have any meaning in an area as rude as the Tibesti). Habre was Oueddei's minister of defense, but the two were rivals for power already and Habre was soon fomenting an armed uprising. In June 1980, Oueddei signed a friendship treaty with Libya which gave the latter the right to intervene against any threat to the internal security of Chad, which Habre clearly was. The Libyans subsequently intervened in force to restore order, and in December 1980 Habre fled to the Sudan, establishing himself in the western border province of Darfur and plotting his return.

In January 1981 Oueddei signed an agreement that was widely interpreted as providing for an eventual merger with Libya (although the Libyans denied that this was the intent), something which caused much concern to a number of African leaders who had begun to fear Libya's ambitions. In October 1981, under OAU and Western pressure, and fearing that Qadhdhafi was backing one of his rivals, Oueddei asked Qadhdhafi to withdraw his troops. Much to everyone's surprise, the Libyans began withdrawing almost immediately. Habre then began to advance on Chad with an irregular army he had assembled in Darfur. He had the support of Sudanese and Egyptians in this effort (and of the Americans as well for at least part of the time).

An OAU peacekeeping force that had been brought in to keep order as the Libyans withdrew was unable or unwilling to confront Habre seriously, and he took Ndjamena, the capital, in June 1982. Oueddei fled to Cameroun and then Libya, where he emulated Habre's example and gathered his own army, with Libyan support, and began a countermarch against the capital in July 1983. Habre's forces proved unable to stop them at the battle of Faya-Largeau, largely because of Libyan air support to Oueddei, and both the French and Americans moved to bolster the government forces. The French committed troops and aircraft in limited numbers, but they sufficed to stop Oueddei's advance. The Libyans have advanced no further, but they are governing northern Chad and Qadhdhafi is speaking of Chad as an "extension" of Libya.

While there have been some notable differences between French and U.S. attitudes toward the problem, President Mitterrand has also spoken of Qadhdhafi's imperialist ambitions, and he seems to share the U.S. view that Qadhdhafi plans to turn Chad into a base for subversion against other states of the region, including the Sudan. The pro-Libyan coup in Upper Volta in August 1983 added to Franco-U.S. concerns in this respect. The French have not taken further measures against Libya, however, and seem to have accepted the Chad stalemate, at least tacitly.

There are several points to bear in mind about this imbroglio. The first is that although the Americans, and conservative African regimes, saw the Libyan intervention in Chad in 1980 as destabilizing, some Africans saw it as just the reverse. The Chadians had been unable to govern themselves or settle their differences, and another African state had intervened at the request of the government to restore a degree of order. The Libyans were not popular with the Chadian population, and they used the occasion to spread pro-Libyan propaganda, but they left when asked and did not behave notably worse than other forces that have taken on similar tasks, such as, the Moroccans in Zaire.

The second is that most governments, including those of the United States and France, had recognized and were doing business with Oueddei and his government, and they were urging reconciliation on the factions, that is, they were not urging Oueddei's ouster. Oueddei was overthrown by Habre because he was not willing to effect a reconciliation, according to the Department of State. The implication is that had Oueddei been more flexible, he would still be in power and the United States would be dealing with him in a normal fashion. Thus, the problem is not Oueddei himself; there seems to be little to choose from between him and Habre, although the latter is better educated and more competent to govern. The problem is that Oueddei is supported by Libya. Whether Oueddei or Habre is in power in Ndjamena is largely a matter of indifference; it is the role of Libya that matters for the United States.

There is a good deal of Chicken Little in the U.S. reaction. If Qadhdhafi truly has plans for a Saharan empire, they are unrealistic. He does not have the population resources nor the military power to dominate and control one, and he will eventually exhaust himself in the venture if he undertakes it seriously. What is more important is that the Chad exercise marks another step in the growing conservative-radical polarization in the northern half of Africa. Sides are being drawn and positions staked out, and the Americans are now involved in the politics of this remote region to a new and unusual degree. The Soviets are unlikely to be far behind, if they have anything to say about it.

The Nature of the Revolution

Qadhdhafi's principal achievement, if that is the word, has been the dismantlement of the Libyan power structure and the creation of a new one. He began with the standard ideological baggage of the Arab revolutionary—support for Arabism and Arab unity, opposition to imperialism, both neo and classic, governmental reform, social justice, hatred of Israel, and so forth. He also emerged as a religious conservative, closing churches, banning nightclubs and alcoholic beverages, requiring rigid observance of Ramadan fasting, and causing problems with the substantial resident foreign population in the process.

It soon became apparent, however, that Qadhdhafi was different and that he was going down a new path. In 1973 he launched a popular, or cultural, revolution, and began a purge of government officials and the bourgeoisie, thereby alienating many of his early supporters, and turning some authority for administration of the country over to "Popular Committees." The philosophy behind this move was explained in Volume I of his personal testament, the "Green Book," *The Solution to the Problem of Democracy*, the burden of which was that the representational institutions of parliamentary democracy and its imitators were a sham and a fraud, and that only direct government by the people was just. This was explained in a series of interminable, rambling discourses to large assemblies of Libyans, a process that Qadhdhafi and at least some of his listeners obviously enjoyed.

In 1975 he announced establishment of "Basic Popular Congresses" at the local level to choose delegates to the "General People's Congress," which was an umbrella organization with authority over the Popular Committees, and resigned from the government to become Secretary General of the Congress. In 1977 he resigned all of his official positions to become the Philosopher of the Revolution. (Today he is referred to in the Libyan press as Commander of the Revolution and Supreme Commander of the Libyan Arab Armed Forces.) Meanwhile, he had foiled a serious coup attempt by other members of the Revolutionary Command Council and had purged the power structure of his opponents, who seem to have been numerous. He had also dealt severely with disturbances at the Benghazi branch of the university and hanged seven students publicly.

He also changed the name of the state from Libyan Arab Republic to the Socialist People's Libyan Arab Jamahariya. The latter word was a neologism, coined from the root for "public" or "throng", which is also the root of the word for republic (Jamhuriya). Whether we call it a "state of the masses" or a "peopledom," as Lisa Anderson suggests, it is as hard to understand as it is to translate accurately, because there is considerable confusion about the functioning of the various committees and congresses. While the usual mechanisms of governance have theoretically been subordinated to them, there is still a functioning, more or less conventional, government structure. The committees and congresses obviously have a considerable capability for interfering with its operation, however, aided and abetted by the innumerable "Revolutionary Committees" set up at all levels as ideological watchdogs over the rest of the apparatus. Furthermore, Qadhdhafi's economic philosophy, as revealed in Volume II of the Green Book, which appeared in 1978, meant the dismantling of the economy—no more private retail trade, wages or rent, only something called participation partnerships and worker self-management committees. Private bank accounts were seized and the currency demonetarized, and the outside observer wonders how the economy can function.

Function it does, after a fashion, and life seems to be tolerable at the village level.[5] In the towns, however, much of the bourgeoisie, which had benefited substantially from the early policies of the revolution, has been pretty well dispossessed. One of the Green Book's slogans, for instance, is "The House is for the Occupants," and the dictum is that "a house for profit is the beginning of domination of the need of another." In other words, one may own the house he occupies, but no more. For the Arab, real estate has usually been the safest and the preferred investment, and to deprive him of ownership of private property except for the house or apartment he occupies and the land he works is a severe disincentive to private enterprise. It apparently is still possible to circumvent these strictures, if one has political connections, or a numerous family, the adult members of which may also own houses, but amassing a real estate empire today is difficult.

These measures, although much less drastic and incomparably less inhuman than those undertaken by the Pol Pot regime in Cambodia, have a similar intent—to restructure society. It is an experiment that has generated a great deal of internal opposition, and there are large numbers of disaffected Libyans now living in exile. By and large, they are not supporters of the old monarchical regime, but were early supporters of the revolution who are now disenchanted and have fled to escape Qadhdhafi's wrath or because they do not like conditions in Libya. The assassination of some of their numbers abroad has reportedly stimulated the survivors to organize a unified movement to overthrow Qadhdhafi, but they have the same factional problems as most exile communities and have so far given no evidence that they are in a position to do anything effective. They have been active in various foreign capitals, including Washington and London, where they staged anti-Qadhdhafi demonstrations in April 1984, leading to the Libyan Embassy crisis in London.

Despite the major accomplishments that must be credited to the revolution as far as the redistribution of wealth and the provision of social services and necessities are concerned, the core of Qadhdhafi's supporters today is probably reduced to those who had nothing before the revolution. Such people are not numerous except in the lower age groups. Meanwhile, opposition comes mainly from the urban sector, from those people who have lost the most—the religious establishment that responded enthusiastically to Qadhdhafi's early puritanism but that has now been left in the lurch (the

Green Book having replaced the Quran for the time being as the guide to behavior),[6] the university students who have been denied even the limited freedom of choice and expression they had earlier, the government officials and businessmen who are now on the shelf, and the politicians and intellectuals who rallied around the original revolution only to be excluded from it as time passed.

If we accept the existence, intentions and numerical strength of the opposition as a gauge of instability, Libya is clearly the most unstable of the North African countries. As of May 1984 there were at least half a dozen Libyan exile organizations dedicated to bringing down Qadhdhafi, and one observer estimates that at least 50 percent of the population opposes him. Possession of the means of coercion, however, is usually the most important single card, and Qadhdhafi controls the military and political machinery in Libya. So far he has outmaneuvered his opponents, who have mounted a number of assassination and coup attempts against him over the years.

The most spectacular attempt to date was an armed attack on a military barracks outside Tripoli on May 8, 1984. Exactly what happened is unclear. Qadhdhafi at first denied there had even been an attack, but subsequently the Libyans announced that they had killed the leader of the attackers, and identified him as a Muslim Brother, presumably meaning he was a fundamentalist. Credit for the attack was claimed by a Libyan exile group, the National Front for the Salvation of Libya, but even its role is uncertain. Qadhdhafi escaped unscathed, in any event, and the attack does not seem to have been well planned or coordinated.

Here as elsewhere in North Africa, the military establishment has been the key to stability and survival. For some time Qadhdhafi has shown signs of dissatisfaction with his, and his unhappiness surfaced in March 1983 with some remarkably hostile press commentary about the army, commentary that could only have been printed with Qadhdhafi's blessing. The army seemed to accept the criticism at the time and went on to perform loyally and well in the Chad operation, but the campaign against it was resumed in the spring of 1984, and Qadhdhafi began talking of plans to replace it with a people's army, the first step toward formation of which would be the institution of universal military service for women as well as men. He encountered resistance from conservative elements in the General People's Congress, who objected to obligatory military service for women, and who managed to defeat the draft law on the subject. Qadhdhafi brought together another "Popular Assembly" which then voted the law, but it remains to be seen whether he will in fact be able to carry it out. (He has also proposed abolition of elementary education, which would become a family responsibility, whether for reasons of austerity or placating the conservatives is not clear.)

The army is unlikely to be enjoying the criticism, much of which is cast in very insulting terms. For example, *al-Zahf al Akhdar*, newspaper of the Revolutionary Committees, on March 21, 1983 ran an article entitled "The Army—Hashish and Frivolity" that began thus:

> A stinking, rotten smell, a deep-rooted reactionary mentality, total and murky ignorance and widespread corruption over which silence can no longer be maintained. This is the army.

(The campaign in 1984 has focused more on the fancy automobiles and luxurious offices the army is thought to have, and on one occasion *al-Zahf al-Akhdar* suggested the people should burn the cars.) The army is even less likely to appreciate being set aside for a people's army, and Qadhdhafi is taking serious risks of alienating the people who have kept him in power. The army may not be willing to preside over its own dissolution.

What all this means in terms of Qadhdhafi's survivability is hard to say. He is clever and ruthless, and he may last for decades. But he may be brought down tomorrow. Certainly he has been careless about acquiring enemies, and one of them is likely to get to him sooner or later. He appears to be following classic divide and rule tactics, however, playing one element off against the other, with considerable success. For instance, he relies increasingly for his own security on his personal guard, which includes women as well as men. He also appears to be relying increasingly on militia groups, and it was the Revolutionary Committees, not the army or police, who were given credit for killing the leader of the May 8 attackers.

Economy

At independence Libya was essentially a ward of the United States and Britain. Their subventions and economic and technical assistance programs helped keep the government afloat and permitted some modest social and economic progress. The country was extremely poor, however, and the average Libyan was ill-fed, ill-housed, and ill-clothed. (The favorite men's outer garment was a British army surplus overcoat, and foreign visitors used to wonder what would happen when the stock was exhausted.) There was no immediate prospect that this situation would change dramatically. The best that could be hoped for was a gradual evolution to a somewhat less desperate level of poverty.

It had long been suspected, however, that there was oil beneath the Libyan desert, and a number of U.S. oil companies, encouraged by a liberal, U.S.-drafted oil law, began prospecting in the Libyan desert in the mid-1950s. In 1959, after a number of dry holes, Esso Libya brought in a well called Zelten II in Cyrenaica, which tested at a high 17,500 barrels a day. The oil boom was on.

Within a year, as other wells were brought in and other companies began to make discoveries, the world began to realize that things would never be the same again. Libya was going to have more money than it ever dreamed of, more than it could spend wisely, and in due course would dispense with the Americans and British.

In the meantime, the United States sought to interest the Libyans in the need to start planning rationally how they were going to use their money. In particular, it suggested that they set up a development council to oversee planning and expenditures, and offered to provide them with the experts from the Ford Foundation or elsewhere to help them do it. The Libyans responded politely, but were uninterested, perhaps because they were suspicious of American intentions or were tired of foreigners advising them what to do. In any event, they went their own way.

With the huge amount of money that began coming in, it was impossible for some of it not to trickle down and to benefit the population as a whole. The Libyan public was impatient with the rate of expenditure, however, and it was widely believed money was being wasted. This, plus the corruption referred to earlier, was one of the most serious complaints against the monarchy.

Under Qadhdhafi the record has been both better and worse. Oil revenues have increased geometrically, and this has permitted massive sums to go into economic development projects. The current five-year plan, announced in January 1981, initially provided for expenditures of $62.5 billion, of which agriculture was to get $10.1 billion and industry $13.5 billion. Projects included an iron and steel complex at Misurata, expansion of the petrochemical complex at Ras Lanouf, $7.3 billion for electricity and desalinization projects, $3.6 billion for housing, $4 billion for education and $1.9 billion for health. Agricultural projects included a 400-kilometer water pipeline from Sarir to Marsa Brega on the coast and a milk products and poultry processing plant to cost $129.9 million. Reduced revenues have forced substantial cutbacks in these plans, but impressive amounts are still being spent. Total investment in development projects from 1970 to 1980 is estimated to have been $35.8 billion, compared to $1.9 billion for the period 1962–1969.[7]

All of this spending has had an inevitable effect (although some of the effect has been the inertial impact of earlier spending), and there have been substantial improvements in such matters as nutrition and medical care. These have brought the death rate down to 13 per 1,000, as opposed to 15.8 in 1969. Literacy is up from 30 percent to 50 percent. Per capita GNP was over $8,500 in 1981, the highest in Africa, compared to $1500 at the time of the revolution and $50 at independence in 1951. There should be no poverty and no hunger. Every family can have a dwelling and the Libyan should be able to eat whether he works or not. In terms of income distribution, people are certainly better off than they were before the revolution, but that does not make them happier. Press reports in the spring of 1984 indicated there was widespread internal dissatisfaction with Qadhdhafi's economic and social measures, as well as with the political climate.

As noted above, the oil glut (and not the U.S. embargo) has seriously affected Libyan oil revenues, which account for 99 percent of exports. The impact has not been as drastic as many ill-wishers had hoped, but the conjunction of lower prices and OPEC quotas, which Libya has often ignored in the past, has sharply reduced the Libyan surplus and forced major economies in development and consumer expenditures.

Describing the extent of the cutbacks is made difficult by the absence of reliable data and conflicting estimates given by different sources. The following is an approximation based on private oil industry and U.S. government sources and is intended only to indicate orders of magnitude. Briefly, Libya earned an estimated $22 to $23 billion from oil exports in 1981. In 1982 that figure dropped sharply to an estimated $13 billion and in 1983 was running at an annual rate of $10-$11 billion. This latter figure is based on the assumption that the price for Libyan crude remains firm at $28.50 and that Libya continues to honor its OPEC export ceiling of 1.1 million barrels per day. The first assumption is probably more justified than the second, and U.S. government sources have been using an income figure of $13 billion for 1983 and 1984.

Over against this, the Libyans had scheduled roughly $12 billion per year for development projects under the five-year plan, have signed arms contracts for something between $2 and $4 billion per year for the rest of the century, and need something like $5 to $6 billion for imports, foreign worker remittances, and so on. This gives an annual total of $19 to $22 billion. Squeezing this down to $10-$13 billion has meant cutting development expenditures at least in half and a sharp curtailment of imported consumer goods, and there are numerous signs of cash flow problems: shelves in supermarkets are reported to be bare, there has been talk of devaluation, the price of local produce has risen as much as 50 percent in the past year, payments to contractors have been slowed down, and contractors are being asked to arrange their own financing. The Libyans are also turning increasingly to barter deals, paying for imports with oil rather than cash, particularly with the East Europeans, and are borrowing money to pay for development projects. The Koreans, for instance, have reportedly agreed to take part payment in crude for more than $2 billion worth of construction contracts (although they were stung on a similar transaction earlier), and the Soviets are reported to have agreed to accept limited amounts of crude in payment for arms.

What these figures mean is that Libya is still relatively well off by comparison with its neighbors, but that a degree of austerity has been imposed and Qadhdhafi is not as free to indulge his fantasies as he once was. Nevertheless, he still has enough money to finance terrorism, which does not cost much anyway, to arm the tribes in the Sahara, also a relatively inexpensive undertaking, and to foment trouble in the Sudan. The Chadian adventure has cost a good deal, however, and this has necessitated more economies in other sectors. The question is whether it will affect his continued involvement in destabilization around the globe—in Africa, Europe, Asia, and Central America. (So far there is no word of his involvement in Australia or Antarctica.)

Even were funds unlimited, there are other constraints on Libya's development capabilities. In the case of agriculture, ground water resources are very limited. Oil wealth has permitted installation of too many modern pumps which have lowered the water table disastrously in coastal areas as the Libyans have turned to crops like citrus fruits, which demand much water. A massive agricultural development project at Kufra, deep in the Sahara, is rapidly depleting water resources that are not being replenished because they are fossil, that is, deposited over the millenia when the Sahara was relatively well watered. The water table at Kufra has thus dropped 15 meters. In time the fossil water will be gone, and Kufra will return to desert. The coastal area gets as much as 20 inches of rain per year and dry farming is possible there, but rainfall is variable, and the 18–20,000 square kilometers of arable land will not begin to support Libya's population, which has roughly tripled since independence to 3.3 million, of which 2.9 million are Libyans. Thus, whatever the Libyans do, they are likely to be dependent on imported food.[8] Today oil supplies 99 percent of their export earnings; what happens 30 years from now, when their reserves will be reduced to the point that they can no longer be major exporters?

Plans for industrial expansion also run up against the Libyan work ethic. This is a common malady in the oil states, where a *rentier* attitude is developing. The local citizens tend to clip their coupons and await the fruits of their investments, while the work is largely done by imported labor. Libya's case is not as striking as those of some of the Gulf states, but the figures are impressive. Out of a work force of 800,000, nearly half are foreign, according to one estimate. Another estimate expresses it differently and says that half of the managerial and professional work force and one third of the skilled are foreign. In the process, the Libyan appetite for work, never very strong, has suffered, and the long-term social consequences of reliance on foreign labor to this extent may be serious.

There are also doubts about the marketability of the products Libya plans to make in its plants, and about the economic and technical feasibility of many of its undertakings. It is reasonable to expect that, as in Algeria, there will be a number of industrial white elephants, although the Libyans actually seem to be more realistic about their capabilities than the Algerians were in the early stages of their industrialization program.

More important than these limitations and doubts, however, is the loss of political freedom that has accompanied economic gains. The atmosphere in Libya today is oppressive. Measuring the degree of oppression is difficult, given the lack of access and the unwillingness of people to talk, but what does come out indicates that Qadhdhafi is running a police state in which no one is safe.

Military

Libya has regular armed forces estimated to total 55–65,000 in late 1981, plus a reserve force, called the People's Army, or Popular Militia, which was thought to have trained 45,000 Libyans (and a number of foreigners) by 1980. These forces are well equipped and include women, some of whom are Qadhdhafi's bodyguards. Libya has spent an estimated $20 billion on Soviet arms since 1976.[9] This quantity of weapons, for example, 2,400 tanks, has been far beyond Libya's capacity to use, and a large part of the equipment is in storage, giving rise to speculation that the Soviets are prepositioning arms. That is possible but seems unlikely. If the Soviets were to place arms in Libya with the thought of using them in an emergency, this would require the stationing of logistics personnel and the operation of depots at a state of instant readiness to issue and maintain equipment. This does not seem to have been done. The equipment is under Libyan, not Soviet, control and reportedly is poorly maintained. Prepositioning would furthermore presuppose a Soviet intention to fight a land war in North Africa, which also seems unlikely. (It would also presuppose confidence in Qadhdhafi's support and cooperation with Soviet policies, another doubtful premise that is probably as clear to the Soviets as it is to the Libyans. Soviet support for Libyan policies, on the other hand, is not too farfetched. There is a congruence of interests between them at times. Both, for instance, may see destabilization in Tunisia as in their joint interest. Both certainly see reduction of U.S. influence in the region as being in their interest.)

There are numerous Soviet, East German, and Cuban military advisors and technicians in Libya—upwards of 6,000. (This figure does not include the Bulgarian road crews and other East Europeans in the civilian sector who bring the total up to about 30,000.) They presumably have trained the Libyans in Soviet military doctrine, which seems highly unsuitable for Libya's circumstances. The army has had four occasions on which it could demonstrate its capabilities—a brief, unpublicized border war with Egypt in 1977 (which was provoked by Sadat and in which the Libyans did rather better than expected), an ill-considered and unpopular expedition to aid Idi Amin in Uganda in 1978 (which appears to have been a fiasco), and the interventions in Chad in 1980 and 1983 (in which the Libyans showed pretty well compared to their disorganized competition). In the 1980 operation, they were aided by a number of mercenary pilots, which perhaps detracts from the grade for their airborne capacity, but it did not affect directly the discipline and effectiveness of the troops once they were on the ground, except in the admittedly vital respect of assuring supplies and communications. The first Chadian adventure may have been a political failure, but the Libyans at least attained their military objectives.

In the second Chadian war, the Libyans showed considerable competence in operating modern aircraft under severe desert conditions, with minimal landing and maintenance facilities—conditions the U.S. Air Force probably would be unable to tolerate. They also moved substantial numbers of men and armored equipment over long distances in terrible heat, and Western estimates of Libyan military capabilities have been revised upward as a result.

Drawing conclusions on the basis of the record-to-date is risky, but it is probably safe to assume the Libyans would perform effectively against the Tunisians. Their manpower limitations, and their reliance on foreign maintenance technicians as well as the distances involved, would severely limit their capabilities against Algeria or Sudan.

Although it is always wrong to disregard any military force with such a stock of weapons, the accumulation of a large quantity of equipment that cannot be used effectively seems to be an aspect of Qadhdhafi's megalomania. He wants the equipment because it is new and sophisticated. If quantity x is good, $10x$ is ten times as good. He may plan to provide the Arab arsenal in the next round with Israel, but Arab failure to respond to the Israeli invasion of Lebanon in 1982 casts doubt on the practicality of such ideas. In the meantime, he is using it to supply other radical regimes and dissident groups, such as Arafat's opponents in the PLO. He used large quantities of ammunition and equipment in Chad in 1983, and has been shipping substantial quantities to the Syrians for use in Lebanon. Perhaps that is the ultimate purpose of the arsenal—interference.

Foreign Policy

Qadhdhafi has been one of the most troublesome mavericks in Arab and African politics for some time, and has distanced himself from all but the most radical elements of the region. His only friends, and their friendship is uncertain, are the leaders of countries like South Yemen and Ethiopia. That he has been totally disrespectful of the norms of polite international behavior and good neighborliness is clear; his motivation, on the other hand, is not. There seems to be no rational explanation, for instance, for his assassination of the Lebanese Shi'i leader, the Imam Musa Sadr, and his companions, in 1978. Whatever Sadr had done, or not done, it would not justify earning the enmity of the Shia by eliminating him in cold blood. Qadhdhafi seems not to understand that he cannot ignore all the rules and expect to have friends. Certainly he does not appear prepared to pay the price of respectability in Africa.

Proponents of the view that he is trying to create a unitary state in the Sahara under Libyan domination claim that he is training Tuaregs (the veiled nomads of the Sahara), Malians, and Western Saharans, and maintain that he intends to use them for the takeover of governments in the area. This is hardly designed to win friends among the states concerned, or their neighbors. Aside from his involvement in Chad, he has repeatedly attempted to foment a coup d'etat in the Sudan. We have already read of his attempt to start a revolution in Tunisia with the Gafsa raid. On his other flank he has been deeply involved in supporting dissident groups and plotting assassinations in Egypt. Whether he is seeking to create an expanded zone of influence, or to bring down the leaders he sees as either too conservative or as traitors to the Arab cause, or whether he has no plan at all but is merely an incorrigible trouble-maker, the extent of the enmity he has earned was shown by his inability to get confirmed as president of the Organization of African Unity (OAU). It is furthermore a gauge of his commitment to his radical role that he was unwilling to make the compromises that could have assured him election to that post. Remarks he made on the occasion of the second aborted Tripoli summit, in December 1982, indicate that he no longer thought the game was worth the candle and was turning his back on the OAU.

Qadhdhafi is a member of the Steadfastness and Confrontation Front, along with Algeria, Syria, and South Yemen (and formerly, Iraq). He boycotted the 1982 Fez summit, rejects totally the concept of a political settlement with Israel, and believes that the issue can be settled only by an armed struggle, one that the Arabs win. They must keep on struggling until they do. This position is consistent with the views of Gamal Abdul Nasser and most of the other Arab leaders of the 1960s and 1970s, and in Arab eyes it is still respectable, although dated. The Reagan and Fez initiatives may lead to progress on a peace settlement, but if they do not, the proportion of Arabs believing that political settlement is not honorable and that they must prepare for another round will increase, and Qadhdhafi, now somewhat isolated, will find himself back in the mainstream. This process may be hastened by the American tendency to identify more closely with Israel, manifested in November 1983.

Qadhdhafi, then, has impeccably radical credentials on the Arab-Israel issue. He also has been a very consistent supporter of dissident movements around the world. There has been a great deal of speculation about the extent and nature of such support. He is popularly credited with being behind any terrorist movement one cares to name, and this is usually impossible to disprove. The full extent of such support will perhaps be revealed when he is overthrown, but it is probable that very few people in Libya actually know the details. Given the lack of coordination endemic to such governments, Qadhdhafi himself may not know everything that is going on. It is evident, however, that at a minimum he has aided a large number of individuals and organizations involved in armed action of one kind or another. They include various Palestinian groups, Carlos, the IRA, Tunisian, Chadian, Ghanaian, and Egyptian dissidents, the Moros in the Philippines, Swiss and Corsican terrorists, the Baader-Meinhof gang and the Red Brigade, the Polisario guerillas in the Sahara, and various Saharan tribal groups. Judging by the Brazilian seizure of Libyan arms enroute to Nicaragua in the spring of 1903, he is also involved in Latin America. Whether he has also been involved, as charged, with the Japanese Red Army, the Basque terrorists, the Puerto Rican nationalists, and others, may be harder to prove, but there is nothing implausible about it.

The catalogue of Qadhdhafi's outrages is impressive: he has attempted to have Libyan dissidents assassinated in Europe and the United States and has succeeded on occasion; he wanted to torpedo the QE2 when it was passing through the Mediterranean enroute to Israel; he allegedly sent a hit squad to kill President Reagan; he tried to have the U.S. Ambassador to Egypt assassinated, and so forth. Of these, with regard to the first, he was following an old North African tradition. The Algerians, Moroccans, and Tunisians all have similar actions to their credit (and indeed, looking around at heads of state in the Middle East today, it is remarkable how many have been involved in political assassinations at one time or another). The other charges are supported by intelligence reports that have not been made public and that are therefore difficult to evaluate. For our purposes there is no need to invent such stories; even if only half of them are true, Qadhdhafi is clearly a destabilizing influence, he is clearly embarked on a course antagonistic to both responsible local governments and Western interests in African and elsewhere, and he seems to be restrained by few of the inhibitions a respectable head of state should feel. He is unscrupulous, destructive, and incorrigible.

The question is whether whoever comes after Qadhdhafi will be any better. He could hardly be more erratic or difficult to deal with, and there are many sensible, normal Libyans who would make decent and capable heads of state. Those who have tried to date have lost, but eventually one of them will get through. At that point there will be a new ball game, but the rules may not be totally to our liking. Qadhdhafi's successor may be no friendlier than he is to the United States, which was unpopular among politically articulate younger Libyans well before the revolution. He will certainly not be able to come to power on a pro-U.S. ticket, and he will have to maintain some of the positions staked out by Qadhdhafi both domestically and abroad. U.S. troubles with Libya will not end with the departure of the Philosopher of the Revolution.

Notes

[1]State Department drafters of the late 1950s used to refer to him in policy papers as "the *aging* King Idris" until someone in the White House pointed out that he and Eisenhower were the same age and told them to stop it.

[2]The officer in charge of the U.S. embassy's branch office in Benghazi, George Lane, had the first official contact with Qadhdhafi. Trying to locate someone in authority in order to get a curfew pass, he went to the radio station, which was broadcasting revolutionary communiqués. Qadhdhafi, then a lieutenant, was directing traffic in the street in front of the station. The person he identified as being in charge was a nameless officer inside.

[3] The Sudanese, for example, are allowing opposition groups to broadcast anti-Qadhdhafi radio programs beamed at Libya. The Moroccan position is ambiguous. Libyan dissidents were being trained there in 1982, but Hassan allegedly undertook to stop supporting them as part of his June 1983 understanding with Qadhdhafi. He has since been accused of betraying one prominent dissident to the Libyans.

[4] For a detailed discussion of the Chad problem, see *Africa Notes*, no. 18 (August 31, 1983), by Alex Rondos, Georgetown University Center for Strategic and International Studies.

[5] See the article "Qadhdhafi's Revolution" and "Change in a Libyan Oasis Community," by John Mason in the Summer 1982 issue of the *Middle East Journal*.

[6] The measure of Qadhdhafi's heresy is given by his ordering the Libyan calendar to be adjusted to start with Muhammad's *death* in 632, not the Hegira of 622, which has been the rule for 1,300 years. This innovation, while not without logic, is a rejection of tradition that many Muslims find profoundly disturbing.

[7] In retrospect, the monarchy was considerably wiser in some economic policies, in the field of agricultural development for instance, than the revolutionary regime has been.

[8] In Roman times Libya exported grain to Europe. Today, after 20 years of serious investment in agricultural development, it imports 60 percent of its food requirements.

[9] See *The Libyan Problem*, State Department Special Report No. 111 (October 1983), p. 2.

6

The Islamic Revival

Since the Iranian revolution the Western world has become increasingly aware of Islam as a political force in the Muslim world. A good deal has been written about this phenomenon, but there has been little agreement about what is taking place.

To begin with, there is a question as to whether there is in fact an Islamic *revival* underway. Various other words have been suggested, such as renewal and resurgence, but all are objected to by one authority or another as implying that Islam was somehow dormant and has now been resuscitated. On the contrary, it is argued, it has simply been following its normal and customary course. The manifestations that have caught the Western eye are not all that new, or unusual, or different from what has gone on in the recent past, acccording to this argument.

It is nevertheless apparent that over the past ten years we have witnessed a transformation in the political role Islam plays in a number of Muslim countries. This may be a normal and recurring phase, but it has produced a situation which is different from that which prevailed before. The question is not, has there been a change?, but, what caused it? and how much importance should we attach to it?

To understand what has happened it is necessary to bear in mind some fundamental characteristics of Islam. The first is that it is a *revealed* religion. Like Judaism and Christianity, it requires the acceptance of certain articles of faith that have been disclosed by divine wisdom to gifted interlocutors, and those who have seen the light tend to be intolerant of other explanations of the universe. The second is that it is *universalist* rather than *nationalist*. It is closely identified with the Arabs because it was they who brought the message to the rest of the world, and theirs is the only language in which the scripture can be written and still be scripture, but it is not doctrinally exclusive with them or any other race of people. Of the 750 million Muslims, only about 130 million are Arab. Most of the rest are South Asian, and Indonesia has the largest Muslim population of any single country.

Thus, while the primary articles of faith accepted by all Muslims—that there is but one God and Muhammad was his Prophet, that the Quran is the literal word of God and was revealed to, not written by, Muhammad, who was a mortal man, and that he was the seal, or last, of the Prophets—are the same throughout the world, the diversity of peoples and cultures within the house of Islam is fully as great as that found in Christianity, and there are important sectarian, doctrinal, and behavioral differences among them. It is therefore just as dangerous to generalize about Islam, or even Islam in North Africa, as it is to generalize about Christianity.

Having said this, I proceed to make a few generalizations. One is that, in principle, Islam is a way of life as well as a religion. It is not something that can be left in the mosque after the Friday prayers, to be resumed the following week, or something concerned only with the spiritual. It is a guide to daily life, and an ever-present determinant in the lives of the devout. It provides the answers one needs for deciding questions of personal status, such as marriage, divorce, and inheritance, for judging disputes and crimes, for regulating the rhythm of the day, for setting sanitary routines, for establishing the norms for rulers as well as ruled. Theoretically there is no area of human activity that is barred to it by belief or practice, and all answers can be found in the Quran, the *Hadith*, or sayings of the Prophet, and the body of religious law that has been built on them.

It is therefore natural for Islam to have a political role, for the Friday sermon in the mosque to touch on political and economic subjects as well as the spiritual, for the mosque to be a platform for protest as well as contemplation, for one's religion to be of direct concern to the government, and for the religion of the government to be of direct concern to the people. The separation of church and state that is fundamental to Western democracy is incompatible with Islam strictly observed.

A second is that Islam has no overarching hierarchy like that of the Catholic church. There are revered centers of religious learning, such as the universities or schools of al-Azhar in Cairo, al-Qarawiyin in Fez, and al-Zeitouna in Tunis, which are regarded as authoritative sources of opinion on religious matters by millions of people, but there is no supreme religious authority or leader, no chain of cardinals, bishops, and priests, no line of religious command from one country to another. Rather, there are autonomous congregations that may accept the guidance of al-Azhar or of al-Qarawiyin or of certain learned authorities in their own town or country, and that may respect the opinions of learned figures elsewhere, but there is no one person who speaks for all of Islam, or even most of it. There are many people who speak for many segments.

There is, nevertheless, what for lack of a better phrase is called the *religious establishment* in each country and town, composed of people of varying degrees of religious erudition who perform fairly standard functions for the community. These people vary from place to place, but in Sunni Islam generally include *imams*, or prayer leaders, in mosques, *qadis*, or religious judges, where religious courts still function, *muftis*, or jurisconsults, who give opinions on questions of religious law, and the *ulama*, or learned men, a body of theologians who are recognized as the final authority on matters of religious law within the polity.

The composition of the establishment and the functions of its members vary from place to place, depending on local practice and the role of the government in religious affairs. While the people described above have traditionally relied for their living on the proceeds from religious endowments and the charity of their families and congregations, as well as sometimes having remunerative, nonreligious occupations or trades, many of them today are on government payrolls, are supervised by a ministry of religious affairs, and display the universal stigmata of the civil servant. Their establishment has, in effect, been nationalized, or bureaucratized.

A third is that in Sunni, as opposed to Shi'i, Islam the religious establishment, with certain obvious exceptions over the centuries, is generally seen as part of the governing elite and tends to support the temporal ruler, good or bad. This is a matter of doctrine as well as practical politics. The Shia, who have a more structured clerical organization and different views on the role of the clergy, are more likely to challenge temporal rulers (although this common conception is now being questioned). North Africa is overwhelmingly Sunni, and this has something to do with the attitude of local religious establishments toward their governments.

Finally, current Islamic attitudes are inevitably affected by the history of the past two hundred years, which has changed the Muslim world in ways that have been profound and traumatic. To understand this one must start with the realization that from the death of the Prophet in 632 until the eighteenth century, while the Muslims had their ups and downs, there was little reason to question the superiority of their faith and practices. Their civilization and their military capabilities were superior in many respects to those of the Europeans, and they saw the latter as crude and inferior.

In retrospect, the tide had begun to turn against them in the fifteenth century, with the expulsion of the Moors from Spain and the Portuguese discovery of the trade routes to India, which had long been monopolized by the Muslims. This was not apparent to the world, however, until the defeats suffered by the Ottoman Turks in Europe in the eighteenth century. In retrospect, the siege of Vienna in 1683 was the high water mark of Islamic power in Europe. By the time of Napoleon's invasion of Egypt in 1798, the decay of the Islamic East was evident to European travelers, who reported that the area was ripe for the plucking. Indeed, Muslim India had already been plucked. By the end of World War I, most Muslim lands had either been occupied by the Europeans or placed under their tutelage. This process of conquest stimulated a good deal of soul-searching among the Muslims, who had already begun to question many of the practices and doctrines of conventional Islam as preached by the establishment theologians and mystic brotherhoods. This self-questioning preceded the European advance but became more intense and relevant to government as the organizational and technological inferiority of the Muslims became more apparent.

The question was, how should they respond to the challenge? With considerable oversimplification, there were two basic responses—that of the secular modernizer and that of the religious reformer. The former argued that Islam and the Muslim world must adapt to the changing circumstances of the modern age. This meant the introduction of European methods and industry and such changes in the role of Islam as were necessary to permit modernization. Among other things, as far as the Ottoman Turks were concerned, this meant the introduction of European-type law codes in civil, commercial, and penal matters to supplement the sharia court system, which was eventually restricted to questions of personal status and religion, and the establishment of a modern, secular school system and civil service.

The reformers, on the other hand, argued that the defeat of the Muslims by the Europeans was the result of backsliding, or divergence from the original Islam of the Prophet. Salvation lay in sloughing off accretions and returning to original sources of inspiration and to strict observance of Muslim precepts (hence the term *fundamentalist*, by analogy with Christian terminology). This did not necessarily mean a rejection of European technology, some of which was useful and could serve God's purpose, but it did mean a rejection of European political philosophies and social practices, which were contrary to Islam and which were gradually creeping into the Muslim world as a result of the wave of secular modernization. The problem posed to the reformers was how to accept Western technology without the behavior patterns that accompanied it.

The dominant ideas that changed the nature of government and society in the Muslim world in the nineteenth and twentieth centuries, however, were by and large the ideas of political rather than religious figures. Whether it was a case of a colonial administration imposing European legal concepts, or of Westernized local officials throughout the Muslim lands seeking to import Western methods, the traditional religious establishment made little contribution: it was essentially an obstacle to be circumvented.

As a result, Islam became a marginal factor in increasingly secular politics. It remained the state religion in most places that had avoided the colonial grasp, but even there it was often something to be taken into account and propitiated rather than be a partner in power. Certain areas of government were normally set aside as the domain of the religious establishment, principally the administration of the sharia, the management of religious endowments, the operation of mosques and religious schools, and sometimes a continuing role of consultation on the licitness of government decisions and actions, but even these areas were not always sacrosanct. The religious courts could be reduced to dealing with matters of personal status by the introduction of civil and criminal codes, or could even be abolished. Religious endowments could be confiscated or nationalized. Religious education could be, and almost universally was, pushed far into the background by increasing popular demand for secular education. Consultation could become a polite fiction. By the end of World War II, in much of the Islamic world the religious establishment had little or no authority and most intellectuals, community leaders and government officials thought this a good thing, because they shared the European view that politically and intellectually, Islam was irrelevant, obscurantist, and reactionary, and the state would have to modernize in spite of it.

As William Zartman points out in *Political Elites in Arab North Africa*:

> Religious figures are absent from the core elite and are minor members of the general elite. Leading 'ulema' (theologians) have access to the core elite but do not provide a major influence on matters of political decision. . . . General religious concerns and sensitivity to Muslim symbols are matters of political culture . . . but the elite do not govern according to specific religious principles. . . . Elites will use Muslim references and signs of identity in their discourse, but this does not mean they are about to rule according to the Qur'an.

The attitudes of the elite that made Islam marginal to political decisions also made it progressively less inhibiting to the transformation of social behavior. Women went out in the street and dropped the veil, they went to the university and entered the job market, they appeared on the beach in bikinis, and they agitated for equal, or nearly equal, rights. Educated people relaxed their observance of the Ramadan fast, ate pork, rarely if ever prayed, and rarely entered a mosque. They had largely turned their back on Islam as a dominating force in their life, although remaining steadfast in their self-image as Muslims. As one observer put it, they were cultural Muslims but not pious believers. To many of them religion meant reaction and secularism meant progress. They left religiosity to the lower classes and the aged.

Throughout the period of secular modernist dominance, the reformers kept up a continuing counterpoint of opposition and criticism, much like their counterparts in the United States. Often so submerged by the tide of progress as to be ignored, they occasionally surfaced with surprising vehemence. Such manifestations as the Mahdist uprising in the Sudan 100 years ago, the foundation and growth of groups like the Muslim Brotherhood in Egypt and the Tahrir, or Liberation, Party in Jordan, and the activities of mystic religious orders across the breadth of Islam gave evidence of a strong and unceasing current of traditional religiosity behind the secular façade. That this current was beginning to come to the surface again was apparent well before Khomeini burst upon the world scene. It was evident in Egypt in the early 1970s, for instance, that the Muslim Brotherhood was alive and well in spite of earlier repression by the Egyptian government. There were also indications of increased religiosity among university students throughout the Arab world, as evidenced by the emergence of new Muslim associations on campuses and of radical Islamic groups (such as the Takfir wal-Hijra in Egypt) which went well beyond the Muslim Brotherhood in their demands, and one of which was ultimately responsible for the assassination of Sadat. Some university students began shedding jeans and miniskirts for "traditional," or "Islamic," dress, which in the case of women was likely to be an enveloping set of garments that concealed the figure but was significantly different from the traditional dress of conservative Muslim women in the same society, while the incidence of beards, considered a sign of religiosity, increased among men.[1] It was becoming acceptable, even innovative and revolutionary, to be pious in a milieu where religion had until recently been largely considered irrelevant.

What is unusual and significant about this revival, if that is the word, is its attraction for secularly educated youth. Far from being a movement led by traditional, religiously educated conservatives, its leaders across the Arab world are to be found among university science students and lay professionals. Reformist agitation is not confined to the bazaar merchants and laborers, the traditional members of religious orders or brotherhoods; rather, it has attracted the educated and skilled. This may make it more ephemeral, as the attitudes of youth change with maturity, but for the time being it gives the movement more dynamic potential than it would have if it were essentially a protest by the elders.

The manifestations of this movement have been spotty, being more apparent in Egypt and Syria than in Jordan or Lebanon, and taking different forms in different places. There are certain common features, however: the proliferation of unofficial Islamic organizations outside the establishment, the appearance of Islamic dress in unexpected places such as universities, the inveighing against, and even attacking of, women who are considered to be dressed immodestly, strict observance of fasting and dietary restrictions by people heretofore relaxed about them, attacks on symbols of corruption and immorality, increased public demand for a return to "true" Islam, or the setting up of an Islamic state, or simply closer adherence to traditional values, and perhaps most important of all, an educated interest in and intellectual commitment to the preachings of reformist ideologues. This is a very different intellectual diet from that of university students 10 or 15 years ago.

The rise of Khomeini was a symptom rather than a cause of this movement, but his overwhelming success undoubtedly gave added momentum to it and suddenly forced the governments of the area to take it seriously. He has shown what can be done with organization and commitment in the right circumstances, and by the revolutionary nature of his accomplishments has freed the reformists, at least in their own minds, from the reactionary label heretofore successfully pinned on them by the secular elite. His success has given them legitimacy as revolutionaries.

What is it the reformists are seeking? Again, there are doctrinal differences between them, and they often display uncharitable, even murderous, views toward each other. There is no overall umbrella organization that speaks for them, and the autonomy of the Muslim congregation is reflected in their anarchy. In general, however, they are seeking basic social, economic and political reforms, and if they are truly fundamentalist, by definition they depend on a literal interpretation of the Quran as a guide for the building of a better society. To this end, they may demand creation of an Islamic state, as Khomeini has done in Iran, or they may not. They certainly demand a rejection of those Western (and non-Western) practices that are incompatible with Islam conservatively interpreted. If they have their way, society will function and governments will run in accordance with the teachings of the Quran, and not secular humanism. Whether this can be reconciled with the needs of sovereign states in the modern world remains to be seen.

Saudi Arabia today perhaps comes as close as any state outside Iran to having Quranic rule. It is the beneficiary of a puritanical reform movement that began in the eighteenth century and that has resulted in a very influential role for the ulama. Yet even there the religious establishment is something to be managed and reconciled to the requirements of modernization. It is by no means certain that this can be done. The effort may succeed in this case because Saudi Arabia is sheltered from financial realities that constrain most Muslim states, and it can afford to run banks that in theory charge no interest, but other states may find it hard even impossible, to do so.

The governments of the Islamic states have reacted in different ways to the reformist challenge, from embracing it as Zia al-Haqq has done in Pakistan, to wary suppression in Tunisia. Except in Iran, no religious group has taken over a government, and it is unlikely that any will, because the process of secularization has gone too far. That a conjunction of circumstances similar to that which occurred in Iran could happen elsewhere is not impossible, but it is unlikely for a variety of reasons, beginning with the high incidence of mullahs or clerics in Iran as compared with other Muslim states. Nevertheless, the increased religiosity of important segments of the population is not something that can be ignored, particularly given the "sensitivity to Muslim symbols which are matters of political culture" mentioned by Zartman. A Muslim government must take account of such stirrings, and must somehow deal with them before they get out of hand. Although reformist agitation is often perceived as anti-Western, it is directed in the first instance against the local power structure, which is at best only slightly less reprehensible than Western imperialism, and a good deal nearer to hand.

An important factor is the dislocation caused by the modernization process. The drift of people to the cities, the declining role of the extended family in urban/industrial settings, the loosening of morals that urban life promotes (or is thought to promote), and the rootlessness of the wage earner, not to mention the crises of slum housing, unemployment, and loss of identity in a larger community, all create a need for security and certainty. Islam provides a rationale for dealing with the inevitable and a standard to which one can repair in uncertainty. It also provides an unequivocal guide to behavior and a social context in which the individual may regain some of his identity and have some sense of solidarity with others. It is one of the few fixed points in a rapidly changing universe, and as such has considerable attraction. More importantly for our discussion, it also gives the answers to why things are going badly and what to do about it—the trouble is corruption and immorality at the top, and the remedy is puritanical reform. With this message Islam begins to lose its marginality.

A second important factor is the failure of the Western models—of parliamentary democracy, of socialism, Ba'athism, and various other formulas for governance—to solve the basic problems of Islamic society in the modern world. This failure has been highlighted by the inability of the Arab nation states to confront successfully their greatest challenge, the creation of Israel in their midst. In that respect, the Egyptian defeat of 1967 was something of a catalyst, marking as it did the utter failure of Nasser's secular policies to cope with the problem of Israel and causing a good deal of soul-searching among Arab intellectuals.

Certainly another cause has been the corroding effect of Western values on traditional behavior. Whether those values were imported by students sent abroad, or by colonial administrators, or by local reformers, they have been attractive because they promise solutions to problems of underdevelopment and economic dependence, but they also pose a threat to Muslim standards of proper behavior and morality. The process of importation has been going on since the eighteenth century, and the Muslims have shown considerable sophistication in dealing with it over the generations. They have reached the point, however, where the attractiveness of these values has dimmed; they have seen the ills of Western civilization and some of them have concluded that its benefits do not justify the disruption brought to their society. Many of their students are returning home convinced that traditional Islam provides answers that are more compatible with human dignity, and their own, than those they found in the Western world.

In brief, religious reformism comes to the surface today as a result of developments that are inherent in the process of modernization or Westernization.[2] Whether it would have surfaced sooner or later anyway is difficult to say. What does seem clear in retrospect is that its appearance in the present circumstances was inevitable.

North Africa

For all its cultural differences, the Maghrib has reacted to the reformist movement in ways very similar to the Mashriq. There has been less violence and less noise, but the Maghribis have been listening to the same preachers and ideas that have moved their eastern brethren, and while their response has perhaps differed in amplitude, the frequency has been the same.

The Maghrib, however, presents a somewhat different religious landscape than the Mashriq. The innate conservatism of the Berbers has meant survival of more pre-Islamic beliefs than in the Mashriq, and has preserved a thicker layer of folklore and custom affecting religious outlook. Thus, while there are tombs of holy men or local saints that are centers of pilgrimage or devotion throughout the Mashriq, they are much more common in the Maghrib and they play a more important role in popular religion. In particular, they symbolize an inability to accept the austere unitarianism that is imposed by Islam strictly observed. Early Islamic coinage, for instance, commonly carried the legend, "There is but one God; he has no associate," that is, there are no saints or intercessors with God.

The poor North African and his wife, however, would prefer to have such an intercessor who will cure their sick child. Accordingly, they will visit the tomb of a local saint and ask him to intervene on their behalf. (Saint worship in North Africa has undoubtedly diminished under the impact of education and secularization, but is still common, particularly among women. Whether it is more or less common than in, say, Italy or Spain is hard to say.)

In contrast to the early Islamic coiners, the newly independent Algerians put the hand of Fatima, the universal Maghribi good luck symbol, on their first coinage and on their national seal. The leaders of the revolution were certainly men of the twentieth century, but they also came from a society in which that talisman against the evil eye was as meaningful as any pious injunction others might choose to put on their coins and bills. (The hand is still to be seen on the seal, but not on newer coins.)

How North African folk religion will eventually react to the reformers is hard to predict. Properly led and inspired, people have a way of shucking off old habits in exchange for salvation. North Africans are no exception, and have done it in the past. Barring the emergence of a modern Mahdi, however, the attachment to folk religion is likely to dilute the strongly unitarian message of the reformers, particularly once it leaves the cities, and to make it less appealing than it might otherwise be.

In North Africa today, reformist activity is most evident in Tunisia and Algeria and least apparent in Morocco, but appearances are deceiving. The ferment is probably just as deep, if not deeper, in Morocco than in the others, but its public manifestations have been less remarkable. Libya is a case apart. There the leader of the revolution has been legislating his own brand of Islamic fundamentalism based on his own interpretation of the Quran. In contrast to the other North African states, in Libya the religious establishment is disaffected and the reformists, if that term can be used properly in this instance, are in charge. Unfortunately, we do not know enough about what is happening in this respect in Libya to describe it accurately. The following survey is therefore limited to the three Francophone states.

Morocco

In Morocco, as elsewhere in the Arab World, the activities of the reformists are outside the framework of the traditional religious establishment. Although the latter has often been known to challenge the monarchy, it is itself part of the ruling elite, linked to other members of that group by family ties and economic interest. Comprising a wide range of religious dignitaries and functionaries, operating a ministry of religious affairs and a network of schools, pious foundations and mosques, publishing journals and participating in the legal system, even though the sharia courts are no longer operating, it is essentially conservative in temperament and unlikely to be involved in revolutionary activity.

The king, in his capacity as Commander of the Faithful, presides over the ulama and is very punctilious about manifesting his religiosity and preserving the establishment. The *habus*, or religious endowments, for instance, have not been nationalized as they have in Tunisia and Algeria, and this is an important source of revenue and influence for the religious establishment. This is but one of the ties of mutual interest that make the establishment an ally of the king, who in turn derives legitimacy from its support.

Outside, and generally looked down on by, the establishment is an alternate, largely rural and working class assortment of religious groups, orders and brotherhoods, many of whom are *sufi* or mystical in purpose, who operate prayer halls, shrines, and *zawias*, or religious centers, that are popular places of visitation by those seeking religious instruction or divine intervention.[3] They are to the religious establishment somewhat as the pentecostal churches are to the so-called mainstream churches in the United States, undoubtedly pious but suspect because of the emotional and superstitious content in their practices. But this is the level of religion that is most relevant to the poor Moroccan, who has not fully abandoned the pagan practices of the pre-Islamic period. The king also derives legitimacy from this popular religious stratum, which generally professes to ascribe baraka to him as well as to various local saints. Historically, however, the zawias have often been sources of opposition and resistance, and many of these religious elements do not accept the King's right to rule, particularly given common perceptions that there is much corruption and immorality in the palace.

The rural Moroccan who is distressed by his condition in the city or town is likely to turn to one of these popular orders for support and guidance. He will find that they have a cell or prayer hall in the quarter in which he lives and will encounter in it people in the same station of life with a background similar to his own. Although the order may spend its time in religious practices, notably the repetition of formulas designed to induce communion with God or ecstasy, and may be apolitical, it has a capacity for building a solidarity of resentment or support that gives it a certain political potential. That potential seems to be largely unutilized today.

Distinct from both these traditional bodies is an assortment of clandestine, or semi-clandestine organizations that are preaching subversive, fundamentalist doctrines. They are particularly active among the university students, who are the traditional reservoir of political opposition. Details about them are fuzzy and inexact, but a knowledgeable source in Rabat estimated in 1982 that there were 15 such groups on the campus of Mohamed V University at Rabat, that 3 percent of the student body was involved, and that an inordinate number of women students belonged, making up perhaps 30 percent of the membership. While the security authorities apparently believe they have these organizations thoroughly penetrated, the Egyptian experience has shown the difficulty of repressing a movement that has as its ideology the official religion of the state.

In this case, student reformists are taking judo and distributing inflammatory tracts from Libya, Pakistan, Iran, and Egypt. They are influenced by the doctrines of the Egyptian Muslim Brotherhood and particularly by the writings of the late Sayyid Qutb, perhaps the most popular and influential of the Brotherhood writers, who was executed in 1966 for advocating an Islamic revolution in Egypt.

The best known of these organizations, and apparently the only one of any size, is the League of Islamic Youth (Jama'at al-Shabiba al-Islamiya). Originally supported by the government as a counter to leftists, it was disbanded after its members assassinated Umar Benjelloun, one of the leaders of the Socialist Union of Popular Forces (USFP) in 1975. One of its leaders reportedly said under questioning that the organization had been established to liquidate politicians and intellectuals whom it considered to be enemies of Islam.

Although the perpetrators of the Benjelloun murder were subsequently tried and sentenced to death or imprisonment for life, and although the organization was officially shut down, it is said to be operating clandestinely and to have several thousand members in Casablanca, Fez, and Marrakesh. Its leaders continue to espouse violence and describe themselves as "Kharijites," a reference to an early sect of dissenters in Islam. The leadership of the league is alleged to be composed of lay professionals—teachers, engineers, physicians, lawyers, and students—not people from either the traditional establishment or the brotherhoods.

The surface manifestations of these activities are similar to those encountered elsewhere—the sprouting of beards, women students wearing Islamic dress and some putting on the veil, the circulation and trading of cassette recordings of inflammatory sermons and religious discourses, pro-Khomeini graffiti and slogans, increased mosque attendance by youths, and increased membership in religious orders by rural youth.

How much significance should be attached to this movement, if it can be called that, is difficult to determine. Given the king's close alliance with traditional religious leaders, his claim to descent from the Prophet, and the continued role of traditional religious institutions in Moroccan society, many writers have assumed that fundamentalist reform has been deprived of much of its appeal. This is a misreading. Certainly the reformists do not have the support of traditional religious elements that Khomeini had in Iran. On the other hand, by all reports the government is taking the movement seriously, formation of an official Popular Islamic Reform Movement as a counter to the reformists being one evidence of this. Other signs are the government's decision to increase the religious content of the school curriculum and the fact that the security authorities have apparently taken the pains to penetrate the reformist organizations. (It is difficult to reconcile their claim that they have done so with reports of the continued activities of the League of Islamic Youth in particular, unless they are using that organization for their own purposes.)

Particularly with what amounts to the suspension of the leftist Confédération Démocratique du Travail following the Casablanca riots, thus closing the principal overt channel of dissent, it is to be expected that clandestine organizations will have an accretion of members from among the urban intellectuals who oppose the regime for one reason or another. While it is commonly said that people no longer question the king's rule but are resigned to it because they know that the alternatives would be, if anything, worse, the religious dissenters have an ideology that goes beyond questioning the nature of his rule on the grounds of human rights or corruption in high places. They are questioning the fundamental assumptions of what is, official religiosity to the contrary notwithstanding, an essentially secular, Westernizing governmental system. It seems unlikely that they will have the numerical strength to do anything effective about it any time soon, but they constitute a new reservoir of disaffection that could create serious problems at all levels of society. They reportedly were among the leaders of the January 1984 riots, and we will hear more of them.

Algeria

In the colonial period Islam was the rallying cry of Algerian nationalism. Adherence to Islam and observance of its practices was one way of asserting one's identity and defying Frenchification. Muslim learned men, or shaykhs, maintained the only schools where Arabic was taught and supplied the principal intellectual and ideological leadership of resistance to the French, preaching that there was an Algerian nationality that should be asserted.

The revolution itself was made by laymen whose motives were secular, not religious, but when independence came, Islam was recognized as the state religion and a good deal of lip service was later paid to Boumediene's slogan that there could be no real independence without socialism and no socialism without Islam. Both assertions are questionable, and, in point of fact, the religious establishment was given no role to speak of in running the government, which was left to the technocrats, few of whom ever went near a mosque. Indeed, in Boumediene's time, mosque attendance in Algeria was like church attendance in Moscow—the old, the infirm, and the idle made up the congregation. This has changed in the last five years—there is a marked increase in the number of young men congregating at mosques, and on a Friday morning they have the aspect of loungers outside the corner drug store in an American town. It has become the hangout for some.

Boumediene nevertheless was obviously influenced by his own traditional Islamic education, and although it was never quite clear whether his rationale was religious or political, or both, he did such things as insisting on rigid observance of the Ramadan fast, cutting wine production and discouraging its consumption, and changing the weekend from Saturday–Sunday to Thursday–Friday, much to the dismay of the technocrats. The latter argued vigorously that this would mean cutting them off from their vital contacts with Europe four days out of seven and that this was contrary to Algeria's national interests. Boumediene was undeterred and insisted that the country should observe the Muslim sabbath, not the Christian. He was on unassailable ground; no one dared defy him and the country converted. This happened in the mid-1970s, an indication that even then, conservative Islamic opinion was a factor in Algerian politics.

Similarly, Boumediene in 1976 ordered the almost overnight Arabization of all the street and shop signs, in spite of the fact that 90 percent of the population could not read Arabic. While his motive appeared to be primarily political (he was attempting to increase the pressure on the population to learn Arabic), Arabization has strong religious as well as political overtones, and this was another measure that had support from traditional Islamic elements in the non-Berber portion of the population.

Since Boumediene's death, Islam has become much more of a political factor than it was. The manifestations, as in Morocco and Tunisia, involve principally the young. For them, Islam has become the language of dissent, of protest against Westernization and the established order, just as it was earlier the language of resistance to colonial rule. Again, as in Tunisia and Morocco, there seems to be no unified organization or movement, but rather a number of scattered groups across the country. In addition to the usual signs—the adoption of Islamic dress by university women, increased interest in pilgrimage, the trade in cassette recordings of sermons—unofficial imams have appeared and organized a network of unofficial mosques, at least one in every city or large town, where the preaching and instruction is fundamentalist. (Although the situation varies from place to place, in most of the Arab world mosques are staffed by imams or prayer leaders who are paid by the establishment or the government and whose Friday sermon is subject to a greater or lesser degree of official guidance. In some places a complete text is distributed, in others broad outlines of subjects and themes are provided. The unofficial imams reject such guidance and preach sermons that are subversive.)

These unofficial mosques have attracted young men in particular, and on occasion in the early 1980s members of the congregation raided hotels and other establishments of ill repute, smashing liquor bottles and throwing acid on women they thought improperly dressed. Both actions are strikingly similar to what fundamentalist groups have done in Egypt and elsewhere in the Middle East from time to time over the past 30 years. The Algerian press tends to label these people loosely as members of the Muslim Brotherhood, even though there seems to be no organizational connection between that group, that is, the Ikhwan al-Muslimin in Egypt, and any of the groups in North Africa (or elsewhere outside Egypt). Thus, in October 1981 the media reported a clash between the "Brotherhood" and the authorities in Laghouat, 250 miles southeast of Algiers, where religious dissidents seized a mosque in protest against the arrest of their leader and called for a *jihad* against the authorities. The Superior Islamic Council, which runs the religious establishment, denounced the seizure and the teachings of the dissidents, and the police eventually seized the mosque and ejected them. (It is interesting that the Algerian media reported this incident at all, since it reflects adversely on national unity.)

Another focus of such activity has been the universities, where students have demanded that rooms in dormitories be set aside as mosques and have joined Islamic youth groups that are neither official nor approved. Similar demands for mosque rooms have been made in factories and government offices and have been met. The provision of mosque spaces in the work place is not unusual in the Levant, but has been in North Africa. In the past, the average Algerian was not thought to worry unduly about his soul while at work, his mind being more preoccupied with earning a living and the price of cigarettes. It is difficult to tell whether this attitude has changed, or was misunderstood, or whether the demand for mosques is simply the product of an active minority that no one can oppose because it is promoting orthodox piety.

These developments, and what appears to be a general increased interest in religiosity, have obliged the government to make various responses. Friday television programs are now almost exclusively religious, all major Muslim holidays now receive much more attention than they did in the past, electronic amplification of the call to prayer is increasingly strident, and more and more mosques are being built by the state. The latter has also set up institutes for the training of imams, and the day is coming when no one will be permitted, at least officially, to lead the prayers unless he has a certificate from such an institute. Most significantly, a long-awaited family status law has been very much under debate, and the religious conservatives have so far managed to exercise a veto over a liberal approach, insisting that its provisions must be compatible with a stricter adherence to Islamic law than had been the original intention of the government and the technocrats. This implies that while the religious establishment may oppose the reformists, its conservative members have drawn strength from their preachings.

The Saudis, Libyans, and Iranians are all alleged to be in some way involved in supporting the reformists, and there is obvious room for foreign manipulation for what appears to be a growing cult. The trading of cassette recordings of sermons and speeches by eastern theologians at the unofficial mosques, for instance, means that the religiously active in Algeria are able to follow trends in similar movements farther to the east. There is no need to look for foreign inspiration, however. There is evidently enough home-grown talent and money to support the reformist movement, and while Khomeini may provide an inspiring example, including the use of cassettes, Shi'i missionaries from Iran do not appear to be active in Sunni Algeria, and it is doubtful they would have a following if they did. They may be having some impact on Algerians in Europe, but that is hard to measure.

The Algerian government, in addition to the steps mentioned above, has also undertaken a morality campaign of its own, at least partially in re-sponse to the reformist agitation, and a number of senior officials and politi-cal figures have been dismissed or arrested for corruption. Meanwhile, the religious establishment has been active in preaching against the subversive doctrines of the unofficial imams and their associates. While the establish-ment has the means and the machinery to propagate its message more thoroughly than the reformists do, it lacks the revolutionary élan of the latter and it probably means considerably less than the latter to Algerian youth who, like most youth, are attracted by anything that challenges the established order.

Just how serious that challenge is remains to be seen. At this writing, the reformists do not look like a threat to the regime, but they are obviously able to provoke a reaction from it, and they are not under control. In con-junction with the social problems of modernization, they could stimulate or add to serious unrest at some point.

Tunisia

When President Bourguiba came to power at independence he embarked on an unprecedented program to modernize the state religion. A personal sta-tus code suppressing polygamy was enacted, religious courts were sup-pressed, the religious endowments were nationalized, the status of the his-toric Zeitouna University, a major religious school, was downgraded, and workers were encouraged to break the Ramadan fast, one of the five pillars of Islam. In his most notorious action, Bourguiba publicly drank a glass of orange juice during the fast and explained that those who were working, like himself, were excused from fasting.

Although some of these measures, and particulary the orange juice epi-sode, scandalized the rest of the Arab world, they received a good deal of popular support in Tunisia, where the dynamic Neo-Destour party was instrumental in gaining public acceptance of Bourguiba's modernist ideas. Meanwhile, as in Algeria, the religious establishment was nationalized and became an administrative body that, in Jean-Claude Vatin's words, func-tioned as an "ideological intermediary of the central power."[4]

In the early 1970s the government supported a politico-religious organization called the Association to Protect the Quran as a counter to growing leftist activities. This organization eventually developed a life of its own, and by November 1979 something emerged from it called the Islamic Revival Movement, which had intellectual as well as working class sympathizers—two lawyers and a philosophy professor were among its first leaders. As it grew, dissension over ideology, tactics, and leadership developed, and the movement split into smaller groups, the most important of which is called the Islamic Tendency Movement (MTI), which sought recognition as a political party in 1981, with Islam as its ideological platform.

Meanwhile, these groups began engaging in familiar activities of the sort we have seen in Morocco and Algeria, including occasional acts of violence carried out under religious slogans, the wearing of Islamic, or "denominational," dress, circulation of cassettes, and so on. The true extent and nature of the alleged acts of violence are difficult to ascertain, but the final provocation as far as the government was concerned was an attack on a Club Méditerranée resort in September 1981. This incident, which was seized on by the foreign press and commentators as evidence of the seriousness of the problem in Tunisia, seems to have been taken somewhat out of context. A demonstration against the club was sparked by the playing of the Israeli national anthem, *Hatikvah*, by an insensitive expatriate social director. The demonstration was composed of people from a nearby village, not confined to members of the MTI, and got out of hand when the police tried to stop it. In any event, the government reacted by banning denominational clothing and sentencing 107 leading members of the movement to prison for up to 11 years. There is some question whether the Club Méditerranée incident was not used as a pretext to cripple the organization.

In September 1982, informed Tunisians were divided in their views as to whether the Islamic Tendency Movement still had a clandestine, cellular organization that was operating outside the prison. All were agreed that it was a serious movement or its leaders would not be in jail, and there was some doubt as to whether that was the way to deal with it. One government official said that although there was no cellular network, reformists were still in control of a number of mosques and were preaching unauthorized sermons. (In Tunisia the government gives the imams the outline of remarks they are to make.) The government was unable to touch them, even though it owned the mosques, because the unauthorized imams were too popular with the congregations in question and it could not risk the political problems seizure and arrest would create. It was seeking more subtle ways of dealing with the problem. The official emphasized the danger of extremist appeals to youth in a moderate society like Tunisia's and said that although the reformists were a minority, they were profiting from Bourguiba's errors in projecting an image that gave many people the impression he was an atheist. The official indicated that he himself was not sure that impression was wrong.

A second man, a political figure, said there was indeed a clandestine MTI network operating outside the prison, that acts of violence by its members were continuing, that it had sympathizers in the army and the government, and that it was profiting from the mistakes of Bourguiba and the reaction against the inevitable loss of identity which modernization caused. A third man, a university professor, agreed that the MTI was serious and described its members as being of two types, sincere nationalists and opportunists. He said a recent opinion poll had shown considerable support for Muslim ideals. People were arguing that morality should be restored to society and were asking detailed questions of imams about how they must behave. Women asked, for instance, whether they could be forbidden to wear denominational dress (the ban has not been observed) and what they should do about being pinched while riding the buses. Could they refuse to ride them?

In the event, those maintaining the MTI was still alive were vindicated by press reports of the arrest of religious militants in early January 1983[5] and by the active role it allegedly played in the January 1984 riots. Although members of the MTI deny any organizational role in the riots, they are popularly believed to have exploited them once they began. That there is considerable support for the MTI, and that it has the potential for being an important political force in the country, was demonstrated by the fact that although it refused to participate in the November 1981 elections after its leaders were arrested, all the parties that did participate, including the Communists, solicited its votes. It seems clear that the reformists have struck a resonant note in Tunisia and it is significant that the movement seems strongest in the most open and progressive of the states under discussion. One explanation is that there has been more importation of Western ideas and attitudes into Tunisia than elsewhere in North Africa, particularly by the chief of state, and this has presented a broader target. The relative freedom of Tunisian society also makes the activities of the reformists easier to carry out and to be seen, and this may give them the appearance of more importance than they actually deserve. It could also be that reformism in Tunisia is no stronger than it is in Algeria and Morocco but that we simply do not know as much about what is going on in the latter two.

Conclusion

Given the events of the past 30 years, it is not surprising to find religious revival a current theme in the Muslim world. Although the concerns of the fundamentalist reformers are broader than those of the Moral Majority in the United States, there is some similarity. There is a nostalgia for old-time religion as a cure-all in both places, and a desire to do something about the destruction of moral standards that once were thought to guarantee human dignity and safety. The Tunisian woman who must commute to work wants protection against the men on the bus, and the businessman who sees his son going to perdition at the Club Méditerranée wants something done about the sex life there. No one knows the inherent limits of modernization. Perhaps there are none, but at least in Islam there are certain sign posts along the way that can be ignored only at one's peril.

That any of these movements constitutes an imminent threat to any state in North Africa is unlikely. Tunisia is the only one in which they seem to have much political potential as of now. In all three the governments possess the means to contain the movement, but one of those means is adaptation of government policies to the new ideology. The demands of the reformists are being taken into consideration and government attitudes modified accordingly. The question today is whether a workable balance can be struck that will mollify the reformists, or at least deprive them of support, and still permit the sort of Westernizing progress that is implicit in economic and social planning now underway. Can religious education, for instance, be increased without detracting from education in technology? Can women be mobilized for the work force without transgressing Muslim moral standards?

Satisfactory answers may be found to all these questions, but they all require a degree of compromise that has not always been a prominent feature of government attitudes in North Africa. Thus, while the problem is under control for the moment, the movements are not, and a failure to understand the deep currents they represent could have serious consequences for the regimes in question. We have not seen the last of Islamic revival as a factor in political change in North Africa.

What are the foreign policy implications of the above? Many Americans, brought up on a TV diet of flag burnings in Teheran, are inclined to equate fundamentalism with hostility to the West and to envisage hordes of Muslims coming over the horizon with scimitars in one hand and Qurans in the other. There is undoubtedly an important element of anti-Westernism in the reformist appeal, which rejects Western values and Western imperialism as injurious to Islam, and the record shows that this hostility can quickly find expression in acts of violence. The reformists, however, seem to be more concerned with their internal than with their external enemies, and in North Africa, at least, their movement is more one of domestic purification than of expansion. Those of their representatives with whom American officials have been in contact usually profess a moderate approach to political issues.

There is no question, however, that fundamentalist ideology will affect the foreign policy of the governments concerned. All foreign policy must reflect domestic realities to some extent, and the reformist current will make governments more sensitive to matters that touch on religious issues. On the Palestine question, for instance, the reformists can be expected to urge against compromise with Israel, and this will be a factor host governments may feel compelled to take into account. Similarly, the stands governments take on social issues at the United Nations, or on such questions as the presence of foreign fleets in the Mediterranean, are likely to be affected by the knowledge that an active minority of the population is waiting to criticize them for aping or giving in to the West. At this point concern about reformist attitudes is unlikely to be critical, because the reformists do not yet constitute factions that are powerful enough to bring down governments. If no progress (in Arab terms) is made in the Arab-Israel issue, however, we can expect an accretion of membership and strength to the reformists, who have preached for some time that Arab inability to bring Israel and the Americans to terms is the fruit of impiety.

Notes

[1]For a discussion of the Islamic dress phenomenon, see the article "Veiling in Egypt" by John A. Williams, in *Islam and Development*, edited by John L. Esposito (Syracuse: Syracuse University Press, 1980), pp. 71–85.

[2]Although the two terms *modernization* and *Westernization* are often used as if they were synonomous, they are not. In theory, at least, modernization, whatever that term means, can be accomplished without adopting Western norms and behavior.

[3]For a detailed discussion of a visitation or pilgrimage center, see *Moroccan Islam* by Dale F. Eickelman (Austin: University of Texas, 1976).

[4]* Unpublished paper presented to the North African Study Group at the Council on Foreign Relations in New York on March 11, 1982.

[5]Additionally, a number of junior officers and noncoms of the air force, reportedly connected with the MTI, were arrested for reformist activities in the summer of 1983.

7

The Problem of the Western Sahara

The conflict over the former Spanish Sahara opposes two states, Morocco and Algeria, with whom we would like to have friendly relations, and offers scope for troublemaking to a third, Libya, which the United States regards as hostile to its interests. Hardly a headline struggle in the American media, the guerrilla war in the Sahara has been a serious drain on the resources of Morocco and a continuing threat to stability in the region and to the survival of the Organization of African Unity (OAU). In particular, the fate of the Moroccan regime is closely bound up with the Sahara, and failure to find a peaceful resolution of the problem will have serious repercussions for King Hassan. The conflict also impedes the United States in developing closer relations with Algeria, and opens an avenue for Soviet penetration into an area that could, with proper development, provide important support to Soviet naval operations in the western Mediterranean and the Atlantic.

Opinions as to what the United States should do about it are divided. For the Ford and Carter administrations this dispute posed a classic dilemma between support for the principle of self-determination on the one hand, and a desire to support a close friend, Morocco, on the other. As usual, the dilemma was posed in terms of decisions regarding material aid and political support for local governments. The Reagan administration has been less inhibited by the self-determination question and sees the issue as one in which a friendly power must be supported, but it too has had to take into consideration the impact of such an approach on our relations with Algeria.

Background

The territory in question is about the size of Colorado and lies between Morocco and Mauritania on the Atlantic coast. Its largely nomadic, Arab-Berber population was put by the 1974 Spanish census at 73,497. This figure is disputed, and the Spanish, who made a serious effort to be comprehen-

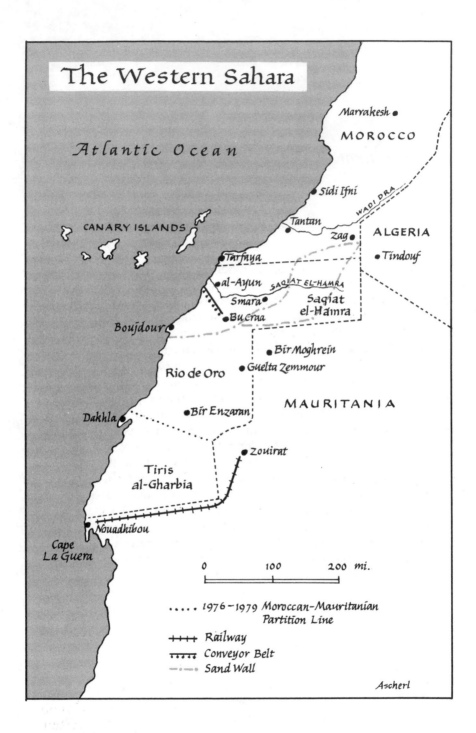

The Western Sahara

Atlantic Ocean

MOROCCO

Marrakesh

Sidi Ifni

Tantan

Zag

ALGERIA

Tindouf

CANARY ISLANDS

Tarfaya

al-Ayun

Smara

Bu Craa

SAQIAT EL-HAMRA

WADI DRA

Saqiat
el-Hamra

Boujdour

Bir Moghrein

Guelta Zemmour

Rio de Oro

MAURITANIA

Dakhla

Bir Enzaran

Zouirat

Tiris
al-Gharbia

Nouadhibou

Cape
La Guera

| 0 | 100 | 200 mi. |

..... 1976–1979 Moroccan–Mauritanian
          Partition Line

+++++ Railway

┬┬┬┬┬ Conveyor Belt

─·─·─ Sand Wall

Ascherl

sive and accurate, admit that their results were not entirely reliable. More recent estimates by students of the problem put the probable total of native Saharans, as opposed to Moroccans and other nonindigenous inhabitants, at 125–150,000.[1] The sparseness of the population reflects the harsh desert climate (2 inches per year average precipitation) and lack of agricultural resources of the region.

Considered by the Moroccans to be part of their territory, the Western Sahara was not effectively controlled by them and they were unable to prevent Spanish merchants from operating in the area known as Rio de Oro (south of Cape Bojador or Boujdor) in the mid-nineteenth century. The Spanish government subsequently claimed a protectorate over the coastal zone, but further Spanish penetration was hindered by French claims to Mauritania and the opposition of local tribes. In 1904 the French ceded to Spain, in a secret agreement, the region north of Rio de Oro, called the Saqiat al-Hamra, or Red Rivulet. The French subsequently tried to negate this agreement, perhaps because it was in conflict with their Treaty of 1912 with the Moroccan sultan, but under British pressure finally agreed in March 1912 to French and Spanish "zones of control," and in November 1912 gave Spain the Saqiat al-Hamra and control over the area between it and the Oued Draa or Draa River, a region loosely called Tarfaya. At the time the Spanish also controlled Northern Morocco, Ifni, on the Atlantic Coast, and the enclaves on the Mediterranean coast mentioned earlier.

Maintained as the colony of Spanish Sahara until 1958, the two regions of Rio de Oro and Saqiat al-Hamra then became a province of Spain. Tarfaya and Ifni were ceded to Morocco in 1958 and 1969, respectively.

The Spanish put almost no money or effort into the Sahara, which they regarded as important primarily because of its strategic position opposite the Canaries. They were interested in denying it to unfriendly powers, and that was about all.

In the late 1960s, however, they began to develop the mammoth phosphate deposits at Bou Craa, and made a substantial investment ($400–500 million) in infrastructure, including the world's longest conveyor belt and a good deal of special excavating equipment from the United States.

Meanwhile, the Spanish Sahara was included on the great list of places to be decolonized in the wave of independence that swept over Africa and Asia in the late 1950s and early 1960s, and the first of numerous UN resolutions calling for self-determination for the Sahrawis, or Saharan people, was passed by the General Assembly's Fourth Committee on October 16, 1964. This was followed by other resolutions in the same vein, to which the Spanish responded that the Western Sahara was a province of metropolitan Spain and therefore not subject to decolonization. Meanwhile, Morocco, Mauritania, and Algeria, while supporting the principle of decolonization, were concerned that it be implemented in a manner that would safeguard their own national interests.

The Moroccans in particular had long claimed the area in question, tracing their claim back to the Almoravid Empire (the Almoravids, 1060–1145, were nomadic Berber tribesmen from the region in question who ruled Morocco, Spain, and western Algeria at one time), to their much later control of all the territory south to Timbuctu, and to the fact that the Moroccan sultan had long appointed *caids* or district officers among certain tribes of Saqiat al-Hamra, that his name was mentioned in the Friday prayers in that area, that his religious authority was recognized there, and that tribes of the area took the *bay'a*, or oath of allegiance to the sultan, in the nineteenth century. Judging by their statements, the Moroccans apparently assumed that if a free vote were to be held, the population would opt for integration with Morocco. Thus, in 1970 their official posture was that there could be no question but that a referendum should be held in the colony. The only question was how to ensure that it was free. This meant that the Spanish would have to depart and let the United Nations supervise it.

During this period the Moroccans were educating a number of young Saharans at Mohamed V University in Rabat, and apparently visualized them as the ruling elite of the province when annexation occurred. By 1973, however, it had begun to dawn on the Moroccans that given a choice, the Saharans would probably opt for independence and that few of them wanted to be part of Morocco. Revelation of this state of affairs came via the students at Mohamed V University, who began expressing anti-Moroccan sentiments, to the distress of the Moroccan authorities.[2] Soon thereafter the latter stopped talking about referenda and began casting about for a negotiated settlement between themselves, the Algerians, the Mauritanians, and the Spanish. The realization that the Sahrawis might choose independence presumably was a factor in Moroccan support for UN General Assembly Resolution 3162 of December 14, 1973, calling on Spain to consult with Morocco, Mauritania, and "any other interested powers" on the organization of a referendum in the province.

Algeria was another "interested power," and its position on the question went through several apparent and puzzling changes, discussed below, but one consistent theme in public and private statements was that Algeria had no claim on the area itself, but merely wanted, (a) to see its people given a chance to determine their own future and (b) to support the OAU position on the sanctity of colonial borders. It has been claimed, particularly in Moroccan circles, that the Algerians were motivated primarily by a desire to have a corridor to the Atlantic from Tindouf, in southwestern Algeria, where there are substantial iron ore deposits, and to have a weak Saharan state which they could dominate. Similarly, Moroccan actions are often ascribed simply to a desire to control Saharan phosphates.

Access to the Atlantic and control of phosphates were undoubtedly of importance to the Algerians and Moroccans respectively, but it would be a mistake to deduce their behavior therefrom. In both instances the prime motivations, as seen by observers on the ground at the time, were political, not economic. Although some observers question the sincerity of Hassan's motives and maintain that his purpose was to divert attention from internal problems, the Sahara is for Moroccan nationalists a piece of sacred *terra irredenta* which was torn from them in the nineteenth century by Spain and which must be united with the homeland. Their claim is historic and long antedates the discovery of phosphates. The phosphate deposits were a very welcome bonus, but they were not the first motive. Similarly, while the Algerians at one time were interested in an arrangement to get their iron ore out of Tindouf and to the Atlantic, they already had a reasonable offer of one from Rabat in a 1972 border agreement. They undoubtedly could have lived with what the Moroccans proposed then, and reiterated in 1975, but said they were not interested. In fact, they claimed in 1976 that it would be cheaper to build a railroad south to Tindouf and freight the ore from there to the point south of Oran where they proposed to build a steel plant, than to take it out via the Atlantic coast. These calculations may have been erroneous, they may even have been sour grapes, but exploitation of the Tindouf ores was far in the future in any event. The Algerians could conceivably (but improbably) go to war because they wanted a weak Saharan state, but not because of access to the sea. There was no need for them to do so.[3]

The Mauritanian position was motivated as much by fear of Moroccan intentions as by anything else. The Mauritanians, who were considered to be in the Algerian orbit in the early 1970s, did not look forward to the idea of Morocco extending to their border and would have liked some buffer between them. (Morocco had originally claimed all the coast as far as Senegal and did not relinquish its claim to Mauritania until 1969.)

Although there had been a number of skirmishes between Spanish troops and nationalist elements in the Sahara in the early 1970s, the pace of the issue had been fairly leisurely until the summer of 1974, when the Spanish informed Morocco, Mauritania, and Algeria that they were going to publish a *status* whose goal was *self-determination* for the Sahara. Then, in August 1974, Spain announced that there would be a referendum under UN auspices to determine the future of the colony. Spanish expectations were not entirely clear, but there was evidently a substantial body of Spanish officials who hoped that the referendum would lead to creation of an independent state that would maintain a special relationship with Spain. King Hassan countered by proposing on September 17, 1974, that the Spanish and Moroccans settle the problem either through referral to the International Court of Justice or through annexation by Morocco. There would be no option for independence. Spain rejected the proposal.

In late October 1974, a summit of Arab chiefs of state was held at Rabat. President Boumediene of Algeria, as well as Hassan and President Ould Daddah of Mauritania, attended. At some point prior to, or during, this meeting, Hassan and Ould Daddah reached an agreement on dividing the Sahara between them. The Moroccans claimed subsequently that Boumediene had been informed and had approved of this deal and produced a tape recording of his remarks to the conference to prove it. The speaker on the tape sounds very much like Boumediene; he regrets that he must leave early to return to Algiers to prepare for the twentieth anniversary of the revolution, expresses pleasure at the agreement that has been reached between Mauritania and Morocco, and specifically mentions the "piece" (jiz'a) that will go to each of those states. Senior non-Moroccan Arab diplomats in Algiers a year later maintained that the tape was authentic and that the chiefs of state who were present had understood Boumediene's remarks to mean that he had accepted a division of the territory between Morocco and Mauritania.

Published accounts of the Rabat Summit do not mention these reported remarks of Boumediene, which were made in executive session, and the Moroccans did not come forward with the tape until much later, when the problem was already out of control. It is not certain why he made them, if he did. The Moroccans claimed he was counting on the Spanish to prevent the agreement from taking effect on the ground. He may also have counted on Mauritanian-Moroccan differences making it impossible to implement, but that seems very imprudent and unlike Boumediene. In the fall of 1975 Boumediene claimed vehemently to the author not to have known of the Moroccan-Mauritanian agreement at the time it was negotiated, but other Algerians are vague in their responses to questions as to whether he in fact made the taped remarks. They maintain that in any event, Algerian policy on the question has been constant and perceptions of inconsistency are the result of misinterpretation. This is hard to swallow.

Whatever Boumediene did or did not say, the Moroccans and Mauritanians, who had been at bitter odds over the Sahara a few months earlier, were to be seen collaborating after the Rabat Summit on a resolution at the UN General Assembly (3292 of December 13, 1974) that called for referral of the question to the International Court of Justice to determine whether when the Spanish came in 1884 the territory had been *res nullius*, that is, belonging to no one, as the Spanish claimed, and if not, what legal ties existed between the territory and Morocco and Mauritania. There was a good deal of support for the resolution, which would postpone the crisis for a while, but it was generally regarded as pro-Moroccan and the Spanish were unhappy with American support of it.

The court then became seized of the problem, and the Spanish, under pressure of increased guerrilla activities and world opinion, announced on May 23, 1975, that they were going to transfer power as soon as possible after the court announced its findings. This increased pressure on Hassan to reach a negotiated solution. In the late spring there was a visit to the Sahara by a group from the UN Committee of 24, who announced in October that they had found the Saharans wanted independence. The Algerians made much of this, while the Moroccans belittled it.

Meanwhile, in early July, Algerian Foreign Minister Bouteflika went to Rabat and met with Hassan. A communiqué was published on July 4 that was read by observers in Algiers and elsewhere as indicating agreement had been reached by the two sides.[4] It was known that Boumediene had personally cleared the language of the communiqué. He had even changed some of it. The language was vague, but it clearly implied that in exchange for Moroccan ratification of the Hassan-Boumediene border accord signed at Rabat in June 1972 (which recognized Algerian ownership of Tindouf—a territory originally Moroccan but gerrymandered into Algeria by the French) and agreement on the modalities of Algerian access to the Atlantic, the Algerians would not cavil at Moroccan-Mauritanian acquisition of the Sahara.

Observers were therefore surprised when, a few weeks later, the Algerian delegate at the court vigorously attacked the Moroccan claim to the Sahara. It seemed Bouteflika had been repudiated, and according to the then Moroccan ambassador to Algeria, who was sent to the General Assembly to lobby, Bouteflika subsequently admitted as much when braced by him in the delegates lounge.

There were no further switches. Algeria remained firmly opposed to Moroccan acquisition of the Sahara. This was reported to be a personal position of Boumediene, and one which was unpopular within the Algerian government and the Council of the Revolution. Unlike the situation in Morocco, the Sahara was not a vital issue to the Algerian man in the street, and the Algerian technocrat deplored the diversion of resources which commitment to oppose Morocco meant. This attitude still persists.

The Green March

The International Court of Justice handed down its opinion on October 16, 1975, shortly after the Committee of 24 gave its report. It declared that while Morocco had "ties of allegiance" with the Sahara, they did not constitute sovereignty and should not stand in the way of self-determination. In other words, they found against Morocco.

Hassan had meanwhile been making preparations for what became the Green March. He had ordered the stockpiling of supplies and transport at various points throughout the kingdom, and when the court decision was published he went on the air and informed his people that they had won— the court had found that the Sahara had ties of allegiance to Morocco and under Islamic law allegiance was tantamount to sovereignty, since it meant loyalty and faithfulness to the sovereign. Therefore, it only remained for the Moroccans to march in peacefully and reclaim what was theirs. To that end, he was organizing a march of 350,000 unarmed citizens to the Sahara. It is indicative of the popularity of the issue that even educated Moroccans did not question the king's selective interpretation of the court's opinion.[5]

The response was electric. Never has there been a more dramatic demonstration of the royal baraka. The king's political fortunes soared. Everyone rallied round—Communists, USFP, Itiqlal, rich and poor, countryman and urbanite, opposition, and supporters. There was a dramatic change in political atmosphere; the Sahara issue had roots deep in the Moroccan nationalist psyche.

Meanwhile, the Spanish and Algerians were in a state of agitation. Franco lay on his deathbed and there was disarray in Madrid. Although much remains to be told about this period, there were several Spanish factions urging different courses of action. The diplomats supported self-determination, the military were opposed to ceding the territory to Morocco, and conservative Falangists favored Morocco.[6] On November 2, Prince Juan Carlos announced in al-Ayun that Spain would protect the legitimate rights of the Saharan people, while the Spanish delegate at the UN told the Security Council that Spain "would repel with all means" the Moroccan march into the Sahara, statements much applauded by the Algerians. Then, on November 6, when the Moroccan mass approached, the Spanish army withdrew 12 kilometers from the border rather than risk the opprobrium of firing on unarmed civilians. Juan Carlos's words had been repudiated by inaction. Hassan's followers (he was not physically leading them but directed the march from a command post safely in the rear) penetrated 11 kilometers and stopped. Both sides had preserved their honor. On November 14 it was announced that Spain, Morocco, and Mauritania had reached agreement on shared administration of the Sahara until the end of February 1976, when the Spanish would withdraw. A deal had been made.

Boumediene was furious and blamed the United States. He claimed that Hassan would never have moved without a green light from the Americans and that the Spanish would not have reversed themselves except under U.S. pressure. The U.S. government, through the author, denied this, as did the Spaniards, but Boumediene was unconvinced. To him, the Green March would not have been possible without U.S. connivance and support.[7]

Boumediene made it explicit to the author at the time that his opposition was political—Algeria had no territorial claims, but it was a party to the question, something that had been recognized by both Mauritania and Morocco. It had something to say, and it was not going to stand idly by while the map of North Africa was changed this way; its security was affected and it could not accept that. The world would see. Hassan had bitten off more than he could chew.

Boumediene was apparently counting on the Moroccan opposition to rise up against Hassan with Algerian help and in late 1975 and early 1976 made an abortive effort to prod it into doing so. He evidently did not understand the extent to which Hassan had rallied, or pre-empted, the opposition, which genuinely supported the Moroccan claim. When an attempt to organize an anti-Hassan movement failed, he turned to the Polisario (Popular Front for the Liberation of Saqiat al-Hamra and Rio de Oro) and made it his chosen instrument, supplying it with arms, vehicles, food, and other supplies, training its troops and giving them sanctuary in and around Tindouf.[8] In February 1976 one of his senior advisors told visiting American officials, "We're going to bleed Hassan white."

The rest of the world paid little attention to Algerian and Polisario capabilities at this point, however, and there was general acclaim in the international press for the brilliance of Hassan's bold move. He had the other Arabs on his side (they saw his actions as consistent with the concept of Arab unity) as well as most of the Africans, in spite of his apparent violation of the OAU doctrine on the sanctity of colonial borders. He also seemed to have the U.S. government on his side, or at least not opposing him. The world apparently had consented to the *fait accompli*. The Moroccans proceeded to occupy the Sahara and seemed to be masters of the situation, in spite of Polisario pinpricks.

The Polisario

The Polisario was formed by Saharan students and intellectuals in May 1973, and made its first strike against the Spanish on May 20 of that year. Demanding independence from Spain, it continued to mount armed attacks and demonstrations against the Spanish over the next two years until the Green March, when it turned its energies against the Moroccans. While not a great deal was heard about its activities against the Spanish, they undoubtedly were one factor in the Spanish decision to vacate the territory. Polisario chagrin at seeing the prize go to the Moroccans is therefore understandable.[9]

The tribal situation in the Western Sahara is confused and complex, but in simplified terms, there are three major tribal confederations: the Reguibat, the Tekna, and the Ouled Delim. The Reguibat, although some of their number raise sheep and goats in the coastal region and have limited mobility, are camel nomads who have always ranged over great areas of the desert in the Western Sahara, southern Morocco, Algeria and Mauritania. They are redoubtable fighters and the French and Spanish did not subdue them until the mid 1930s. Their experience and tribal organization prepare them well for guerrilla fighting. Traditionally, they are anti-Moroccan.

Some Tekna, on the other hand, are traditionally labeled as pro-Moroccan, while the Ouled Delim are supposed to be politically as well as geographically closer to Mauritania. Both are traditional rivals of the Reguibat. The Polisario draws its strength primarily from the Reguibat, but it has also drawn members from other tribes in the territory. It is presumably from the ranks of the Tekna and Ouled Delim that many of the Saharans who greet visiting American congressmen with affirmation of their loyalty to Morocco are drawn, but Reguibat can also be found who will do the same. (There are no reliable data on the numbers of members in the various tribes, but based on empirical evidence, that is, the estimated number of refugees at Tindouf, at least half the population must be Reguibat or allied tribes.)

One basic issue is whether the Saharans are Moroccans. The Moroccans maintain that they are, pointing to tribal areas that include Moroccan territory, ties of family relationship, cultural similarities, historical relationships, and declaration of loyalty from a wide variety of Saharans. The Saharan members of the Polisario, on the other hand, maintain that they are not, that their language, customs, and tribal organization are quite different from those of the Moroccan tribes, that they have never accepted Moroccan suzerainty and that those swearing loyalty to Morocco are either Quislings or not true Saharans. The Polisario thus represents a nationalist movement in the basic sense of that term—a group claiming to be a distinct people. Since it is unlikely to win the military contest, the success or failure of the movement depends largely on the extent of its recognition by external powers.

The first foreign power to aid the Polisario was Libya, which gave it unspecified amounts of financial and arms aid as far back as 1973. Indeed, Qadhdhafi has claimed that Libya founded the Polisario in 1972, but that is not taken seriously. It did not begin to constitute a serious military force until the Algerians began giving it support in 1975–76. In the succeeding eight years, arms supply relationships have gone through various phases, with the Libyans at one point being the principal suppliers. The Algerians are the principal suppliers today, but no reliable figures on amounts and types are available. In the early stages of the conflict some Algerian troops were actively engaged on the side of the Polisario, but after a disastrous engagement at Amgala in January 1976 (for which Boumediene was blamed by some of the survivors because he refused to authorize air support for the surrounded garrison) this ceased.

The Polisario has also gained recognition, but little material support, from many states of the Third World, including a majority (28 out of 50) of the members of the OAU. It has not been recognized by the United States or by major European powers (including the Soviets), however, and this has been a significant political obstacle which it has so far been unable to overcome. The current status of the Saharans is somewhat like that of the Kurds, admirable fighters the world wishes would make their peace with their overlords and stop posing inconvenient questions about self-determination.

Polisario armed strength is another area of controversy. As of September 1982, U.S. intelligence officials in the area estimated that the Polisario numbered 7,000 armed fighters, and one official source in 1984 put them at 3,500. Other estimates have gone as high as 20,000. A well-placed Polisario figure told the author in 1983 the number was 10–15,000. Whatever figure is used, it is testimony to the remarkable fighting abilities of the Saharans that a body of irregular troops that size is holding down 40–50,000 regular Moroccan troops sheltered behind a fortified wall. The Polisario is armed with largely Soviet materiel—light modern weapons and some heavy equipment, including track-mounted SAM-6 missiles. These have presumably been supplied to the Polisario by the Algerians and Libyans with Soviet knowledge, but the Soviets have not been supplying weapons directly. Polisario tactics have been built around the use of jeep-like vehicles for long-range patrols and hit-and-run raids, and the Moroccans have been unable to defeat them on their own ground.

Most of the Polisario's fighters come from the large number of Saharan refugees living in the camps around Tindouf. Again, there is no agreement on the number of these refugees. The Saharans claim 150,000, the Moroccans say there are only 15,000 and independent relief agencies put the number at 80,000 in early 1977.

Drawing on the testimony of defectors, the Moroccans have routinely claimed, almost from the beginning of the fight, that there were substantial numbers of Cubans, Malians, Libyans, and various other non-Saharans fighting with the Polisario, but have not brought forward any convincing evidence. In particular, they have not produced any non-Saharan prisoners.[10] Given the regularity with which nomadic tribes of the Sahara ignore national borders, it is quite likely that there are Malian tribesmen in Polisario. There have also been a few Cuban medical personnel at Tindouf. By and large, however, the Polisario seems to be of Saharan origin as advertised.

Although the difference is sometimes more apparent than real, the Polisario is in theory the political wing of the Saharan provisional government, the Saharan Democratic Arab Republic (SDAR), while military activities are the responsibility of the Saharan Popular Liberation Army. The term Polisario is used locally to cover all three, but the distinction between it and the SDAR should be kept in mind. It is the latter that maintains diplomatic contacts and the framework of a state. Its headquarters are in the Tindouf area, but it maintains representatives in Algiers, Madrid, and various other capitals as well as at the United Nations.

The War

On February 27, 1976, the day after the Spanish withdrew completely from the Sahara, the Saharan Democratic Arab Republic was proclaimed by the Polisario. According to the Algerian media, which devoted a good deal of attention to the event, this transpired at Bir Lahlou on the eastern edge of the territory, but the foreign correspondents who attended were not sure where they were and suspected that the ceremony took place on the Algerian side of the border. The new republic was recognized by Algeria a week later and Morocco immediately broke relations in retaliation, announcing that it would do the same with all other governments that followed Algeria's example.

In April 1976 the Moroccans took Guelta Zammour, the last hamlet in the Western Sahara still controlled by the Polisario, and reached agreement with Mauritania delimiting their respective holdings. In June there was an audacious Polisario attack on Nouakchott, and President Ould Daddah then asked for Moroccan military help to defend Mauritania. The fact that the Polisario could project a force of 500–600 men from Tindouf to Nouakchott, a distance of 1,000 miles, was sobering, but it did not deter the Moroccans from consolidating their position, and there seemed little question but that they would succeed in imposing their control throughout the area.

The Polisario gradually grew in strength, however, and by mid-1978 the Moroccans were in trouble. Ould Daddah was overthrown by a military coup on July 10 and the new Mauritanian junta entered into a ceasefire arrangement with the Polisario and subsequently opted out of the fighting. Meanwhile the Polisario had begun attacking Moroccan positions within Moroccan territory, that is, not in the Sahara.

Moroccan performance in response to these attacks was spotty, and there were obvious problems of organization, leadership, and supply. In particular, Moroccan air support was not as effective as it should have been, in part because the command structure was too centralized, with the king making decisions that should have been made routinely by local commanders, and partly because the F-5 aircraft in the Moroccan inventory were not designed for antiguerrilla operations. King Hassan saw the problem as being one of equipment, and turned to the United States with a request for more, including OV-10 reconnaissance aircraft, helicopter gunships, and more F-5s.

By this time, however, two developments were affecting U.S. willingness to respond. The first was the declining support for the Moroccan position in the Third World, particularly in the OAU and in the U.S. Congress.[11] The second was a matching disinclination within the Carter administration to get too heavily involved in supporting the Moroccans.

Briefly, although the United States recognized the Madrid agreement of November 14, 1975, which conferred administrative authority over part of the Sahara on Morocco, it was also on record as voting for various UN resolutions calling for an act of self-determination by the Saharans. These included 3458 (A) of December 10, 1975, which reaffirmed the inalienable right to self-determination " . . . of all the Saharan population originating in the territory." Although the Moroccans claimed that the Saharan territorial assembly, or Jemaa, had met on February 26, 1976, and that the 65 members (out of a total of 102) who were present had voted unanimously to integrate the Western Sahara into Morocco and Mauritania, and that this constituted an act of self-determination, neither Spain nor the United Nations recognized the vote as valid. Neither did the United States.

Under the Carter administration, a close look was taken at the problem, and the Department of State's legal advisor issued an opinion saying that the use of American arms against the Polisario in the Sahara would contravene the U.S. military assistance agreement with Morocco, since arms were supposed to be supplied only for the defense of Moroccan territory, and the United States did not recognize the Sahara as being Moroccan. The Moroccans, however, were obviously using U.S. equipment in the Sahara, particularly the F-5s supplied some time earlier. Meanwhile, the United States was in the process of shipping them $500,000,000 worth of arms under a modernization program begun in 1974 and designed to equip two brigades to fight against Algerian armor. There was no doubt the Moroccans would use this equipment in the Sahara if it suited their purpose. The American military aid mission had no control over its disposition.

Nevertheless, a series of efforts was made to get some sort of meaningful commitment from the Moroccans not to use American arms in the Sahara. On one occasion, in the summer of 1978, visiting American officials thought they had a commitment from the king himself, only to be told later by one of his advisers that they had misunderstood his remarks. By October 1978 this had become a serious issue in bilateral relations, and the Americans hoped to resolve it during the King's November visit to Washington. No agreement was reached there, however, and the issue dragged on until the fall of 1979, when President Carter agreed to sell $232.5 million worth of equipment, including 20 F-5Es, 24 Hughes 500 MD helicopters, and six OV-10s to Morocco, and to relax the U.S. position on the use of such arms in the Sahara.[12] Meanwhile, the Moroccans had occupied the remainder of the Western Sahara after the Mauritanians signed a peace treaty with the Polisario and withdrew from their portion in August 1979.

At the time the United States agreed to the 1979 arms package it was accepted wisdom that the equipment involved would not dramatically alter the course of the war, in which the Moroccans had just suffered damaging losses at widely scattered points in Morocco and the Sahara. It was hoped, however, that it would give a salutary lift to Moroccan morale, which was beginning to suffer from the armed forces' inability to deal effectively with the Polisario and from the increasing isolation that Morocco was facing from the rest of the Third World. In any event, Moroccan performance improved in the spring of 1980, more because of improved operational procedures than because of new equipment, and a new strategy was developed for consolidating Moroccan positions in what was called "the useful triangle" of the Sahara, roughly the northwestern half of Saqiat al-Hamra. To that end, a 400-mile fortified barrier, called The Sand Wall (U.S. military call it The Berm), was built from Zag to al-Ayun and Boujdour passing by Smara and Bou Craa (see map). As of early 1984, the wall was being supplemented by extensions taking it closer to the Algerian frontier, and the Moroccans apparently plan to enclose most of Saqiat al-Hamra. Within the wall, security is much improved and the barrier has forced the Polisario, which had grown increasingly bold in attacking Moroccan towns and garrisons, to rethink its strategy, hitherto dependent on the unrestricted, rapid movement of lightly armed men over long distances.

The Moroccans originally maintained some garrisons outside the wall, but the risks of doing so were illustrated by what was perhaps the most serious incident of the war, an overwhelming Polisario attack, October 13,

1981, on the garrison at Guelta Zammour, which lies a good 100 miles beyond the wall and is very close to the Mauritanian frontier. As noted earlier, this was the last Saharan hamlet held by the Polisario in early 1976, and it has been the scene of several engagements since then. Judging by Moroccan press photos, it was heavily defended. The *New York Times* on November 15, 1981 put the number of Moroccan troops there at 2,400 (other sources say 1,500), some 200 of whom were captured by the Polisario and 200 of whom were killed, according to the *Times*. The Moroccans subsequently evacuated both Guelta az-Zemmour and Bir Enzaran, and the only town outside the wall that was still garrisoned, as of the spring of 1984, was Dakhla (Villa Cisneros).

More serious than the loss of troops at Guelta Zammour was the effective air defense put up by the Polisario during the engagement. It momentarily neutralized the Moroccan air arm, which had been the most useful tool in the Moroccan arsenal, claiming to have shot down a C-130 transport, which had been the workhorse of the campaign, two Mirage F-1s, an F-5E fighter, and a helicopter. The Moroccans claimed that the guerrillas employed Soviet T-54 and T-55 tanks and, more importantly, radar-guided SAM-6 missiles, which are mounted on tracked vehicles. Washington sources subsequently confirmed the presence of SAM-6s and speculated that the Saharans may also have been using the much simpler SAM-9, a heat-seeking missile. The Moroccans maintained that the Saharans did not have the capability of operating the SAM-6 and complained to the Soviets about the presence of "non-Africans" operating these weapons against the Moroccans. The Polisario denied that they had SAM-6s or that any outside forces were involved in the attack.

As a result of this incident, the Moroccan air force was for some time hesitant to expose itself to more of the same, and this was affecting its operations. The Moroccans asked for U.S. help with electronic countermeasures against the SAM-6s and received a positive response. Putting such measures into effect took training and time, however, and did not provide an immediate solution. In the meantime, the Moroccans found unspecified "other expedients" for coping with the problem, at least temporarily, with the help of the French.

As noted above, the Reagan administration has shown itself to be considerably less inhibited than its predecessors in supporting Moroccan policy in the Sahara militarily. Although there has been no quantum jump in the amount of military equipment being sold, in part because the Moroccans do not have the funds to buy more and in part because of congressional limitations, there has been a good deal of verbal support in the form of declarations by a stream of high-level visiting firemen and U.S. officials in Rabat that has created an impression of close U.S. identification with Moroccan policies. The impression has been strengthened by the various signs of military cooperation—the facilities access agreement, joint maneuvers, frequent visits to the Sahara by U.S. military personnel, the supply of U.S.

sensors for the sand wall, and formation of a joint military committee. The Moroccans have come to expect such support and to regard it as a gauge of friendship. Fortunately, their military situation has not deteriorated further so as to stimulate demands for a greater U.S. commitment of personnel and equipment.

Although there were a number of minor skirmishes after Guelta Zammour, with both sides issuing claims of victory, there was little serious fighting for almost two years. As of June 1983 the Moroccans were feeling secure behind their wall and had effectively abandoned the rest of the Sahara to the Polisario, going out on interdictory air raids and doing some patrolling, but not making any real attempt to control or administer the territory. The Polisario, meanwhile, was roaming the open spaces, presumably considering new tactics to circumvent the Moroccan barrier. Military and diplomatic observers in Rabat thought the Moroccans could sit out the war indefinitely, and that their strategy had paid off. There were, of course, obvious parallels with other static defenses and mentalities that raised questions about the long-term desirability of the Moroccan approach, but the Moroccans did not seem to mind, and their casualty rate was much lower than it had been. The Polisario had not paraded a new batch of Moroccan prisoners for some time,[13] and there was a general belief in Washington that the war was all but over.

For its part, the Polisario had not been talking about military victories for some time and did not sound as though it thought it was winning the contest. Following the international hue and cry over Israeli use of cluster bombs in Lebanon in the summer of 1982, the Polisario began making an issue of Moroccan use of the same weapon in the Sahara, claiming that the Moroccans were striking at civilians and livestock for lack of better targets. A House Foreign Affairs Committee staff study mission was shown the American-made canisters from which the bomblets came in September 1982, and there seemed to be no doubt that the Moroccans had used the weapon in question.[14] More to the point, however, it was complaints about cluster bombs, not claims of decisive engagements, that one heard from the Polisario, and this was taken as a sign of lowered military expectations.

This relatively calm scene was suddenly shattered by a heavy Polisario attack on the Moroccan hamlet of Lemsid, or al-Msayyid, on July 10, 1983, followed by other attacks at different points along the wall, and involving the occupation of part of the town of Samara at one point. Although initial Moroccan reports spoke of only a few casualties, the Polisario claimed to have killed 300 Moroccans and wounded 300. The truth probably will never be known, but the importance of these engagements was in their scale (the Moroccans claimed the Polisario used 170 vehicles), their duration (skirmishing went on for weeks), and the fact that Lemsid is partially protected by the sand wall defenses in historic, that is, pre-Saharan, Morocco. The Polisario evidently found a way to penetrate those defenses, and this was a serious development for the Moroccans. The latter responded in late October with a large-scale (18,000 men) search-and-destroy operation outside the wall that was impressive but ineffective in terms of suppressing the Polisario, and intermittent skirmishes have occurred since then.

In spite of the skirmishes, there is no sign yet that the Polisario is able to maintain a prolonged campaign at the same force level it used at Lemsid. On the other hand, it is clear that Morocco's defensive strategy cannot prevent the Polisario from attacking more or less at the time and place of its choosing, provided it has the supplies and equipment. Thus neither side has the ability to win a decisive military victory. As long as the Polisario enjoys a privileged sanctuary in and logistics support from Algeria, and as long as it can operate freely in the undefended wastes of Northern Mauritania, Morocco will be unable to control it. Conversely, it is also clear that the Polisario does not have the military capacity to impose its will on Morocco. It cannot establish a functioning Saharan state without Moroccan acquiescence. The outlook then is for a continued military stalemate, until and unless a political settlement can be found.

Political Settlement

Efforts to mediate a settlement began almost as soon as the crisis was precipitated by the Green March. The Saudis, Egyptians, Sengalese, and the Arab League in particular made efforts in 1976, and the OAU has been seized of the problem ever since. The last individual attempt, by King Fahd of Saudi Arabia in November 1982, was as unsuccessful as the first. These efforts have invariably come up against the fact that the parties were not yet ready for the very serious compromises needed for a settlement. The Algerians have continued to say the problem is between the Saharans and Moroccans and that they are merely supporting the universally recognized right of self-determination. The Moroccans maintain that they have simply erased a sequel of colonialism, that the file is closed and they are not prepared to negotiate the status of the Sahara, which is an internal matter. In their view, the way to stop the fighting is for the Algerians to stop supporting the Polisario, which would evanesce as soon as that happened. The Polisario says it is prepared to negotiate with the Moroccans, but since the Moroccans refuse even to recognize its existence, it has no alternative but to fight.

The one multilateral initiative that holds out some hope of breaking this deadlock is the OAU referendum proposal discussed below, but it will require concessions, particularly from the Moroccans, which the latter are unlikely to make freely. The story of OAU involvement is complex, but its efforts have generally pointed to a cease-fire and referendum as the solution. In February 1981, the Polisario, apparently relying on favorable prospects for admission to the OAU under Algerian sponsorship, announced that the time for a referendum had passed. At the next OAU summit at Nairobi from June 24 to 27, however, King Hassan surprised everyone by proposing that a "supervised" referendum be held in the Sahara.[15] The summit, expressing its gratification at this statesman-like initiative, established an implementation committee composed of Guinea, Kenya, Mali, Nigeria, Sierra Leone, Sudan, and Tanzania to work out the terms and conditions. It was given until the end of August to do so. Meanwhile, the parties were called upon to observe an immediate cease-fire, the details of which were to be worked out by the committee.

The Polisario reacted negatively to the resolution, but the Algerians, who had welcomed it, put pressure on it to accept. In mid-July the Polisario agreed, provided certain conditions were met. They included direct negotiations between the Polisario and Morocco to work out the modalities of the referendum and cease-fire, withdrawal of all Moroccan forces from the Western Sahara to a distance of 150 kilometers north of the Oued Draa, the complete withdrawal of Moroccan administration, the return of all Saharans, including those in Algeria, to their native villages, the establishment in the Sahara of a provisional international administration made up of the UN and the OAU in collaboration with the SDAR, operation of this administration for at least three months prior to the referendum, and the liberation of all Saharans held by the Moroccans. These conditions were, of course, unacceptable to Morocco, which has consistently refused to negotiate with the Polisario over anything, and which was not called upon by the OAU to remove its troops and administration from the territory, something it would have refused to accept in any event.[16]

In August the OAU implementation committee met in Nairobi and issued its decision on the referendum. It provides for a general and free referendum on self-determination that will allow the Saharans to express themselves freely and democratically on the future of their territory, to be held in the Western Sahara (and not Algeria, Morocco, or Mauritania), with the eligible voters being all Saharans listed in the Spanish census of 1974 who have attained the age of 18 or above. Voting is to be by secret ballot, with a choice between independence or integration with Morocco. The referendum is to be administered by an impartial interim administration supported by civilian, military, and police components. There is no mention of the composition of these components, and no mention of the withdrawal of Moroccan forces. The committee also urged the parties to agree on a cease-fire through negotiations under its auspices.

The Moroccans accepted these terms, although insisting that they could not negotiate directly with the Polisario, but were prepared to negotiate indirectly through the committee. At the same time, the Moroccans made it clear that what they had in mind was a "confirmatory" exercise, in which the Saharans would be allowed to ratify their adherence to Morocco, and that they would not accept the idea that there could be an independent Saharan state. How this position was to be reconciled with the specific choice between independence or integration given in the committee's decision was not made clear. The Moroccans simply let it be known that they would not countenance a situation in which the vote could go against them. Thus, in a televised speech before the (Moroccan) Consultative Council for Saharan Affairs on November 6, 1981, the sixth anniversary of the Green March, King Hassan said the referendum would not consist of asking the inhabitants whether they would or would not prefer to remain Moroccan. Rather, it would involve a confirmation of the Saharans' allegiance to the king of Morocco:

> The question will be phrased as follows: "Do you confirm the act of allegiance (the bay'a) that ties you with His Majesty and King of Morocco, and which indicates that you are a part of the Kingdom of Morocco?" The King explained that any formulation of the referendary question which questions the desire of the Sahrawis to remain Moroccan would be inconsistent with the very premise of the bay'a, which is founded on a reciprocal agreement between the Sovereign and his subjects. In return for the people's pledge of support for the Sovereign, the King, in turn, pledges to defend the rights of his citizens, first and foremost of which is their right to remain Moroccan. A King is granted many powers, but he does not have the right to take an action which would exclude a Moroccan citizen from the Moroccan community. Thus, in accepting the referendum, Morocco cannot deviate from Islamic constitutional law, and the Sovereign cannot ask his citizens whether or not they would like to remain Moroccan.[17]

As noted above, it is unclear how this interpretation is to be reconciled with the general and free choice proposed in the Committee of Implementation decision. In fact, it is impossible, and events since then have revolved around this fundamental contradiction.

In June 1983 the OAU addressed the problem again at Addis Ababa, passing a resolution naming Morocco and the Polisario as the parties to the dispute and urging them to negotiate directly on a cease fire and a referendum to be held by the end of the year. The Moroccans refused to negotiate with the Polisario, of course, and the Implementation Committee was unable to put the resolution into effect. The Moroccans, however, continue to state their readiness to have a referendum. In a speech on July 9, 1983, Hassan implied that the resolution might go against Morocco but said nothing would compel him to give the Sahara to a group of mercenaries, that is, the Polisario. He reaffirmed his willingness to accept a referendum in his speech to the UN General Assembly on September 28, 1983, but this did little to dissipate widespread skepticism about the sincerity of his protestations. There is growing impatience among the African states with what is seen as Moroccan dilatoriness in refusing to negotiate with the Polisario, and this issue may again prevent the holding of an OAU summit in 1984.[18]

The Moroccans have long argued that the key to settlement is in the hands of the Algerians, and the possibility that the latter might make a deal at their expense has been a constant apprehension of the Saharans. In material terms, the Algerians have very little to gain by continuation of the war. They are reported to be tired of it but to feel obliged to continue support for the Polisario for ideological reasons. After the commitment of resources and political influence the Algerians have brought to bear on the problem in the past, they would face severe criticism both domestically and internationally if they suddenly abandoned the fight. It would indeed be a significant defeat for the proponents of the view that wars of national liberation must inevitably succeed.

Speculation that such a deal was in the works was heightened by the previously unannounced meeting between King Hassan and President Benjedid near Oujda on February 26, 1983, the first such meeting since the early 1970s. Although various portents were read into the language of the communiqués—the Moroccans reported that Hassan had reiterated Morocco's adherence to the Nairobi resolutions and his definite wish to implement them as soon as possible, while the Algerians reaffirmed their willingness to bring about a rapprochement between Morocco and "our brothers in the western Sahara," without mentioning the Polisario or SDAR by name—there has been no further development that would indicate that there has been a breakthrough on this front. Indeed, in spite of some high-level visits between the two countries, relations have cooled and Benjedid's reported remarks while on a state visit to France in November 1983 indicated that there had been no softening of Algerian support for the Sahrawis. Furthermore, continuing Polisario attacks, which could not have taken place without Algerian permission, have shown that the Algerians are not yet prepared to sacrifice the Polisario for the sake of improved relations with Morocco. In late 1983 there were rumors that impending changes in the Algerian power structure which might presage a more flexible attitude, but this did not come to pass.

Nevertheless, a number of important developments in intra-Maghrib relations did follow the Hassan-Benjedid meeting. In April 1983 restoration of Algerian-Moroccan relations was reported (prematurely) to be imminent, and partial re-opening of the border between them was announced on April 7. There was a flurry of visits at the cabinet minister level between the various capitals of the region, including Tripoli, and an intra-Maghrib conference was held at Tangier the last weekend in April to lay the groundwork for a Maghrib summit that was to discuss intra-Maghrib relations. The summit has yet to be held, however, and there is no expectation that it will be any time soon. Bilateral problems, and notably the Sahara, have gotten in the way.

The most remarkable episode in these exchanges was a sudden visit to Rabat by Qadhdhafi in late June 1983. He and Hassan were reported to have discussed then current problems within the PLO, Chad, and the Western Sahara. The meeting was said to have been at Qadhdhafi's initiative, and he announced that his purpose was to mobilize all the Arabs against Israel. Although the Delphic quality of Qadhdhafi's utterances makes it difficult to know what he means, the lack of Moroccan reaction to his Chadian venture supports the speculation that a deal was made: Libya would withhold support from the Polisario if Morocco would not react against his attempt to restore Goukouni Oueddei to power in Chad. Although there was considerable skepticism that Hassan would make such an agreement, given the effect on the interests of some of his African allies and the United States, or that Qadhdhafi would honor one for long, the speculation apparently was well-founded. In November 1983 Moroccan officials were maintaining that Qadhdhafi had shut off aid to the Polisario in June and had not resumed it. This had not affected Polisario ability to strike at Lemsid, but it obviously has implications for the future of that organization, which for the present has no alternative to Algerian support. As of May 1984, Libyan support for the Polisario apparently had not been resumed, at least not on a noticeable scale.

The Moroccans had hoped that in an improved climate the proposed Maghrib summit would pave the way for resolution of the Saharan conflict "in the Greater Maghrib context." This rather vague formula meant that they would be prepared for substantial concessions in the way of local autonomy for the Saharans within an overarching Maghribi federation, a federation which might well exist only on paper but which would give legal and political justification for an act of devolution in the Sahara. Whether such a formula would satisfy the Saharans is not clear.

The nature of a settlement that stops short of a full act of self-determination for the Saharans is something that has been debated for years, and the discussion normally comes around eventually to either a territorial or a political compromise, or both. Under the first heading, part of the Sahara would be turned over to the SDAR, and the rest would remain Moroccan. One variant would be a Saharan-Mauritanian federation. Various proposals of this nature are discussed in Chapter 5 of John Damis' Conflict in Northwest Africa, but all that have been put forward to date have been rejected by both the Moroccans and the Saharans. One of the problems with the territorial approach is that almost all of the useful portion would be left in Moroccan hands, while the Saharans would wind up with the town of Dakhla, on the coast, and an empty wilderness behind it.

Political, as opposed to territorial, compromise would be based on some arrangement that gave regional autonomy to the Saharans. While the Moroccans may be ready for substantial compromises in this respect, they will insist on retaining sovereignty. The post-Camp David negotiations between Egypt and Israel have illustrated how ambiguous the term autonomy can be, and maintenance of meaningful local autonomy, even under a federal system, is difficult. Whether the Saharans would be willing to settle for half a loaf will depend in the final analysis on what their alternatives are, and what they can expect to get from the Moroccans. It is not inconceivable that they would eventually accept such an arrangement, particularly if their external support began to dry up.

For the moment, however, there is no sign of real movement on the substance of the issue, and the Sahara conflict will be with us for some time to come unless there is a radical change in the positions of one or more of the parties.

Conclusion

It is fashionable to see the Sahara war as being primarily a manifestation of a struggle between Morocco and Algeria for dominance in Northwest Africa. While their rivalry undoubtedly plays an important part, and the Algerians probably would not have supported the Polisario as they did had they not been angry with the Moroccans, the fundamental, irreducible issue is self-determination for a colonial people. The problem is how to accommodate Morocco's quest for sovereignty with the rights of the indigenous inhabitants. Were those rights not considered legitimate, there would be little support for the Polisario in the OAU or elsewhere. This gives an ideological cast to the problem that limits the flexibility of both the Algerians and Saharans and prolongs the war. While the Algerian man in the street might be willing to jettison the Polisario tomorrow, Algeria's leaders have to be more concerned about the political implications of doing so. They have a reputation to maintain, just as other leaders of sovereign states do. As for the Saharans, to abandon their search for full self-determination means to abandon their case entirely. It may come to that in time, but the record to date indicates that they are unlikely to give up without a struggle.

Meanwhile, the continuing military stalemate and the massive sums being spent on urban infrastructure in Saharan towns are a heavy drain on Morocco's limited resources and have contributed importantly to the present economic crisis in that country. Although the conquest of the Sahara was popular, the war is not, and indefinite continuation is likely to turn the political atmosphere in Morocco sour, and to present Morocco's friends with some unpleasant dilemmas—they may find themselves being pressured to increase their commitment in order to bring about a military solution, even though the best judgment of most outsiders is that such a solution is not possible.

At the same time, divisions among African states and political tensions over this question are likely to increase rather than diminish if there is not some substantial progress either toward implementation of the OAU's referendum proposals or toward a negotiated settlement. To the extent that the OAU is a force for stability in Africa, anything that weakens it is contrary to the general interest. By the same token, an early solution is something devoutly to be wished for.

Implications for the United States

The United States has a direct interest in good relations with both Algeria and Morocco, and resolution of the conflict between them over the Sahara would be a very favorable development for it. Its ability to play a role in reaching such a settlement is limited by the same factors that have frustrated various would-be mediators—the unwillingness or unreadiness of the parties to make compromises, and the fact that the Maghribis communicate better with each other than they do with outsiders. Now that the parties have moved somewhat on their own, the United States should do everything it can to encourage the process. To this end, its support for Morocco should be qualified and measured to make it clear to the Moroccans that they have no blank check from America, and that American military support will be conditioned on progress toward a settlement.

Notes

[1]As of 1983 there were alleged to be 100,000 Saharans in al-Ayun alone. The Polisario claims 150,000 are living in the Tindouf area. This would make the total over 250,000.

[2]They were perhaps stimulated by the founding of the Polisario in that year.

[3]For a detailed discussion of the phosphate and iron ore factors, see pp. 14–38 of John Damis, *Conflict in Northwest Africa* (Stanford: Hoover Institution Press, 1983).

[4]*Al-Moujahid*, the French-language journal of the Algerian government, carried the text of the communiqué in its edition of July 5, 1975. It said that Algeria had noted "with great satisfaction the understanding reached" by Morocco and Mauritania on the Sahara.

[5]The text of the king's speech can be found in the FBIS bulletin for October 17, 1975.

[6]For a further account, see John Damis, *op. cit.*, pp. 64–65.

[7]An article in The *New York Times* (December 6, 1981), reports "Congressional sources" as saying that then deputy director of the CIA, Vernon Walters, was sent to Spain by Secretary of State Kissinger in late 1975 to convince Juan Carlos to accede to Moroccan desires in the Sahara. There is circumstantial evidence, including U.S. lack of support for UN resolutions against the Green March, that lends credence to the allegation. The Spaniards, for their part, were convinced that Hassan could not have organized the Green March without outside help, and suspected the Americans. The official record will never reveal the full truth, but Secretary Kissinger, intentionally or otherwise, may have given Hassan what the latter took to be a green light during a conversation in the summer of 1975. This may come out in someone's memoirs. Anything was possible in that era, and American officials on the spot were usually the last to know, but to the best of the author's knowledge, there was no American involvement in preparations for the Green March.

[8]He may have begun supporting the Polisario earlier, but that support became much more substantial after the Green March.

[9]For further details about the origins and composition of the Polisario, see John Damis, *op. cit.*, pp. 38–44. Moroccan description of them as mercenaries is not to be taken seriously. See also Tony Hodges, *Western Sahara, The Roots of a Desert War* (Westport, Connecticut: Laurence Hill & Co., 1984).

[10]Polisario sources say there is no truth to the Moroccan allegations and point to racial and linguistic differences between the Sahrawis and other peoples of the area as something that would be difficult to conceal if such outsiders were present.

[11]See, for instance, the article by New York Congressman Stephen Solarz in the Winter 1979/80 issue of *Foreign Affairs*.

[12]The arms were supposed to be supplied contingent on Hassan's moving toward a negotiated settlement. It is not clear from the public record that this was made explicit to him, but in

any event he made it clear that he had no intention of modifying his position vis-à-vis the Polisario and that he thought he would get the arms anyway, which he did.

[13]In December 1983 a Polisario official informed the author that his organization was holding 1,500 Moroccan prisoners in the Tindouf area, while 200 Sahrawis were being held by the Moroccans in a damp cavern in the Tarfaya area. He described the cavern as being "under the sea."

[14]The study mission report, *U.S. Policy Toward the Conflict in the Western Sahara*, was issued in March, 1983 by the Government Printing Office, Washington, DC.

[15]The word he used was the French *controlé*, which means verified or supervised, but not *controlled* in the English sense. This has given rise to a misunderstanding. He is widely thought to be advocating a *rigged* referendum. This is probably what he has in mind, but that is not the way he is describing it in public.

[16]The Polisario maintains that its conditions are the same, *mutatis mutandis*, that the Moroccans put forward when they were demanding a referendum in the pre-1973 period.

[17]Morocco News Summary, Embassy of Morocco (Washington, D.C., November 1981).

[18]Hassan's ambiguity regarding the referendum is brought out clearly in pages 40–43 of the report of a congressional study mission by the House Subcommittee on Africa, issued by the Government Printing Office on March 9, 1984.

8

North Africa and the Powers

North Africa was for many years the hunting preserve of colonial powers, notably France, Italy, and Spain. This experience not only marked local psyches and cultures, it also established patterns of communication and trade that still persist in unexpected ways. The love-hate relationship that commonly springs up between the ex-colony and the ex-metropole is manifested daily in the relations between the North African states and Europe, and France in particular.

As noted earlier, commerce among the countries of the Maghrib (and between that region and Africa and the rest of the Third World) is minimal. Their principal trading partners are Western Europe and the United States. This is illustrated in Tables B and C. As Table B shows, industrial countries (Western Europe, the United States, Canada, Japan, New Zealand, and Australia) get two-thirds to three-fourths of North Africa's trade, while the rest of Africa and the non-oil exporting Middle East get about 2 percent.

Looking at the value of exports and imports exchanged with the countries of North Africa (Table C) we find that up through 1981 the United States was far and away the most important trading partner of the region as a whole because of its massive purchases of Libyan and Algerian oil. With the imposition of the U.S. embargo on Libyan oil, and reduction of purchases from Algeria because of the oil glut to an estimated $2.792 billion in 1982, that has changed, and the United States probably ranks fourth or fifth today. In the period 1979–81, Germany, Italy, and France competed for second, third and fourth place. Italy's total for 1981 was a surprising $11.773 billion, just under the United States' $12.918 billion (probably a low figure), but France emerged as the leader in 1982, with a total volume of trade of $10.131 billion, followed by Italy, Germany and the United States, in that order.

These figures do not include arms sales, at least from the Soviet bloc, but even if we include them, with an arbitrary figure of $1 billion per year, the

Table B. Trade Distribution of North African Countries—1982 (percentages)

EXPORTS	MOROCCO	ALGERIA	TUNISIA	LIBYA
INDUSTRIAL COUNTRIES (Western Europe, USA, Canada, Japan, Australia, New Zealand)	64.4	93.4	79.8	75.9
OIL EXPORTING COUNTRIES	5.1	—	6.6	—
NON-OIL, DEVELOPING	17.8	6.1	10.8	21.1
AFRICA	2.7	1.3	1.6	.1
ASIA	7.7	.4	3.7	.9
EUROPE*	5.1	2.0	5.0	15.9
MIDDLE EAST	.6	negligible	.4	.7
WESTERN HEMISPHERE	1.7	2.5	.1	3.6
USSR, EASTERN EUROPE, etc.**	6.8	.5	1.5	2.4

* Cyprus, Malta, Greece, Hungary, Portugal, Romania, Turkey, Yugoslavia
** USSR plus Bulgaria, Cuba, Czechoslovakia, East Germany, North Korea, and Poland

IMPORTS	MOROCCO	ALGERIA	TUNISIA	LIBYA
INDUSTRIAL COUNTRIES	64.9	82.5	81.8	80.0
OIL EXPORTING COUNTRIES	20.2	.1	4.5	—
NON-OIL, DEVELOPING	7.6	12.8	10.7	15.2
AFRICA	1.0	2.3	1.3	1.3
ASIA	2.7	2.1	1.5	4.9
EUROPE	2.0	5.2	5.7	8.5
MIDDLE EAST	.1	.3	.6	.3
WESTERN HEM.	1.9	2.9	1.5	.2
USSR/EASTERN EUROPE	6.6	2.5	2.3	2.7

Source: *Direction of Trade Statistics Yearbook—1983*, International Monetary Fund

Soviets would rank at or next to the bottom of the list. Spain is a strong fifth throughout the period, and the UK usually ranks with or after Japan, a surprisingly weak performance. The UK's small share of the market seems to reflect a decision, conscious or otherwise, not to compete. Japan's probably reflects lack of familiarity.

The most surprising revelation of these figures is that France is not in as dominant a position as one would expect. Although it is the biggest supplier to the region, it is not the biggest customer for its products. The United States, on the other hand, which is the biggest customer, or was until 1982, is far from being the biggest supplier. It has been running a large trade deficit with the region, unlike the Europeans, except Germany. This disparity is somewhat diminished today by the reduction in purchases of North African oil, but the region remains an area where the United States buys a good deal more than it sells.

European cultural influences continue to be strong. In the three western

Table C.   North Africa's Principal Trading Partners
(millions of dollars)

| | 1980 | | 1981 | | 1982 | | |
	Exports	Imports	Exports	Imports	Exports	Imports	
FRANCE	1188	773	1201	645	1131	613	Morocco
	2626	1718	2371	2349	2124	3896	Algeria
	933	389	966	434	933	391	Tunisia
	671	666	907	506	428	615	Libya
SPAIN	370	213	307	190	326	197	Morocco
	458	547	557	488	685	670	Algeria
	122	14	118	12	146	36	Tunisia
	35.8	1265	427	1326	267	1081	Libya
ITALY	261	130	235	161	198	146	Morocco
	1289	713	1426	1179	665	1516	Algeria
	339	414	525	613	509	480	Tunisia
	2545	3469	4297	3337	2141	2758	Libya
GERMANY	237	277	219	216	215	222	Morocco
	1374	2281	1254	2359	1350	1574	Algeria
	374	315	358	220	402	240	Tunisia
	1251	4325	1486	3304	1173	2957	Libya

Source: *Direction of Trade Statistics Yearbook—1983*, International Monetary Fund

Table C.1

| | 1980 | | 1981 | | 1982 | | |
	Exports	Imports	Exports	Imports	Exports	Imports	
UK	161	145	114	125	164	106	Morocco
	331	265	351	320	348	310	Algeria
	69	41	71	44	68	22	Tunisia
	670	108	1067	149	460	595	Libya
US	344	41	429	41	397	51	Morocco
	542	6881	717	5208	909	2792	Algeria
	173	63	222	12	214	62	Tunisia
	509	8905	813	5476	301	533	Libya
JAPAN	45	85	68	103	81	107	Morocco
	457	456	472	697	677	522	Algeria
	68	1	93	1	66	1	Tunisia
	527	361	1059	349	285	46	Libya
USSR, EASTERN EUROPE, etc.	275.9	247	287.9	240.4	287.3	144.6	Morocco
	76	265	76	292	65	277	Algeria
	103.3	31.0	96.5	26.8	76.2	29.4	Tunisia
	252	215	236	370	225	315	Libya

Table C.2

	1980		1981		1982		
	Exports	Imports	Exports	Imports	Exports	Imports	
	52.9	48.0	47.2	64.9	67.4	50.3	Morocco
POLAND	57	23	63	23	60	20	Algeria
	22	5.2	34.9	8.8	32.2	5.7	Tunisia
	40	92	39	—	37	—	Libya
	323	24.9	656	34.4	561	33	Morocco
SAUDI	68	33.82	.75	33.82	.71	28.74	Algeria
ARABIA	304.8	1.2	421.4	1.3	124.3	4.1	Tunisia
	—	—	—	—	1	—	Libya
	86	55	36	14	56	2	Morocco
BRAZIL	167	83	267	303	125	185	Algeria
	25	3	17	—	35	—	Tunisia
	35	140	11	369	11	350	Libya

Note: Data for USSR, Poland, Libya, and Algeria partly based on extrapolation. Other data vary with source. The U.S. Embassy in Algiers, for instance, estimates 1981 imports from Algeria at $6 billion, not the $5.2 billion shown above.

states French remains the language of refinement, and education in French as opposed to Arabic is still the ticket to professional advancement. French culture has affected thought processes and given an indelible stamp to the way the elite live, work, and play. The Italian impress on Libya is today much fainter than that of the French on their former colonies, but that historic connection is also still alive, if somewhat attenuated.

Europe, as North Africa's closest neighbor and principal trading partner, has a potential for playing a role in trans-Mediterranean affairs that has yet to be exploited. Except for France, the European powers are secondary political actors in North Africa today, and they evince little desire to take on greater responsibilities. They are happy enough to compete for contracts and commerce, but tend to regard North Africa as an area of low priority and interest. Except for the French and Italian, and to a lesser extent the British, European diplomatic establishments in these countries tend to be undistinguished. Their diplomats do not bother to learn Arabic and generally take little interest in the country. In part this is a problem of limited means, but the Europeans could do considerably better in the allocation of interest and personnel, and it is surprising that they do not.

While there is frequent working-level contact between U.S. and European diplomatic representatives about political and economic conditions in North Africa, it is ad hoc and there is no institutional mechanism for regular or consistent consultation. The region is rarely high on the agenda of senior European visitors to Washington, or of senior American visitors in Europe, and there is very little coordination of policy. Indeed, the Europeans would just as soon avoid publicized coordination with the United States in this area, since they do not want to identify themselves with U.S. policies in the Arab world.

The Americans, for their part, generally reciprocate by not taking the Europeans seriously enough, by rarely bothering to consult them, and by not seeking to promote a more active European role. This is unfortunate, and something should be done both to improve the level and intensity of consultation, and to improve attitudes between these friendly powers, who have many common interests in this area. There are strong territorial instincts to be overcome on all sides, and there will be resistance to closer cooperation from many quarters, but the task cries out to be done.

France

The once important French communities in the Maghrib have shrunk to a shadow of their former selves, down to 45,000 in Morocco, 15,000 in Tunisia, and 45,000 in Algeria. They nevertheless remain the largest single foreign communities in these countries and continue to provide trained cadres in surprising places. In particular, they can be found in schools and hospitals throughout the region, and the preeminence of French as the language of technical discourse gives them an enormous advantage over foreigners speaking lesser tongues such as English and Russian. The French aid programs that provide young *cooperants*, many of whom are fulfilling their national service obligations, to work in the schools and hospitals, also make available military and civilian advisers of more elevated status whose activities are often oriented toward market development—the French military adviser (there are some 250 in Morocco and 40 in Tunisia) normally recommends acquisition of French equipment, just as the American adviser sells his own national products.

French aid and trade data for North Africa vary depending on one's source and the rate of exchange used. The figures shown in Table C indicate that the volume of trade in both directions with Algeria is roughly two-and-a-half to three times what it is with each of Morocco, Tunisia, and Libya, and that French exports to all the countries of North Africa except Libya are three to four times American exports. In 1981, the French extended economic and financial aid, mostly in the form of loans and financial facilities, of $200–300 million to Morocco and $100 million to Tunisia. They also have an impressive number of technicians and *cooperants* in the Francophone states—8,000 in Morocco, 2,300 in Algeria, and 840 in Tunisia. These figures compare with a total American official presence (including the Peace Corps) of about 300 in Morocco, 25 in Algeria, and 200 in Tunisia.

The reverse of this coin is the large Maghribi presence in France (and lesser numbers in other European countries). There is a wide divergence in figures from different sources, but as of September 1982, according to the French Foreign Ministry, there were over 1.5 million North Africans in France. Of these, 450,000 were Moroccans, 830,000 Algerians (1.5 million if one counts French nationals who also have a claim to Algerian nationality), and 250,000 Tunisians. Judging by figures for the total foreign community in France, perhaps 45 percent of the North Africans are employed or seeking employment. The remittances they send home are important, particularly for Morocco, where they amounted to an estimated $1 billion in 1981 and $852 million in 1982. The Algerians, because many of them have brought their families to France in recent years, have remitted a good deal less, dropping from about $1,200 million in 1970 to perhaps $450 million in 1981 and $250 million in 1982. As noted earlier, Tunisian remittances in 1982 totaled $342 million. More important than the remittances is the employment offered to the surplus laborers of North Africa. Whether the dependence on foreign employment that this breeds is healthy is another question, and experience in labor-exporting countries shows that the way in which such remittances are spent often has unfavorable consequences for the economy.

In the usual pattern of such migrations from the Third World, many villages and regions of the Maghrib have established a habit of sending workers to particular industries or towns in France (and elsewhere in Europe), where they perform essential functions at the lowest rung of the social and job scale. Your porter at the intown terminal of Charles De Gaulle Airport, for instance, is likely to be an Algerian, and on the Paris metro you can hear Maghribi Arabic or Berber more than any other single language, except possibly French.

The conditions in which these workers live, and the social problems arising from their presence, have been a source of serious concern to successive French governments, and under President Mitterrand steps have been taken to regularize the presence of large numbers of illegal immigrants from Africa, including the Maghrib. While the French have shown considerable generosity in according regular status to many of these people, the process has not been easy. Particularly in a period of recession, the existence of so many foreign workers competing for employment has been a source of civil strife, with violence erupting from time to time, and the question of migration and work permits has long been a contentious issue, especially in French relations with Algeria. The French today are trying to encourage foreign workers to return home, offering them what amounts to severance pay for doing so. Success to date has been limited, but a more restrictive European approach to the hiring of such workers is already affecting job markets in North Africa.

French interests in North Africa today are primarily economic and strategic. Like the Americans, the French want to maintain access to the oil and gas of this region on reasonable terms, they want to maintain a continuing market for French products and technology, including arms, and they want to have a respectable share of the very large contracts being let (by the Algerian and Libyan governments in particular) for development projects. They have also been active in seeking participation in major hydraulic and industrial projects in Morocco and Tunisia. They find that their long-standing *mission civilisatrice*, that is, spreading French culture, is not only a national interest in itself, but a means to facilitate commercial penetration.

French strategic interests, as indicated earlier, are largely a function of geography. North African oil is important, but not vital, provided other oil is available. North African real estate, on the other hand, has vital implications for French security. The basing of a Soviet fleet at, say, Mers el-Kebir in Algeria, or Tangiers, would pose a direct threat to the French fleet, and require significant changes in military dispositions taken for the defense of France.

France is, furthermore, of all the European powers, the most directly concerned with air access to Africa through the northern corridor, which is controlled by the Maghribis. France could not be indifferent to the domination of any Maghrib state by forces hostile to it. While the United States has similar concerns, the immediate impact on its security of such a development is less than it would be for France.

The direct importance of North Africa explains in part the unwillingness of the French to join the American anti-Qadhdhafi crusade which began in the spring of 1982, even though they have ample reason to want him neutralized, since he has caused them much trouble in the Sahel and Chad. Aside from their trade and financial stakes in these countries, the French cannot afford to alienate any of them politically. Like the Spanish and Italians, they make a point of saying that U.S. relations with Libya are an American affair, but they think it would be a mistake to close all the western doors to Qadhdhafi and force him into the arms of the Soviets. They therefore have no intention of following the American example. (The 1983 Chad crisis put severe strains on this resolve, and the French came close to open hostilities with Qadhdhafi. This may yet come to pass if the current stalemate breaks down.)

The French have also been very anxious to stress the "balanced" nature of their policy toward Algeria and Morocco. French officials all speak of that policy as being *equilibré*. This is obviously put forward to counter the popular view that President Mitterrand, as a Socialist, has at least corrected, if not reversed, the pro-Moroccan tilt displayed by Giscard d'Estaing, and that he is tilted toward Algeria. Early in Mitterrand's term there was a good deal of speculation in this respect, sparked by such events as French agreement to pay an elevated price for Algerian natural gas, the appointment of a foreign minister considered pro-Algerian, the attitude of the French Socialist Party, which was considered anti-Moroccan and pro-Saharan by many Moroccans, and most worrying of all for the Moroccans, French insistence that they pay 2 billion francs in arrearages for arms already delivered if arms shipments were to be continued. This issue was settled in January 1983, but no details were made public, and it can be assumed the Moroccans are still having difficulty making payments.

French officials are quick to point out that although Mitterrand took some 18 months to visit Morocco, he invited Hassan to Paris for a private visit within six months of his election. This was in spite of the intense opposition to the idea within the French Socialist Party, which was upset because Moroccan socialist leader Abderahim Bouabid was still under arrest. The two reportedly had a fruitful discussion of outstanding issues, but seem to have settled nothing.

The Mitterrand visit to Morocco in January 1983 generated a good deal of impressive rhetoric, including a call by Mitterrand for a conference on the western Mediterranean to be held at Paris, but le Monde, in its issue of February 1, 1983, noted: "So many 'triumphal' visits of French officials to the two principal powers of the Maghrib having been followed by disappointments in relations with Rabat as well as Algiers it is well to be particularly circumspect about matters concerning this region."

France today obviously has the most important stake in North Africa of any outside power. It has the most important export trade, the most important human and cultural influence, and the most acute strategic interest. The question is whether the Maghribis see it as the most important power on their horizon. There are some interesting national sterotypes at work in this regard. American officials on the scene are convinced that the United States is the number one foreign power in Tunisia and Morocco, while the French think they are number one, certainly in Morocco, and probably in Algeria and Tunisia as well. The French perennially suspect, however, that the United States is trying to supplant them in this region, and they speak of the "American game" or the "American card" that local governments may play from time to time. This theoretical contest is generally perceived by the French, and many Americans, as a zero sum game, that is, one in which a gain for one side is a loss for the other.

This is a short-sighted and parochial view. Except in the admittedly important field of commercial competition, U.S. interests and those of France in North Africa are congruent. Both have an interest in stable, independent governments that, while they may not be their clients, more importantly are not clients of the Soviets. Any accrual of influence to one Western power promotes Western interests as a whole. Those interests would be served by increased rather than decreased French influence in the area, and it need not be a zero sum game, provided the participants can rise above their territorial reflexes. The U.S. could not possibly match the French commitment in personnel, in any event, and while there has been some interesting reaction against French in favor of Arabic and English across the region, the French cultural connection is today much stronger than the American. There are, for instance, 25,000 Moroccans in French schools today, compared with an estimated 350 in the United States, and the French language will remain the dominant foreign language in Morocco for any period that can usefully be discussed.

Spain

Spain's historic involvement with North Africa long antedates France's. As noted earlier, the Muslim army that first invaded Spain in 711 was commanded by a North African, and the majority of his troops were Berbers. The story of Muslim conquest and rule, and the long struggle of the Spanish *reconquista*, is one of the most passionate and complex episodes of European history and has left a profound imprint on all the parties. Morocco in particular was for centuries the front line in the contest between Islam and Christianity, and Moroccan attitudes and culture were deeply affected by this warfare and by the eventual penetration of North Africa by the Spaniards and Portuguese, commencing with the seizure of Ceuta by the latter in 1415.

Spain at one point controlled most of the North African coast from Tangier to Tunis, and there are surprising remnants of this occupation today. As noted in Chapter 1, Spain occupies, and regards as sovereign territory, five small enclaves on the Moroccan coast—Ceuta, Melilla, Penon de al-Hucemas, Penon de Velez, and the Chafarinas Islands. Penon de al-Hucemas is a small, fortified rock a few hundred yards off the coast and is used as a military disciplinary barracks. Penon de Velez is a minuscule rocky eminence which shelters a tiny fishing village and a small garrison and is connected to the coast by a narrow sand bar. The Chafarinas Islands had only 195 inhabitants in 1977. Ceuta and Melilla, however, are sizeable Spanish towns (occupying nine and four square miles respectively, and having populations of about 66,500 and 55,000 in 1982).

None of these possessions is on the high road to any place (although they are on the tourist track to Morocco), and they have about as much economic and military value for Spain as the Falklands do for Britain. To the Moroccans, these enclaves are part of the national territory, and they maintain that their position is like Spain's with regard to Gibraltar—they support the principle of the integrity of national territory and say that when Gibraltar is returned to Spain they will demand return of the enclaves. Ceding them to Morocco would cause serious domestic problems in Spain, however, and this is a very difficult and contentious issue in Spanish-Moroccan relations. For instance, the Spanish ministers of agriculture and fisheries and of transport and communications cancelled a visit to Morocco scheduled for February 1983, because the Moroccans had raised the enclave issue in a meeting of the Arab Interparliamentary Union in Rabat, calling on Spain to enter negotiations on the subject, and because one of King Hassan's courtiers, Ahmad al-Alaoui, had written in his newspaper that the Moroccans could not let the problem drag on indefinitely. The Spanish foreign minister responded in a press conference that there was no question the enclaves belonged to Spain. This contretemps passed in time and the Spanish prime minister visited Morocco in March 1983. Radio Madrid reported that he did not discuss the enclave issue with the Moroccans. Perhaps that was a condition of the visit.

Spanish officials freely admit that the enclaves have no strategic or economic value and that they represent a net drain on the budget. In theory, Ceuta and Melilla, which are free ports, could be developed further as such, but the Spanish have not shown much imagination in this regard, and it is questionable whether the necessary customers could be found if they did, since both places have no hinterland and tourist traffic is only moderate. The same officials also emphasize, however, the very deep sentimental attachment that the Spanish military, and many civilians, have for the enclaves. One of the Spanish Socialists' criticisms of Spanish adherence to NATO, for instance, is that NATO's defense frontier does not include the enclaves, and this is one reason they have not proceded to seek full membership.

When asked why there is this attachment, the Spaniard is likely to say that almost every Spanish officer, or someone in his family, has either been born or served in one of these *presidios*, that Melilla was Franco's last stop en route back to Spain during the civil war, that there is a symbolism about these remote outposts seized from the infidels and held at great sacrifice over the centuries, that the Spanish are no more prepared to sacrifice the resident Spanish population than the British are to sacrifice the Gibraltarians, and that these have been Spanish property for so long as to have been always so.

The Spanish will not admit a parallel between their enclaves and Gibraltar, but fear that the Moroccans are going to agitate the issue when they feel the time is ripe, whatever happens to Gibraltar. They have no predictions what Spanish policy will be at that time, but note that Spanish attachment to the enclaves is much stronger than the attachment was to the Western Sahara and that the Spanish military will want to fight rather than give them up. In 1982 they had a total of about 20,000 troops stationed in the enclaves, which would give them considerable defensive capability.

Because of proximity, the enclaves, and economic and fishing interests, Morocco is the most important of the North African states to Spain, although its trade with Algeria and Libya is larger. Of the estimated 20,000 Spaniards living in North Africa, about 14,000 are in Morocco. They do not figure largely in the economic life of Morocco today, but other Spaniards do. Spain is a minority partner in the Bou Craa phosphate deposits in the Sahara, now controlled by Morocco, and the fishing grounds off the Moroccan and Saharan coasts, among the richest in the world, are of great interest to Spain. Some 16,000 Spanish fishermen in roughly 1,000 boats, mostly from southern Spain and the Canaries but also from Galicia, fish in these waters. While the net proceeds of their activities, estimated at $500 million in 1981, may not be vital to the Spanish economy (although the Spaniards are, surprisingly, the largest consumers of fish in Europe), their jobs and livelihoods are of intense political sensitivity. Entire Spanish communities are dependent on them, and prolonged interruption of their fishing in these waters would have very serious political repercussions in Spain. After long, and sometimes acrimonious, negotiations, the Spanish and Moroccans finally reached agreement in the summer of 1983 on a long-term fishing accord. This was an important and encouraging development because heretofore the Spanish had ignored Morocco economically. They do not, for instance, permit Moroccan citrus to transit Spain freely, since they see the Moroccans as competitors.

Spain was one of the major players in the early phases of the Western Sahara dispute and has been managing a difficult balancing act between Morocco and Algeria ever since. For a period during the late 1970s, in response to Spanish policies perceived as pro-Moroccan, Algeria was giving support, in the form of radio time, to the Canary Islands liberation front (The Movement for the Self-Determination and Independence of the Canary Archipelago or MPAIAC). The movement, which was erroneously thought to consist only of a man named Antonio Cubillo, his wife, and a typewriter, carried out a number of bomb attacks in the Canaries in 1977 and 1978, and one of its bomb threats was partially responsible for a collision of two commercial airliners that killed several hundred tourists.[1] Algerian support for the front was withdrawn after Spanish Prime Minister Suarez visited Algiers in the Spring of 1979 and in his capacity as president of the ruling Central Democratic Union (and not as prime minister) met with the secretary general of the Polisario, Muhammad Abdul Aziz. The Spanish maintain that this did not constitute official recognition.

MPAIAC is not a movement of native peoples. The original Berber inhabitants of the Canaries, known as the Guanches, were almost entirely eliminated by the Spanish, who took possession of the islands in 1496. While a few people may still claim descent from the Guanches, the MPAIAC represents the "old" Spaniards on the islands as opposed to the "new" and not the Guanches.

Spain also has important interests in Algeria, including a projected gas pipeline across the Mediterranean that would supply the southwest European market. Bechtel has made a survey of the proposed line, which would cut across a small corner of Morocco and is therefore a long way into the future. The Spanish are already buying a limited quantity of Algerian liquefied natural gas, which is being re-gasified at Barcelona. They are also seeking to market military equipment and other items in Algeria. Spain was the fifth ranking supplier of Algerian imports in 1979, but in 1982 it was behind France, the United States, Germany, Italy, Japan, and Austria, in that order, as a trading partner. The Spanish have important contracts in Libya as well as in Morocco and are in the process of trying to develop markets in Tunisia. They do not have major economic influence in any of these countries however, and their importance, real and potential, is primarily as a competitor for European citrus and olive oil markets, as noted earlier.

The Spanish, conscious of their special and often unhappy relationship with North Africa, have followed a prudent, low-profile policy in the area, emphasizing their stand on the Arab-Israel issue (they have not recognized Israel) and their interest in trade, and downplaying the colonial past and such issues as the Canary Islands liberation movement. They enjoy generally good relations with the states of the region as a result, but their political influence is limited. As with France, it would be a healthy development if Spain, as a member of the Western community of nations, were more active and influential in this area. Spanish resources may be limited, but Spain has a number of possibilities, as in its dealings with Morocco, to show more interest in North African economic development and to cultivate closer political relations. Perhaps Spain's eventual adherence to NATO will encourage a more active partnership with the other Europeans here and elsewhere.

Italy

Proximity has assured Italy a long-standing connection with North Africa. The link has waxed and waned over the centuries, but it has rarely been severed completely. Like Spain, although to a much lesser degree, Italy (and Sicily in particular) was exposed to Muslim conquest, and there were recurring skirmishes between the Italians and the North Africans until the suppression of the Barbary pirates in the nineteenth century. In spite of the hostilities, the Italians were able to maintain commercial connections with the area, and especially with Tunisia, throughout much of the period from the eleventh to twentieth centuries.

Italy's seizure of Libya in 1911 was a belated assertion of colonial power status, and was one of colonialism's more egregious failures. It took agonizing decades to subdue the country, and its conversion into a productive asset and population outlet had only started when World War II destroyed the dream. Goats graze today in the ruins of houses built for Italian colonists, and the lasting effects of the occupation on Libyan culture seem to be slight. Thirty years ago Tripoli and Benghazi were Italianate cities. They are no more. On the other hand, Libyans still go to Italy for education, recreation and medical treatment, and there is considerable business activity between the two countries.

Italy's economic interests in North Africa today are greatest in Libya and Algeria. The Italians have been actively involved in sizeable economic projects in both countries, and the size of their commitment is indicated by the fact that as of April 1984 the Libyans had been for two years $2–3 billion in arrears on payments to Italy for work completed.[2] There are still some 20,000 Italians in Libya, most of them transients working under contract. The permanent Italian community was deported en masse by Qadhdhafi.

Similarly, the Italians have had a number of important construction and development contracts in Algeria. Their biggest is the Trans-Mediterranean gas pipeline, which goes from Algeria to mainland Italy via Tunisia and Sicily. This undertaking is designed to supply Italy with 12 billion cubic meters of gas per year.

Italy's political role, like Spain's, is limited. This is in part because the Italians, as well as the Spaniards, have tried to avoid initiatives that could affect their commercial relations. In the case of Libya, for instance, the Italians have been unwilling to support American initiatives to isolate Qadhdhafi because their economic interests would suffer. At the same time, they admit that Qadhdhafi is a destabilizing influence and see him as someone who, while not a Soviet client, associates with people who are (such as the South Yemenis and Ethiopians). They feel, however, that to some extent he has been pushed into these relationships by the United States and believe they have an important role to play in providing him with continued access to the West.

As is the case with Spain and France, it would be in the Western interest if Italy were to play a more active role in North Africa, but its means are limited, and it is not clear that it has the capacity to do a great deal more than it already is, although Italy has impressive human resources that could be utilized, for instance, in vocational training and technical assistance programs in places like Algeria and Morocco. Little has been done in that respect so far.

The European Community

While Spain and Italy may not have the military or financial weight needed to play heavy roles in North Africa, the European Community as a whole theoretically has the ability to do so. In the view of the Francophone states of the Maghrib, this would be a desirable development, giving them an alternative to reliance on the superpowers. In seeking a means of stimulating more European involvement, the Maghribis have shown considerable interest in developing a Mediterranean consensus on various issues and made unsuccessful efforts to convene a conference of Mediterranean states in the early 1970s. They also made a determined effort to get Mediterranean issues, and particularly the superpower military presence, placed on the agenda of the Belgrade Conference on Security and Cooperation in Europe. While they managed to get some reference to the matter in the final document of the conference, substantive consideration was postponed until the Madrid Conference, where again nothing happened, in spite of a filibuster by the Maltese delegate. This reflects the disinclination of the superpowers, as well as a number of European states, to further complicate an already complex and difficult negotiation by raising Mediterranean questions that would pose vexing problems for all of them. Neither the Soviets nor the Americans, for instance, would welcome discussion of their naval presence in the Mediterranean, a presence that is regarded by a number of riparians as extraneous and dangerous.

Although the United States was until recently Algeria's largest customer, Western Europe is the largest trading partner of the Maghrib in general. All the states except Libya have "cooperative agreements" with the European Economic Community, meaning they have somewhat less than full access to the Common Market. They enjoy preferences over nonmembers, but their exports to the market are subject to quotas when they compete with the products of European members, for example, Dutch tomatoes. They are also partners in the Euro-Arab Dialogue, which the Arabs had hoped would lead to a remodeling of European-Arab relations and greater European participation in the search for a Middle East settlement, that is, they had hoped for political benefits. The Europeans, however, although they make the right political noises, as in the Venice Declaration on the Arab-Israel issue, tend to see the Dialogue as an exercise in limited technical and economic cooperation, under which the Arabs will supply the money and the Europeans the brains for a series of projects in economic development and cooperation. Results to date have been modest, and the Maghribis have been disappointed in their expectations. While their limited access to the Common Market has been an important benefit, it *has* been limited, and the North Africans see themselves as receiving second class treatment as compared to Spain. The issue of North African vs. Spanish citrus and olive oil is likely to be contentious for some time, as will the issue of European discrimination against North African manufactures. The Moroccans, for instance, are encouraged by foreign advisers to stand on their own feet and produce items such as textiles regarding which they have some comparative advantage, but then find themselves unable to work to capacity because of EEC quotas. Thus, the Europeans have not provided an alternative to the superpowers, have not played the political role they could, and have not provided the economic benefits the Maghribis think they should. While it would be in the long-term interests of everyone to have them do so, if for no other reason than to offer an alternative to polarization of the region between the U.S. and the Soviets, judging by past performance neither Moscow nor Washington would welcome it in fact, whatever they might say publicly. The U.S. government tends to regard European initiatives in the Arab world as unhelpful and irresponsible, while the Soviets tend to regard the Europeans as handmaidens of U.S. imperialism.

The United States

The United States has a long history of friendly relations with North Africa. Morocco was the first foreign state to recognize the infant republic, and the United States has maintained consular representation in Morocco, Algeria, and Tunisia since the end of the eighteenth century. Except for the brief episodes of the war with the Barbary pirates, the United States was not among the powers deeply involved in North Africa, and it was probably its remoteness from the scene that prompted the Sultan of Morocco, Mohamed IV, in 1871 to ask it to extend a protectorate over his country to shelter it from the voracious European powers, who were partitioning Africa. The United States refused, but the request was indicative of an essentially trustful attitude toward the United States that has been a recurrent (if not permanent) theme in relations between the two states. Earlier in this century, the United States, although careful not to alienate its French allies, was generally perceived as sympathetic to Maghribi aspirations for independence, as evidenced by its being the last major power to recognize the French protectorate over Morocco, by President Roosevelt's insisting on meeting then Sultan Mohamed V and his son Hassan at Casablanca in 1943, in spite of the displeasure it caused the French, and by the-then Senator John Kennedy's speech of support for Algerian independence in 1957. American diplomatic representatives maintained contact with Maghribi independence movements at least as far back as World War II, and echoes of those contacts can still be heard today.

American interest deepened greatly in World War II with the commitment of troops to North Africa. Many landed in Morocco, and while most of them passed through the country fairly quickly, the U.S. Navy established a permanent presence at the French airfield at Port Lyautey, just north of Rabat. Renamed Kenitra after independence, this became in time a major communications complex, with the transmitting and receiving done at two outstations and with all communications of the Sixth Fleet eventually channeled through it. In 1951, under agreement with the French, the United States began building three major Strategic Air Command bases at Sidi Slimane (between Kenitra and Meknes), Nouasseur (south of Casablanca) and Ben Guerir (north of Marrakesh), and there was an important air force presence in the country until 1963, when the Moroccans, who had not been consulted about the agreement with the French, finally required the Americans to evacuate them. The Moroccans agreed, however, to continued U.S. use of the Kenitra complex, which was ostensibly converted to a Moroccan training base, but which continued to provide a vital communications link for the Sixth Fleet until the mid-1970s and was not evacuated until 1978.

Arising from this presence was a fluctuating U.S.-Moroccan military relationship under which the Moroccan armed forces will have received by the end of 1984 a total of $600–800 million worth of U.S. military equipment, much of it in the past ten years. Until recently there has been no quid pro quo for this assistance, but the Moroccans have been cooperative on such matters as fleet visits, overflights, and intelligence sharing, and both sides have seen the military relationship as being in their common interest.

This relationship took on a new character after 1975, however, first because of the Sahara war and then, under the Reagan administration, because of a perceived U.S. need for access to Moroccan base facilities for staging the Rapid Deployment Force to points east. As noted in Chapter 5, the Sahara conflict has generated a Moroccan demand for more military assistance and for the use of American weapons in an area that the United States has not recognized as Moroccan sovereign territory, thereby raising the question of whether the arms are being used for legitimate self-defense. While the Carter administration initially had serious doubts about this, it was beginning to resolve them in favor of Morocco as early as 1979, and the Reagan administration, as one of its first acts, moved to demonstrate that it was not concerned about legal issues in its desire to help contain countries perceived as friendly and as supportive of the United States vis-à-vis the Soviets. Morocco is such a country.

U.S. commercial relations with Morocco remain modest. Investment there has gone from $60 million in 1970 to $40 million in 1980, to $60 million in 1982 and down to $50 million in 1984. Given the declining value of the dollar due to inflation, this represents a sharp decline in real terms. U.S. firms are involved in some light industrial operations, notably tire and cork factories, and are interested in contracts for shale oil development and uranium processing. The King Ranch is involved in a stock-raising operation and there are a number of potentially attractive opportunities for investment in agribusiness and elsewhere, but as yet there are none of the highly lucrative prospects found next door in Algeria in the 1970s. Not only do the Moroccans have little money, but they are not all that easy to do business with, and the sometimes predatory tactics of the royal court have dampened the enthusiasm of many entrepreneurs. Furthermore, because of their historic connection and the predominance of French over English as a second language, the French have enjoyed substantial advantages in Morocco that have discouraged U.S. investors.

The United States' most important interest in Morocco is political. King Hassan is perceived as a moderate leader who has been helpful in many matters—arranging initial contacts between Israel and Egypt, supporting the anti-Communist insurgency led by Jonas Savimbi in Angola, twice supplying troops to prop up President Mobutu's rule in Zaire, supplying security personnel to conservative regimes in Africa and the Gulf, and agreeing to limited but significant military cooperation with the United States. The Moroccans have, for instance, supplied valuable intelligence on Soviet weapons captured in the Sahara. They have also let U.S. military aircraft and ships use their airfields and ports with minimal restraints. King Hassan is also regarded, with somewhat less justification, as a counter to extremist currents in the Arab world. (His influence is in fact limited by his remoteness from the center of Arab politics and by his lack of material resources with which to influence the other Arabs. He is furthermore constrained by the realities of domestic as well as Arab politics to avoid taking positions that would be considered pro-American and therefore pro-Israel.)

Algeria, with which the United States has political relations that are usually correct and somewhat distant, is of considerable economic importance. At this writing American firms hold between 1 and 2 billion dollars worth of Algerian government contracts, down from $6 billion three years ago, in part because of the suspension of liquified natural gas contracts. The remaining contracts are principally for the construction of petroleum-related facilities, such as liquefaction plants, gas pipelines, and gas treatment plants. Until 1982 the United States was, as noted earlier, Algeria's biggest single oil customer, taking over 50 percent of its exports in 1980, compared to France's 15 percent share. In exchange, the United States supplied only 6 percent of Algeria's imports, amounting to $595 million, but part of the difference was taken up by contractual services. U.S. exports in 1982 were up to 8 percent of Algeria's imports, still far behind the French.

By and large the contracts mentioned above do not represent capital acquisitions or investments. Although the Algerians are now permitting joint ventures involving foreign firms, in general they do not welcome foreign investment, and the contracts referred to above are for construction and services only. Algeria and the United States have thus avoided burdening their relationship with vested interests. The exception is the liquefied natural gas contracts, which have involved substantial investment in cryogenic tankers and regasification facilities in the United States and elsewhere. This investment has been jeopardized, if not forfeited, by the disagreement over gas prices.

While there has been a good deal of private U.S.-Algerian economic cooperation, and the Export-Import Bank has played an important role in financing it (its current exposure there is about $1.3 billion), there has been very little political cooperation. This is discussed in more detail in Chapter 9, but it is something of a paradox that the United States feels much closer to Morocco, where its material interests are slight, than it does to Algeria, where it has an important financial stake and which has a potential for good and bad considerably outweighing Morocco's. The realities of their different potentials are readily apparent to the Moroccans, who are perpetually looking for signs that the United States will continue to support them for reasons of strategic or material interest rather than just sentiment. The fact is, however, that America's economy and Algeria's are complementary, while America's and Morocco's are not.

The American political relationship with Algeria reflects a persistent irritation with Algerian policies in international fora. Particularly during the mid-1970s, but at other times as well, Algeria has played a leading radical role in the nonaligned movement, and this has led to frequent clashes with the United States over such matters as Vietnam, Palestine, and the New International Economic Order (which was launched by Boumediene). Algerian oppositon to American policies is inevitable on many Third World issues that are important to Algeria and that become matters of ideology and principle. Nevertheless, Benjedid is following more moderate policies than Boumediene did, and the Algerians have indicated a strong interest in improved relations. Modest progress is being made and there is a substantive dialogue between the United States and Algeria today that holds the promise of better understanding.

Tunisia is the least potent of the North African powers, the least difficult to live with, and the one with which the United States has the fewest problems. The Tunisians alone have never antagonized or embarrassed the United States since their independence. They have been open about their need for help, but have not been afraid to do their own work. There are occasional bilateral problems, but they are manageable.

The United States has little economic stake in Tunisia and although it, along with the rest of North Africa, has potential strategic value, there is little likelihood of the United States' trying to benefit from it directly, that is, militarily, short of a cataclysm. U.S. material interests are therefore slight, but the United States has an interest in Tunisia's survival as the most truly moderate of the Arab states. It also has an interest in the success of its modernizing efforts as a demonstration of what can be accomplished through a pragmatic approach.

Libya was originally important to the United States because of the military facilities it had there—Wheelus Air Force Base and related ranges. In exchange for their use the United States paid the Libyan government a small annual subvention. Wheelus, because of the generally clear weather in Triplolitania, was the preferred location for range practice by U.S. Air Force units stationed in Europe. Aircraft would land and take off with high frequency during the practice season, and for many years the readiness of air force units in Europe depended on the availability of Wheelus.

The Libyan revolution of 1969 brought an end to this, and Wheelus was turned over to the Libyans in 1970. By then petroleum had already surpassed Wheelus as the principal U.S. interest in the country. By 1980 Libya was the United States' third largest supplier of imported oil and until late 1981, six U.S. companies were involved in its extraction and export. Because of its high quality and location it was then selling at a premium price of $40 a barrel, long since lowered to a more modest figure because of the oil glut. In addition, a number of other U.S. firms, such as Brown and Root, were working on some $10 billion worth of economic development projects financed by oil revenues, and U.S. exports to Libya were running at about $900 million a year.

The worsening of bilateral relations, which had begun long before, did not begin to affect these operations seriously until mid-December of 1981, when in the midst of the furor over reported Libyan attempts to assassinate President Reagan and other senior officials, the United States called on U.S. companies to leave Libya and then invalidated U.S. passports for travel to that country. As noted in Chapter 5, although many of the 2,000 Americans then resident in Libya were reluctant to leave, and some have stayed, the majority had left by the summer of 1982.

In March 1982 the United States embargoed the importation of Libyan oil. Exxon, the discoverer of Libyan oil, had already announced in November 1981 that it was withdrawing and Mobil followed suit in June 1982, only to reverse itself the following month. The reversal was predicated on an understanding with the Libyans that failed to materialize, and Mobil subsequently announced, in December 1982, that it was definitely pulling out. In both cases the companies advanced economic reasons for their decisions, and the high posted price of Libyan crude, which created marketing difficulties, was one factor. The impact, however, was as much political as economic, and the Libyans see the Americans as trying unsuccessfully to strangle them economically for political reasons.

A fuller discussion of policies toward Libya will be found in Chapter 9. The question posed for U.S. policy makers, simply stated, is whether to respond in kind to Qadhdhafi or to ignore him. The Carter administration tried flexibility and that did not work. The Reagan administration has been trying confrontation. It, too, is unlikely to work.

This is not a matter of indifference. If the other companies still in Libya (Occidental, Amerada Hess, Conoco, and Marathon) follow the Exxon-Mobil example, the direct U.S. stake in Libya will dwindle to almost nothing. The United States will nevertheless have a continuing interest in what Libya does. Given the small size of its population and the isolation of its leadership from the rest of the Arab world, Libya's capacity for bold power moves is very limited. It does have an impressive capacity for mischief, however, and it is located in an area of keen geopolitical interest to the Americans and the Soviets.

The Soviet Union

The Soviet Union's interests in North Africa are as varied as those of the United States. It has a direct or indirect strategic interest in all the countries of the region, and for similar reasons. In particular, the Soviets have long sought base facilities along the North African coast for their Mediterranean fleet.

The permanent Soviet naval presence in the Mediterranean is a phenomenon of the last 20 years. Although Soviet naval activities in these waters began with the basing of submarines at Valona in Albania in 1958, that arrangement was terminated when Albania left the Soviet Bloc in 1961, and from then until 1964 Soviet activities were confined to the occasional dispatch of submarines from their Black Sea or North Sea fleets. There was no separate Soviet Mediterranean command or fleet.

The permanent stationing of naval units in the Mediterranean began in 1964, and a separate Mediterranean command had been set up by 1965. From a handful of vessels in the beginning it grew to a permanent level of 40 to 50 vessels, to be augmented in times of crisis to as many as 96 (at the time of the 1973 Ramadan War).[3] Of these, 34 were surface fighting vessels and 23 were submarines.

While U.S. naval officers are quick to point out the combat superiority of the Sixth Fleet and allied navies, and express confidence that they can deal effectively with the Soviet fleet, they are also quick to recognize that the Soviets have a capacity to impose serious damage on U.S. units, that preventing them from doing so will not be an easy task, and that while the Soviets have yet to challenge the Sixth Fleet directly, they constitute an inhibiting presence. The Mediterranean is no longer America's private lake as it was in 1958.

U.S. naval superiority rests largely on the carrier and its ability to project airpower long distances quickly. That superiority, is also essential to the deployment of amphibious forces. The Marines cannot land safely without it. The Soviets have lagged far behind in carrier development but have structured their Mediterranean fleet to take advantage of the sizable targets that U.S. carriers present. They have concentrated on submarines and short-range missiles, which pose serious problems for the defense of carrier forces. The effectiveness of such tactics was first demonstrated when the Egyptians sank an Israeli destroyer in the fall of 1967, using a small missile boat with relatively primitive surface-to-surface missiles. The most recent demonstration of the effectiveness of air-to-surface missiles was given by the Exocet in the Falklands War, and the vulnerability of large ships to such attack will assure that the next large-scale naval confrontation will be different from those of World War II.

The Soviets have also had to adapt to a difficult logistics, support, and command environment because the Soviet Union is not a riparian state and has no Mediterranean allies as close as those of the United States. Although current difficulties with the Greeks, and longstanding problems with the French, show that the permanence of such arrangements should not be taken for granted, the U.S. Sixth Fleet enjoys full access to a number of first-class naval facilities, and the use of ground installations for command, logistics, and home porting purposes, at various points on the northern shore of the Mediterranean. This greatly facilitates maintaining a permanent naval presence, and even with these facilities the navy is constantly looking for additional access.

The Soviets, on the other hand, have no comparable access. For some time after the June War in 1967 they were allowed by the Egyptians to use base and maintenance facilities at Alexandria and Port Said and to base aircraft at Egyptian airfields, from which they flew surveillance missions against the Sixth Fleet. The Alexandria facilities were particularly important because of the comparative sophistication of Egyptian repair capabilities, and the Soviets had what amounted in time to their own naval base, although they did not enjoy the sort of extraterritoriality the Americans enjoyed at Wheelus, for example. They were also developing facilities at the port of Mersa Matruh, near the Libyan border, and were apparently planning to make heavy use of that port. Soviet use of these facilities was sharply curtailed with the Egyptian expulsion of Soviet military personnel in 1972 and completely terminated in 1976. The Soviets have never found a satisfactory substitute. At the moment they have access to the following facilities:

Yugoslavia: heavy maintenance of auxiliary units and diesel submarines at the ports of Tivat, Bijela, and Tropir.

Syria: light maintenance of diesel submarines at Tartous.

Tunisia: drydocking for auxiliary vessels and submarines at Bizerte (Menzil Bourguiba).

Algeria: light maintenance at Annaba for submarines.

None of these compares with the facilities the Soviets once had at Alexandria or which the Americans enjoy at various European ports such as Rota, Gaeta, and Suda Bay (Crete).

Aside from maintenance and supply services, bases provide, among other things, the possibility of expanded communications and intelligence facilities, a stable platform for command functions, permanent facilities for shore leave and entertainment (an important morale factor), shelter from the elements, and the possibility of home porting. The Soviets, deprived of such facilities, have had to make use of anchorages outside the territorial waters of coastal states, where the bottom may be as deep as 100 meters. Their main anchorages along the North African coast in 1983 were:

- Off Sollum, near the Egyptian-Libyan border.
- Off Hammamet, Tunisia.
- Banco le Sec, off Tabarka, near the Algerian-Libyan border.
- Banco Tofino, between Spain and Morocco.

Of these, Hammamet and Sollum are their principal maintenance anchorages, while the others are used primarily for operational rendezvous.

Soviet ships come to these anchorages for mail, medical, supply, and maintenance services provided by auxiliary vessels. While the arrangement is obviously workable in the sense that the Soviets are able to maintain their fleet in operation this way, it is unsatisfactory in terms of the nature of supply and maintenance services that can be provided afloat, and the Soviets have consistently sought new port facilities ever since their departure from Alexandria. Indeed, they were seeking them along the western Mediterranean coast of North Africa well before that, and their continuing need for them must be taken as one of the constants in the Mediterranean geopolitical equation.

That they have so far not succeeded in finding an alternative to Alexandria along the littoral somewhere says something about the strength of local nationalism and the general desire of the North African states to stay out of East-West confrontational issues. Local resistance to Soviet blandishments in this respect is, however, affected by perceptions of threats posed by other powers. The Egyptians gave the Soviets access to their facilities largely out of desperation following the 1967 war, and Libya or Syria could well do the same if they felt sufficiently threatened by the United States or local powers friendly to it, that is, Egypt or Israel. Remarks by Qadhdhafi to Eric Rouleau of *Le Monde* in July 1983 reflected this possibility. Accusing the United States of trying to transform the war in Chad from a purely internal affair into a confrontation between imperialism and a people striving to achieve freedom, he remarked, "Our relations with the Soviet Union are becoming closer to the extent that threats from the imperialists are multiplying." He has muttered similar threats on subsequent occasions.

The Soviet naval presence has strategic implications that go well beyond the strictly Mediterranean context. To begin with, it represents an outward thrust that is in marked contrast to earlier Soviet naval practice and that has coincided with development of an airborne capacity to project military power beyond the continental frontiers of the Soviet Union. This capability was first revealed, or rather implied, in reports of Soviet preparations to intervene with airborne troops in the 1973 Ramadan War. More obvious evidence was given by their airlift of supplies and personnel to Angola in 1975 and to Ethiopia in 1977.

The Cubans have provided must of the manpower for this projection, and have enabled the Soviets to play the sort of intercontinental interventionary role hitherto reserved to the Western powers. Soviet capabilities in this respect may be less impressive than those of the United States, but they represent a quantum jump from zero, and are something that must now be reckoned with in Western policy calculations. While most of the dramatic projection from the Soviet Union has been done by air, and has not involved the Mediterranean fleet as a carrier, the latter has had an important surveillance and escort function, with an as yet untested capability for interfering with NATO efforts to block the movement of Soviet aircraft or ships across the Mediterranean.

Secondly, Soviet forces that are blocked from moving across Europe by NATO have flanked those defenses to some extent by maintaining a permanent presence in the western Mediterranean, even if it is dependent on unsatisfactory anchorages. That presence at this point is insufficient to represent a major threat to the security of NATO, but it has a potential for growth and, as noted earlier, granting the Soviets base facilities in any of the North African countries would have serious implications for France and Italy in particular, but for all of NATO as well, because it would greatly extend the quality and range of Soviet operational capabilities on their flanks.

The French and the Moroccans periodically float rumors that the Algerians have given the Soviets the use of facilities at the former French naval base of Mers el-Kebir, west of Oran, but there appears to have been no truth to them. Soviet vessels pay occasional visits to Moroccan ports, but enjoy no special privileges there. They used Libyan airfields for their military aircraft on two occasions in 1981, but as of mid-1984 there was still no pattern of regular use.

The Tunisian decision to let the Soviets have access to their naval repair facilities at Bizerte was taken not out of any doctrinal or political sympathy but from the lack of other customers and a need to create employment. Had the Americans or West Europeans been interested, the Soviets would not have an entry there now. Their use of these facilities is reported to be very infrequent in any event, whether because of Tunisian-imposed limitations or because Soviet needs are limited, or because the facilities are not all that attractive, or because the Soviets distrust the Westernized environment, is not clear. Nor have the Soviets been as active as they might be in calling at Algerian and Moroccan ports. This may be in part for operational reasons, but both the Moroccans and Algerians deliberately restrict foreign military visits, Soviet and otherwise. Were those restrictions eased, we probably would see more Soviet naval activity in the ports of those countries. Libya also apparently restricts visits by Soviet as well as non-Soviet naval units, and a change in policy there would also probably bring a change in Soviet practice.

Aside from the activities of their fleet, the Soviets have had some sort of military relationship with all the states of North Africa except Tunisia at one time or another. When King Mohamed V of Morocco, who was one of the leaders of the radical Casablanca bloc, turned to the Soviets for arms in 1960, they rapidly supplied him with what was then considered to be a substantial quantity of modern aircraft and tanks. They have been the almost exclusive supplier of military equipment to Algeria, although the latter has recently turned to the United States for certain items such as radios and C-130 transports. The Soviets have also done considerable advising and training of Algerians, but have not played the dominant role they once played in Egypt. There are an estimated 2,000 Soviet military advisers in Algeria today (compared to 20,000 in Egypt in 1972).

Libya has been a major purchaser of Soviet arms, buying far more than it can use. Most of them are in storage, purportedly for use by the Arabs against Israel. The quantities are so large, however, and Libya is so remote from the battlefield, that, as noted earlier, there has been speculation that the Soviets are prepositioning arms there for their own use, just as it has been proposed that the United States do in Israel and Egypt. Aside from the lack of confirming evidence, this seriously underestimates the strength of Libyan nationalism, but the current U.S. confrontation with Libya could change that, as could a decision actually to pre-position substantial quantities of American arms in Israel (assuming of course, that the Soviets would be interested in doing the same in Libya, which remains to be established).

The Soviets' purpose in selling arms to these countries is to increase their influence. The Soviets' interest in North Africa is not new, as evidenced by their seeking a trusteeship over Libya at the end of World War II. To them the area is important politically as well as militarily. Morocco, Algeria, Tunisia, and now Libya have all played key roles in Third World politics at one time or another, and the Algerian capacity for effective political action is particularly important to the Soviets. There is a frequent congruence of

Table D. The Soviet Presence in North Africa

Soviet and Eastern European Military Technicians—1981		North African Military Personnel Trained in Communist Countries 1955-81	
Algeria	2,000	Algeria	2,395
Other	2,600	Libya	1,990
		Morocco	145

Soviet and Eastern European Economic Technicians—1981		Soviet & Eastern European Economic Aid Extended 1954-81 (in millions of dollars)		Academic Students Being Trained in USSR & Eastern Europe as of December 1981	
Algeria	11,150	Algeria	1,570	Algeria	2,225
Libya	31,700	Morocco	2,315	Libya	275
Morocco	2,350	Tunisia	325	Morocco	650
Tunisia	600			Tunisia	1,055

The U.S. presence is minuscule by comparison:

Table D.1 The United States Presence in North Africa

Military Advisors and Technicians—1983		Military Personnel Trained in U.S. 1950-1983		Military Aid Extended— 1954-1981 (in millions of dollars)	
Morocco	12*	Morocco	3,047	Morocco	800
Algeria	0	Algeria	200	Algeria	0
Tunisia	6*	Tunisia	1,467	Tunisia	200
Libya	0	Libya	567	Libya	17.6

Economic Technicians (Includes private businessmen and Peace Corps)		Economic Aid Extended— 1954-1981 (in millions of dollars)		Academic Students Being Trained in U.S. as of September 1983		
					USG Scholarships	Other
Morocco	250-300	Morocco	1,622	Morocco	106	250
Algeria	150-200	Algeria	50	Algeria	66	2,000
Tunisia	150	Tunisia	1,256	Tunisia	0	150
Libya	600-1,000	Libya	200	Libya	0	3,000

* Does not reflect mobile training teams and other military personnel temporarily detailed to these countries. They probably bring the Moroccan total well above 50 much of the time.

positions, if not interests, between the two, and the Soviets hope for Algerian support on major issues at the United Nations. They are less expectant with regard to Morocco and Tunisia, but the latter also support Soviet positions when they coincide with those of the non-aligned states. (Since non-aligned issues predominate at the UN, *all* of the North African states, including Morocco and Tunisia, vote much more often with the Soviets than they do with the United States.) The Algerian role in promoting such coincidence is often critical, but it very frequently is a case of the Soviets aligning themselves with the Third World rather than vice versa. If anyone is leading in this relationship it is the Algerians, not the Soviets.

Some idea of the degree of Soviet involvement in North Africa is given by the figures in the Department of State's booklet *Soviet and East European Aid to the Third World, 1981*, published in February 1983. While some of its language about Algeria is misleading, the figures are probably no more inaccurate than any other estimates available in the public domain. They come ultimately from the CIA.

Because of Qadhdhafi's eccentric behavior, Libya, for all its arms purchases, must be a source of concern to the Soviets, who do not like surprises. The Soviets have not been involved in Libyan oil ventures and have little material stake in that country. They are earning a good deal of hard currency through their arms sales, but they do not appear to be getting much in the way of influence over Qadhdhafi. Again, there may be a congruence between Soviet and Libyan positions on certain matters, but that is more a reflection of their common opposition to the United States than of any agreement on basic questions of ideology or national goals.

The Soviets have been involved economically in Algeria, supplying equipment and winning contracts for various development projects such as the Annaba steel mill and an aluminum plant. Their technology is often second-rate, however, and the Algerians generally prefer that of the Americans or other Westerners. The Soviets would not have won the contract for the aluminum plant, for instance, if U.S. companies had been prepared to share their technology with the Algerians.

While the Soviets have not had a major aid program in Morocco, they have been actively involved in two important contracts, one for up to 10 million tons of phosphates for 25–30 years under a $5 billion barter agreement announced in 1974, and one for operating and training a Moroccan fishing fleet. Both of these ventures touch sensitive spots in the Moroccan economy, and Soviet performance may lead to other contracts (it may also rule them out). As of today, the Soviets are committed to buy about eight times the value of Moroccan products that the United States buys annually, and their potential involvement in the Moroccan economy is considerably more substantial than that of the United States.

In sum, the Soviets have a sizeable presence of one sort or another in all four countries of the Maghrib. They are major arms suppliers to two of them, and have important economic connections with a third. They have been adept and flexible in meeting the desires of the countries concerned, from their original willingness to supply MIG's to Mohamed V to their willingness to buy his son's phosphates. While they probably have no early expectations of taking over any of these states, they are in a position to exploit opportunities for expanding their influence, opportunities that usually seem to be provided by the actions, or inactions, of the United States rather than by those of the Soviets.

In spite of their numbers, the Soviet presence is not very obtrusive, and except possibly in Libya, and that rather recently, they have not been very active politically. Local Communist parties do not play leading roles in local politics and the Soviets are not perceived as posing a threat to local regimes as they are in other places. They have gone out of their way to avoid taking sides in the Sahara dispute and other local causes through which they might be able to help bring about the downfall of conservative regimes. The Soviets have material interests in Morocco as well as Algeria and apparently do not want to put them at risk. It would be wrong to assume, however, that they are not interested in seeing revolutionary change occur in the states of the region, and that they will not do what they can to promote it when they believe doing so will not harm their interests. They seem to be following an essentially pragmatic and ad hoc policy for the time being, however.

Notes

[1] John Damis, "The Role of Third Parties in the Western Sahara Conflict", *The Maghreb Review*, Vol. 7, Nos. 1–2 (January-April 1982), p. 1.

[2] The Libyans have been talking about not paying these bills at all as a means of obtaining reparations for losses suffered in the colonial period.

[3] Most of the data in this discussion come from *La Flotta Sovietica Nel Mediterraneo* by Admiral Girolamo Fantoni, published by the Centro de Studi Strategici in Rome, in June 1983.

9

United States Policies

For the United States, serious economic and political involvement in the Middle East began with the Iran crisis in 1946 and the Greek-Turkish aid program under the 1947 Truman Doctrine.[1] By late 1947 U.S. policy planners were describing the security of the area as vital to the security of the United States and for at least 30 years policy documents in Washington have been defining U.S. national interests there as being: (a) denial of the area to the Soviets, that is, to Soviet hegemony, and (b) access to the area's petroleum resources on reasonable terms.[2] Since 1967 this formula has been expanded to include the security of Israel, and peace and stability in the area as other interests.

North Africa, on the other hand, has never witnessed large-scale political or economic (as opposed to military) involvement by the United States and has had a more modest role in the calculations of the policy makers. Its security is rarely, if ever, described as vital to that of the United States, and while considered part of the Middle East for bureaucratic and administrative reasons, it is obviously different and separate, and its importance to the United States has been of a different order. The nature, as opposed to the magnitude, of the U.S. interest in North Africa is, however, much like that in the Middle East. Thus, the importance of the area for the defense of Western Europe has already been discussed in the introduction, and while the risks and the nature of the threat are different, the objective of denying the area to the Soviets for security reasons remains as valid here as it does further east. Similarly, while North African petroleum resources are much less important than those of the Gulf, were access to them to be denied to Western Europe for any reason it would pose a serious threat to Western interests, including those of the United States. Basic U.S. interests in denial of the area to the Soviets and access to its petroleum resources on reasonable terms therefore apply to North Africa as well as to the Middle East. It is furthermore in the Western interest that the peoples of the area live in

154

peace, that acceptable political and social values prevail in the region and that the states of the area respect their obligations to their own citizens and to the international community.

There are generally two ways of looking at the question of how these interests are to be secured. The first of these is the *globalist* view, which holds that the world's problems are primarily manifestations of the Soviet-U.S. competition, and that everything else is secondary. Thus, Henry Kissinger reportedly saw the 1973 Ramadan War between Israel and Egypt as essentially a contest between Soviet and U.S. arms that was won by the latter, and the scales did not fall from his eyes until he made his first trip to the area after the war and discovered the Arabs. On the other side are the *regionalists*, who see the world's problems as manifestations of essentially local issues—of underdevelopment and tribal disputes that are related to superpower rivalries only to the extent that interference by those powers is one of the causes of the problem. Their argument is that the way to deal with the Soviets is to help local people solve their problems themselves; then they will show no interest in the Soviets.

Recent U.S. policy in the Middle East and Africa illustrates this dichotomy. Even though he may not have realized it, President Carter was essentially a regionalist, at least with regard to Africa and the Middle East, until the Soviet invasion of Afghanistan. The latter came at a time of growing fears of Soviet military superiority which were being stimulated by various conservative groups as well as of strong criticism of the administration's weakness in the Iran crisis. Carter responded early in 1980 with the Carter Doctrine, a statement saying the United States would resist, with force if necessary, any attempt by outside powers to take over the oil resources of the Persian Gulf, although it was far from clear that any such danger actually existed. This marked a major change in direction away from the regionalist approach. It was a globalist statement, reflecting a new obsession with a possible Soviet drive to the Indian Ocean or the Gulf, which would, among other things, set the stage for blackmailing Europe by cutting off oil supplies. It was accompanied by a perceptible lassitude about following through on the Camp David process, one of the principal accomplishments of the regionalist approach. This lassitude was even more marked during Alexander Haig's tenure as Secretary of State, when efforts were directed toward organizing a "strategic consensus" of Israelis and Arabs against the Soviets, to the almost total disregard of the Arab-Israel problem. The Israeli invasion of Lebanon in the summer of 1982 awakened the administration rudely to the dangers of local disputes and the strategic consensus disappeared from the front pages as the Reagan peace initiative of September 1 took form. The latter was an essentially regionalist initiative. In the fall of 1983, however, the Reagan Administration began speaking again of strategic cooperation with Israel, and its spokesman's remarks about Syria being a Soviet surrogate implied a renewed globalist outlook.

This alternation of regionalist and globalist approaches illustrates the limitations of both. Either one followed to the exclusion of the other eventually leads to error and miscalculation. What is required is a balanced approach, which sees the relevance of local factors without ignoring the global ones. Unfortunately, most of the globalists tend to be Europe-centered and to know very little about the Third World. Once in the saddle they run rough-shod over their opponents and are prone to question the integrity, loyalty and strength of character of those who oppose them. This is often enough to stifle dissent.[3]

U. S. policy in North Africa today tends to be globalist, to see Morocco as an ally against the Soviets and their presumed clients, the Libyans, who are perceived as trying to take over Saharan Africa and as threatening those regimes that are friendly to the United States. Algeria, meanwhile, is perceived as at best unwilling to help, while Tunisia is a spectator. In the globalist view, the game here is to frustrate the Soviets, and the best way to do it is to arm one's friends and try to isolate or otherwise discomfit theirs.

In point of fact, the most effective barrier to Soviet penetration, here as elsewhere, is stable, independent states able to resist pressures and blandishments from outside powers of whatever persuasion. The identity and personality of the leaders of such states is less important than the existence of entities that are secure enough to defend themselves and maintain their political integrity. It is arguable, for instance, that the Western world would be better off with an unfriendly but independent Qadhdhafi than with a weaker leader who became a Soviet client.

In discussing the states of the region, certain realities should be kept in mind. The first is that the western three have a common history both as the Barbary states and as former French colonies, which makes them different from the eastern Arabs and much more European in their outlook in many important respects. This is particularly true of extraregional foreign policy issues such as the Palestine problem. Paradoxically, this often makes it more difficult for Americans to communicate with them. Cartesian logic and French grammar can be greater obstacles to American-Arab communication in the Maghrib than traditional Arab thinking and language are in the Mashriq.

More importantly, the western three are run by mature elites with considerable sophistication, prepared to deal with the United States on a basis of equality, but not to be treated as clients. Libya, the odd man out, is ruled by a relatively inexperienced, revolutionary elite that is difficult to deal with on any terms as a result. All four states are, however, independent and relatively stable. While by no means assured, it is possible to visualize a peaceful succession in any of them. On the other hand, while all four states have institutions that are described as democratic, each of them is an autocracy in fact, and the successor to the current leader in each will certainly be an autocrat, or a committee of autocrats.

All of them, except Libya, have a common set of social and economic problems brought on by high birthrates, the shortage of jobs, and the drift to the cities. Libya's problems are different and relate more to an excess of money than to not enough. All four of them, in spite of their current stability, carry within them the long-term seeds of disorder. Because such disorder would threaten stability and independence, offering the risk of foreign interference and manipulation, it is in the interest of the United States that these seeds not sprout. Even in the case of Libya, it is questionable whether violent upheaval would serve U.S. interests, because one can never predict how such violence will end, or what the consequences will be for the other states of the region.

Finally, the United States has an overriding national interest in maintaining reasonable relations with the states of the region. In the case of Libya under Qadhdhafi, the term "reasonable" probably excludes any relations at all at the moment, but this is certainly not the case with the others. Although U.S. material stakes vary widely from state to state, each is important in its own right and it is axiomatic that good relations are more in the national interest than bad, particularly for a world power whose nationals are engaged in trade and commerce and which has important strategic interests in the region.

All of this may seem self-evident, but we need to know what it is the United States should be seeking. Although peace and stability as national goals are usually taken for granted, policymakers tend to lose sight of them in their search for influence and prestige and in their preoccupation with external causes of internal problems.

Policy Constraints

In dealing with North Africa, the United States is remarkably free of extraregional constraints. The area is marginal to the Arab-Israel dispute, there is no domestic lobby that is passionately interested in what goes on there, there are few U.S. citizens having major claims against North African governments, there are as yet no local wars in which the U.S. military are directly involved as combatants, there is no major ethnic group in the United States that identifies closely with North Africa, and U.S. economic interests, while substantial, are not such as to prevent it from deciding freely what is in the national interest without worrying unduly about jobs in Toledo.

Nor do U.S. interests in the region conflict with those of its allies. Since the end of the Algerian revolution the French and Americans have normally had similar views on North Africa. While they frequently see each other as competitors for influence and contracts, and while there is occasional ill feeling as a result, they do not see each other as threats. On the whole, their competition has been friendly and, except in commercial matters, their interests have been similar if not always identical. Both want a stable and independent North Africa, and neither wishes to be overly burdened with special relationships and responsibilities, even though both sometimes encounter pressures for such relationships in Tunisia and Morocco.

No other U.S. ally, with the possible exception of Spain, has major political (as opposed to economic) interests at stake in the region, but all of them share an interest in peace and stability. The problem of the Spanish enclaves may eventually result in a Falklands-type dilemma for friends of Morocco and Spain, but that does not currently affect U.S. freedom of action. While the Soviets' interests and attitudes are more problematical, and one must be alert to their activities, the role they are playing today does not seriously constrain American policy except in the case of Libya, where there is a risk that U.S. actions will drive the Libyans into their arms.

U.S. freedom of action *is* constrained, however, by changing perceptions of strategic requirements and by established commitments to friends. Thus, events in Iran and Afghanistan have changed U.S. perspectives regarding defense of the Persian Gulf. This in turn has led to greater emphasis on the Rapid Deployment Force and to a desire to have access to Moroccan base facilities in order to stage troops and equipment there en route to the Gulf. This has increased Morocco's strategic importance to the United States, given a greater sense of U.S. commitment to that country, and affected U.S. policy toward the region as a whole by increasing U.S. identification with Morocco.

Meanwhile, U.S. attitudes toward Libya have been deeply influenced by commitments to Sudan and Egypt. The U.S. display of naval and air power directed against Libya in the third week of February 1983, for instance, was stimulated by a Libyan threat against Sudan, not the United States. Similarly, in the summer of 1983 the U.S. involvement in the Chad imbroglio was provoked by fears that if Libya's client Oueddei won the contest it would effect the security of Sudan and Egypt. Thus, the White House spokesman on August 5, 1983, said, "If Libya or Libyan-supported forces were to gain control of Chad, close U.S. allies, such as Egypt and Sudan, would be seriously concerned about their own security. Other states in the region would also be deeply worried." Indeed, the poor state of U.S. relations with Libya is to a significant extent a function of the poor relations between that country and Sudan and Egypt. Were they friendly with Qadhdhafi, it is likely that U.S.-Libyan relations would be a good deal better.

The examples given above are passing phenomena, but they illustrate the truism that sovereign states are rarely free to act as they wish. The web of interests and commitments to other states prevents them from doing what they might otherwise think was in their national interest, narrowly perceived. Foreign relations, like all human intercourse, are bound about by mutual obligations and mutually accepted limits.

Morocco

Morocco is an old friend, but there is a bittersweet quality to the relationship, which has often been uneasy and marked by periods of mutual irritation. It has little real warmth. The United States' traditional support for Morocco has never been spelled out in any formal agreement between them. Rather, there has been a long-standing U.S. habit of finding that because of Morocco's strategic position and cooperative attitude on various matters of common interest, it merits help on a specific issue. This *ad hoc* approach is based on national interest, not treaty or alliance obligation.

An important factor in U.S. attitudes is that both states have shared an inclination to support conservative governments throughout the Third World, without worrying unduly about the political philosophies they may represent. Hassan has gained considerable credit with the United States through his willingness to stand up and be counted in this respect. He has usually so acted because he saw it as being in his own best interest, but in the process he has gained a reputation in Washington as a staunch opponent of radical movements in Africa. In addition to supplying security personnel to a number of African (and Gulf) governments, he has, as noted earlier, twice sent troops to Zaire to help stop invasions of Shaba Province (ex-Katanga) by exiles from Angola and has long been deeply involved with Jonas Savimbi and his UNITA (National Union for the Total Independence of Angola) guerrillas in Angola. In both these instances he was prepared to act when the United States was paralyzed by legislative restraints and public opinion. A number of African specialists have argued that such actions are not in the interest of Africa or the United States, because propping up a corrupt and incompetent Mobutu in Zaire merely delays the evil day and makes it worse when it comes, and the Savimbi connection delays and complicates efforts to work out an understanding with Angola. The Carter administration was divided over whether the Zaire operation was helpful, and the Reagan administration is reported to be ambivalent about the Savimbi operation, which is not helpful to its own efforts to negotiate a settlement in southern Africa. Nevertheless, the United States government, through various agencies, has either helped with or acquiesced in both operations at one time or another.

The Carter administration was initially somewhat reserved in its attitude toward Morocco, largely because of tensions arising from the Western Sahara problem and pervasive doubts about the durability of Hassan's regime. The Reagan administration (and before it the Ford administration), on the other hand, has projected an unabashedly pro-Moroccan image. While this illustrates the swings through which U.S. policy can go, even under Carter there was no question of the United States' basic interest in King Hassan's survival and of military and economic support for his country. The limits of the swing are thus rather narrow. The United States may not support specific Moroccan policies or actions, but there has been no questioning of the principle that it should support friendly governments, particularly when they are in a strategically important location, and Morocco is such a place.

Support for friendly governments, while it sounds unexceptionable, often runs up against conflicts with other interests discussed earlier, as when the friend in question undertakes actions that are destructive, such as the Argentine invasion of the Falklands or the Israeli invasion of Lebanon. Governments are therefore usually cautious about making open ended commitments to support other governments, and U.S. policy toward Morocco observed the traditional restraints in this regard for many years. In the last years of the Carter administration, however, the fall of the shah raised questions around the world as to the seriousness of U.S. purpose and whether it could be counted upon to help its friends. A felt need to reassure people in this respect was one of the reasons for the 1979 arms package for Morocco[4]—the United States was going to show that it stood by its friends, even though it had reservations about how the arms package was going to be used.

This somewhat tepid decision by the Carter administration was subsequently reinforced by the Reagan administration's desire to make contingency arrangements for the use of Moroccan base facilities. Given its access to Portuguese and other European bases, the United States does not have to rely absolutely on Moroccan facilities, but these constitute what the military call a "useful redundancy," particularly given the tendency of the NATO allies to distance themselves from U.S. Middle East policies.[5] While the details of the arrangements made with Morocco, including the nature of any quid pro quos, have not been published, there has been an obvious growth in military relations between the two countries since 1981. In February 1982 Secretary Haig announced that this growth required a more formal structure and that the two states were considering formation of a joint military commission to meet periodically for consultations.[6] The Moroccan foreign minister was careful to downplay the significance of Haig's remarks, reflecting a pervasive Moroccan uneasiness at the closeness of the U.S. embrace, but the commission was established and met for the first time in April 1982. Subsequently a joint economic commission was formed and both sides have begun meeting roughly annually. The military commission, for instance, met again in Washington in May 1983 and in Rabat in May 1984.

The facilities access agreement was initialed during Hassan's visit to Washington in May 1982 and announced by the Department of State spokesman at the noon briefing on May 27 as follows:

> The United States and Morocco have reached agreement on the use and transit by the United States forces of agreed airfields in emergencies and for periodic training. The United States will not permanently station armed forces or establish United States military bases in Morocco in connection with carrying out this agreement. It will have an initial term of six years and will continue thereafter unless terminated on two years notice by either party.

The spokesman also said, under questioning, that the text of the agreement, which did not need Senate ratification because it was not a treaty, would not be released, and refused to be drawn into a discussion of its contents.

It can be assumed, however, that the United States will stockpile supplies at the airfields in question and a small caretaker staff will be needed to monitor their condition and accessibility. This undoubtedly will require an increase in U.S. military personnel in Morocco, the implication of the spokesman's statement to the contrary notwithstanding, but the numbers should not be large, and the job can be done by civilian contract or rotating military personnel in order to keep the spokesman honest. Military upgrading of the airfields in question is expected to cost $28 million, a figure that will undoubtedly be increased substantially in time.

Another indication of increased U.S. military cooperation with Morocco are continuing joint military exercises, the first of which was held in November 1982. They have included amphibious landings on the Moroccan coast and penetration testing of Moroccan radar defenses. They have passed largely unnoticed by the U.S. press, but the Algerians have taken them as another sign that the United States is trying to build up a position of military strength in Morocco. Such exercises have been under discussion for some years and the Sixth Fleet has long been interested in the use of Moroccan beaches for landing exercises. There is considerable military utility to this sort of cooperation, but the question has always been whether it would justify the political effect on the host country and its neighbors, particularly when the states in question are theoretically nonaligned. Such activities inevitably give rise to accusations that the host country is becoming too closely identified with the military power that uses its territory. Thus, Egypt was popularly considered to have become a Soviet client state in the period 1967–1972 because of the facilities the Soviets enjoyed there. American use of Moroccan facilities will raise similar apprehensions on the part of Algeria and the Soviets, as well as from the opposition in Morocco. Indeed, Moroccan ministers and other members of the ruling elite have privately expressed concern to outsiders about the implications of Morocco's military involvement with the United States, and while such cooperation may be superficially popular today because it is seen as meaning the United States will aid the Moroccan war effort in the Sahara, it runs counter to deeply felt nationalistic sentiments. The Moroccans do not want to be too closely identified with anyone.

A fundamental assumption of U.S. policy in Morocco since 1956 has been that the king (first Mohamed V and then Hassan II) is a source of stability and that he would be a better ruler than any likely alternative. Although Hassan has many critics at home and abroad, he has governed Morocco in a way that has maintained order with only a moderate degree of political repression by Third World standards. If he is overthrown, it will be by military coup d'état, perhaps in conjunction with a popular uprising, because only the military have the capability of assuming power in Morocco today. While rule by military leader or junta is a common formula in the Arab world, that is no recommendation. It is normally a response to the inability of civilians to run the country effectively, and there is no such problem in Morocco. The United States would probably be able to deal and maintain satisfactory relations with a military government in Rabat, if it were led by the conservative senior officers now in the Army. But a group of young, radical officers taking over might not be interested in cooperation with the United States. Indeed, they might wish to put as much daylight as possible between themselves and America. In terms of its strategic interests, the United States is probably better off with a known quantity like King Hassan than some successor out of nowhere, but to make this judgment is not to conclude that the United States should undertake to try to secure Hassan's throne for him by direct or indirect intervention in the event of an internal crisis in Morocco.

Aid

Whoever rules Morocco, the United States has a continuing interest in helping the country resolve its social and economic problems in order to promote stability and evolutionary development. While it has also had a political interest in extending military aid at various times, including the present, it is by no means clear that this should be a continuing long-term policy commitment. U.S. economic development assistance, which was down to $11 million per year in FY 1982, has been so small that it would have been terminated some years ago had it not been considered an important political symbol. The amount was increased to $13.5 million in FY 1983 and $19 million in FY 1984, but is still a drop in the bucket—insufficient either to have substantial impact on economic development or to give any significant influence over Moroccan economic policies. (Judging by the experience in Israel and Egypt, not even the most generous aid programs give much influence over the latter.) The FY 1984 AID budget also included $34.5 million in PL 480 commodities and $7 million in economic support funds. Current AID strategy emphasizes improving the quality of life of poorer Moroccans and focuses on improving agricultural productivity, improving the health services delivery system, teaching new, employable skills to women, and making more effective use of Morocco's renewable energy sources. The health services program includes support for Moroccan family planning programs.

The visible accomplishments of the aid program, particularly since the United States stopped financing monumental projects some years ago, are limited, but there is undoubtedly some cumulative effect, particularly from the training of technicians, although impact is hard to measure. For years, for instance, the United States has been training agricultural technicians in Morocco and the United States. After years of disappointing results, this is beginning to pay off in the creation of a cadre of government officials with practical knowledge of American agricultural technology. They will inevitably affect Moroccan agricultural practices, but just how much is difficult to say.

As an adjunct to the economic aid program, there has been a Peace Corps contingent in Morocco for many years. At this writing there are some 150 volunteers in the country, teaching English in secondary schools and working in agricultural extension and vocational training programs. Again, the effect has been modest, particularly when compared with that of the much larger French cooperant presence, but it has increased Moroccan knowledge of English and of Americans in ways that are usually positive. We must admit, however, if we wish to be candid, that the volunteers, not the Moroccans, are usually the principal beneficiaries of the program.

U.S. military aid is on a different scale. Most of it has been in the form of sales, with variable credit terms and facilities. Until 1974 the principal activity had been the supply of a squadron of F-5 fighters and training in their use. In 1974 the United States began the $500 million modernization program mentioned in Chapter 7, and also began discussions on what eventually became a Moroccan-financed $220 million air defense radar project, the commercial contract for which was awarded to Westinghouse and which has now been completed. In 1979 the United States agreed to an additional arms package of $232.5 million, and the FY 1984 aid budget request was for $30 million in grant military assistance and $60 million in Foreign Military Sales (FMS) guarantees. Only $26.8 in FMS was authorized. The 1985 budget calls for $40 million in grant aid and only $10 million in FMS sales. For one reason or another, not all of the sales facilities offered in the past have actually been used by the Moroccans. The FY 1983 Congressional Presentation of the Department of Defense showed total foreign military sales agreements with Morocco for the period 1974–81 as amounting to $811 million, of which only $478 million worth had been delivered. Commercial arms exports, that is, those not going through the U.S.-government-administered FMS program, were put at $68.1 million. The principal problem for the Moroccans has been a lack of resources for payment, particularly since the Saudis reduced their aid.

Although these sums are modest compared to the amounts being poured into the Near East, they are substantial by past standards in Morocco and represent an increased commitment to the defense of that country. The arms have been offered in part to maintain good relations and in part in the hope they will improve Morocco's security situation, i.e., that they will help secure the loyalty of the army to the king, and that they will permit Morocco to defend itself. While these objectives have been met, at least partially, the arms have not made Morocco more flexible on the Sahara, as had been hoped in 1979, and they have involved the United States peripherally but significantly in Morocco's conquest of that territory. U.S. military personnel are regular visitors to the Sahara, they have provided the Moroccans with training and equipment to improve their performance against the Polisario, and at least some military personnel see this as a way of getting at Qadhdhafi and the Soviets, who are visualized as the forces behind the Saharan resistance. Thus, one U.S. service attaché in Rabat told a foreign visitor in 1982, "We are facing the vanguard of Soviet armed forces out there." Under the influence of such attitudes there is always the risk that

Hassan's war will become the United States', in spite of Washington's firm rejection of the idea. Attitudes in such matters are likely to crystallize suddenly and without sufficient forethought in moments of crisis, such as that in Chad in the summer of 1983.[7]

Policy Recommendations

Looking at North Africa from the author's perspective, which goes back 25 years, it is difficult to escape the conclusion that the United States is overcommitted to Morocco, not in the magnitude of its aid programs so much as in the common perception in Washington that Hassan is a unique friend, even an ally (a term used increasingly loosely these days), and that he is defending our interests in Africa and the Middle East. Thus, James Clarity, writing in the February 1, 1983, *New York Times* reported, "The United States is apparently succeeding in its intensified effort to make the Kingdom of Morocco its closest and most useful ally in the Arab World." He quoted the U.S. ambassador in Morocco, Joseph Vernier Reed, as saying, "My mandate is to illustrate to our friends around the globe that the Reagan administration wanted to single out Morocco as the primary example of how America supported a proven ally and friend."

In a meeting with President Carter in 1978 Hassan said that what he wanted from the United States was a clear manifestation of its support for him; he wanted a public commitment. The Carter administration, guided by the wisdom of collective experience among Washington practitioners of foreign policy, would not give it. The Reagan administration, less bothered by the lessons of history, did give it, through the statements of its ambassador in Rabat and those of a variety of senior officials in both Rabat and Washington, and through a series of actions that have been taken locally as evidence of U.S. commitment.

Even were there no problem arising from Morocco's rivalry with Algeria, or no contest over the Sahara, this sort of identification with a local ruler is a mistake. It holds promise of future trouble in relations with Spain, when and if the issues of the enclaves is agitated, and it will eventually threaten the survival of Hassan himself, because the obverse of the U.S. commitment to him is that he is being labeled a U.S. stooge.

Americans are particularly prone to personalize their relations with foreign states, that is, to see them as relations between individuals who happen to be heads of state, and to embrace the foreign ruler who is considered to be pro-American, while reviling those considered pro-Soviet. When a diplomat gets such a fixation, he is said to have *localitis*, meaning that he has lost perspective and thinks the sun revolves around the local leader with whom he is dealing, or, conversely, that he cannot abide the local man and is unable to judge him dispassionately. When the administration as a whole succumbs, it is called *overidentification* if the affliction is in the positive sense, and *obsession* if in the negative.

In either case, the disease is dangerous. The positive syndrome can lead to the destruction of the local leader, and it almost always leads to unrealistic expectations on both sides, which in turn lead to acrimony. There is a common tendency, for instance, to expect the Moroccans, or Saudis, or Egyptians, or Jordanians to take positions on the Arab-Israel issue that are inconsistent with their national interest simply because we want them to. These expectations are founded on the belief that the state, or regime, in question is pro-U.S., or at least pro-Western. That means it should accept U.S. definitions of the common good and follow the latter's utilitarian approach to foreign policy, whatever its own imperatives.

It would be safer to discard forever such labels, and to realize that the local leader's first responsibility is to his own people and country, that he is pro-Moroccan or pro-Saudi and not pro-anyone else. He may be prepared to modify his policies to accommodate the United States on some issue, but if he sacrifices the national interest in doing so, intentionally or otherwise, he is being disloyal to his people and he will not last. He will be considered to have identified his interests with those of a foreign power rather than those of his country. When the overidentified local leader loses, so does his patron, and we can trace a series of disasters across the Middle East in which identification of the local leader as a U.S. client contributed to his downfall and damaged U.S. interests: Iraq and Lebanon in 1958, Libya in 1969, Tehran in 1979, Egypt in 1981, and Lebanon in 1984.

U.S. policy toward Morocco should be based on the tried and tested rules that (a) friendship and support for legitimate aspirations does not mean unqualified support or an uncritical embrace and (b) the embrace has become uncritical at the point when frank criticism of the local leader is no longer welcome at home. This happened with the shah in the 1960s, and the events that followed were due in large part to the unwillingness of the White House, and by extension its ambassadors, to question the wisdom of the shah or what he was demanding. The Americans fed his delusions of grandeur and helped him lose touch with reality. There is a similar aura of unreality about Washington attitudes toward Morocco in Washington, which often expects Hassan to play a constructive role which is beyond his capabilities if he is to remain in power. Morocco is, after all, an Arab state, and its interests and those of the United States are different.

What Hassan expects from his relationship with the United States is support for Morocco in the Sahara as well as more generalized support on other matters, such as his eventual confrontation with Spain over the enclaves. Support for Morocco in the Sahara has meant weapons, training, and votes at the United Nations. He has not requested a security umbrella, but certainly expects that his military cooperation with the United States will at least entitle him to a degree of support equal to that which would be extended to the states of the Persian Gulf. He may even expect that the United States will intervene militarily to protect him if he gets into trouble, if he is indeed its closest Arab ally, as The *New York Times* claims. Whether these expectations are realistic in the long term is something else. There is unlikely to be any political support in the United States for military intervention anywhere in North Africa except in the event of a gross and large-scale intervention in Tunisia or Morocco by Libya, and even then there would be no assurance that it would be forthcoming. It would furthermore be most unwise for the United States to involve itself in a domestic power struggle in Morocco or elsewhere in North Africa, tempting as the urge to do so might be. The longer-term U.S. interest in the region is in its people and its governments, not their individual rulers.

These expectations on both sides are likely to be unmet when the chips are down, and the United States should revert to its traditional policy of friendly relations based on mutual respect for national interests, without any illusions that Hassan is an ally or that he can afford to be identified as United States' chosen instrument. A failure to do so will bring eventual disaster. U.S. interests lie with friendly relations with Morocco, not with a particular ruler or government. A wise U.S. policy, while recognizing that we must deal with the government in power, will constantly bear in mind the possibility that the government may change, but U.S. interest in a friendly Morocco will not.

Algeria

As opposed to Morocco, the problem here is one of underidentification. Although the United States has important economic interests in Algeria, the most important in North Africa, political relations between the two countries have been at best correct and more often cool because the two find themselves on opposite sides of so many international fences. The Algerians are not communists, they are not even Marxists,[8] but they are often committed to change and revolution while the United States is usually committed to preservation of existing political systems. Their policies and interests inevitably collide as a result.

While Algeria and the United States have different ideologies and different perceptions of reality, there is a substantial middle ground where both of them can operate in reasonable comfort, provided both of them are prepared to exercise a certain amount of discipline and flexibility. The first step for Americans is to disabuse themselves of the notion that Algeria is a Soviet client. This is easier said than done. In the first place, Algerian and Soviet world views usually seem considerably closer to each other than those of Algeria and the United States. Algeria, as a Third World leader, feels compelled by its ideology and history to oppose imperialism, which means the capitalistic West. On the other hand, whatever they may say publicly, the Algerians have no illusions about Soviet motives, and they do not take orders from the Soviets. As leaders, the Algerians are not disposed to follow anyone, whatever camp they may belong to. As suggested in Chapter 8, the fact that the Soviets and Algerians vote together on many issues at the United Nations is more a reflection of Soviet alignment with the Third World than Third World imitation of the Soviets.

In the second place, as noted earlier, the Algerians have been major purchasers of Soviet arms and have bought an estimated $4–5 billion worth since 1975. They have recently begun to diversify their sources and have bought some $200 million worth of C-130 transport aircraft (a total of 14 planes) from the United States, but Algeria still ranks as the fourth largest purchaser of Soviet weapons among Third World countries. Also as noted earlier, the acquisition of these arms has been accompanied (as of 1981) by the presence of an estimated 2,000 Soviet and East European military advisors. In addition, as many as 11,150 Soviet and East European technicians were working in various sectors of the Algerian economy.[9]

For their part, the Algerians maintain that they need these weapons for defense of their extensive territory against the Moroccans and Libyans and that they have no alternative to reliance on the Soviets for arms, because they have standardized on them and cannot get them in the same quantity or on the same terms elsewhere. They point to the fact that over 85 percent of their trade is with the West and less than 5 percent with the Soviets and Eastern Europe, to the impressive record of private U.S.-Algerian economic cooperation, and to the remarkable role they played in negotiating the release of the Tehran captives, and say they are ready for a "new phase" of cooperation with the United States and want to improve relations.[10]

The Algerians have not felt their attitude is fully reciprocated by Washington. They maintain that the United States is building up positions of strength in Morocco and Tunisia as part of a policy of strategic cooperation and confrontation and that continued U.S. support for Hassan is permitting him to avoid making the concessions that are necessary for peaceful settlement of the Sahara problem. Their perception is that the United States is firmly on Hassan's side and has insufficient time for Algeria.

In part this is a question of words and gestures rather than substance. The Algerians hear pro-Moroccan statements made by U.S. officials and take them seriously. They note the steady stream of high-level official and unofficial visitors to Morocco, arriving with the full blare of Moroccan and U.S. official publicity, whereas they had only unadvertised visits by lesser fry until Vice President Bush went to Algeria in September 1983. (A brief visit by Secretary of State Shultz, planned for December 1983, was postponed at Algerian request because insufficient time was allotted for it and because it would have come during intense preparations for an FLN party congress the same month.) In the opposite direction, although there have been brief visits by senior Algerians to Washington in the past, there has been no really high-level visit since independence, except for a quick trip by Boumediene in connection with a UN meeting in New York in 1974. Meanwhile, King Hassan has been to Washington three times since 1978, and there has been a great deal of high level Moroccan-U.S. speech-making, all of it prominently reported by the Moroccan press as evidence of U.S. support for Morocco's just claims in the Sahara. The Algerians, unfortunately, follow the Moroccan press and take it seriously.

Counterpoint to this is provided by the consistently anti-U.S. tone of the Algerian media and the apparent inability of the Algerians to comprehend that unnecessarily confrontational tactics on issues such as the Arab-Israel problem or the North-South dialogue, or silence on the shooting down of the Korean airliner in 1983, alienate Americans. The Algerians explained their sabotaging of the U.S. position in favor of family planning at a UN conference in 1974, for instance, by saying they were tired of being patronized on this issue by the United States. One can understand their irritation with sometimes condescending U.S. attitudes, but one must also realize that gratuitous opposition generates unwanted antagonisms.

The Algerians have also been unable to overcome their conspiratorial attitudes, born partly of their independence struggle, but also reflecting cultural patterns established well before the coming of the French. They are suspicious of foreigners as well as each other and have not been sufficiently interested in improving relations with the Americans to show much trust in them. It is axiomatic that such trust is a prerequisite to friendship, and that it must be generated somehow if relationships are ever to get off the ground. The Americans are not alone in this experience. The Algerians are not warmly friendly with anyone—not the Soviets, nor the Chinese, nor the Vietnamese, nor any of the other peoples of the Third World. They may have good relations with them, but there is little affection to be found. They are very much loners in the international field, and while they may be respected, they are not loved. Respect is all a state should aspire to, but unless there is some personal warmth in human relations, they are likely to be lacking in substance, and that is the U.S. situation with the Algerians today.

The situation is complicated, of course, by Algerian support for the Polisario against Morocco. The latter having been identified as a friend of the United States, it is difficult to be friendly with its apparent enemy, particularly when Americans think they see their own enemies, the Soviets and Libyans, involved in the affair on Algeria's side. The United States should be interested in seeing the Sahara problem settled almost as much because of what it would do for Algerian-U.S. relations as because of what it would do for Morocco. Solution would not end the ideological differences between Algeria and the United States, but it would make the middle ground easier to occupy by removing a major irritant.

In deciding what its policy toward Algeria should be, the United States should not lose sight of the former's politico-economic potential. By virtue of its revolutionary past, activist policies, wealth and economic capacity,

Algeria already has a good deal more influence outside its borders than any other state in North Africa, and that influence will grow rather than diminish with time. Although their development efforts have fallen well short of original expectations, the Algerians are beginning to benefit from their massive investments in industrial infrastructure and eventually will be a regional economic force to be reckoned with, at least in northern Africa, if for no other reason than that they have no meaningful local competition. The United States need not subscribe to Algerian views, or try to ingratiate itself, but it has a long-term political and economic interest in reasonable relations with this state and should act accordingly.

Policy Recommendations

Specifically, the United States should bear in mind the importance of gestures and the need to strike a balance between what it does for Morocco and what it does for Algeria. Striking a balance does not necessarily mean giving equal treatment; it does mean giving the Algerians a chance to show the sincerity of their desire to improve relations and taking their views into consideration when doing things for Morocco.

The United States cannot be expected to overturn its relationship with Morocco in order to cultivate Algeria, nor are the Algerians asking for that. They are rather seeking less biased treatment. Ideally, the United States should openly proclaim, like the French, that its policy toward Morocco and Algeria is *equilibré*, or evenhanded. This would require a Pauline conversion on the part of those officials in Washington who are victims of their own preconceptions about the nature of Algeria and its policies. The most effective method of promoting such a conversion is greater contact at the upper levels on substantive problems such as the Sahara, the Tunisian succession, the Arab-Israel problem, and the North-South dialogue.

There has been some encouraging movement in this respect since 1982, starting with a more active exchange between the Algerian ambassador in Washington and officials of the Department of State, but the dialogue that has been opened is well below the top level in both countries. In Algeria, as elsewhere in the Third World, there is no substitute for contact at the chief-of-state level, and the Bush visit to Algeria should be followed by a visit to the United States by President Benjedid.

At the same time, a determined effort should be made to find areas of cooperation with Algeria in the field of cultural, technical, and scientific exchanges and educational programs. There is great interest in the United States on the part of young Algerians, but it is largely untapped. The 2,000 or so Algerian students in the United States today (compared to a handful in 1974) should be helped and encouraged to learn more about this country and to take back with them a better understanding of U.S. attitudes and reactions. There is also considerable scope for exchanges in the medical field, and Algerian doctors are interested in alternatives to reliance on

French or domestic medical training. Indeed, in all fields of intellectual endeavor, as a general proposition, the Algerians have been too dependent on European expertise and methodology. A much expanded Fulbright program, operating in both directions, could help remedy this.

Tunisia

U.S. interest is in the survival of a stable and moderate Tunisia. The most pressing mutual concern for some time has been the succession to Bourguiba and the outlook for the future after that transition is made. The two states have no serious bilateral problems and have many interests in common. There is enough trust and friendship between them so that they can speak to each other frankly and can cooperate on many issues. Tunisia is entering a stage, however, at which preservation of these mutual interests is by no means assured. As in Morocco and Algeria, current social and economic trends pose serious challenges to the government and affect the outlook for continued stability. The dangers are heightened by the need to transfer power, and by the possibility of foreign interference designed to affect the outcome.

Unfortunately, there is not a great deal outside powers can do about internal situations in the absence of requisite actions by local leaders and their followers. It has been suggested, for instance, that the United States should urge political liberalization and early departure from office on President Bourguiba, but there is no assurance that such advice, if accepted, would be correct. It is, furthermore, questionable whether the Americans, as outsiders, have the right to urge a course of action when they do not have to live with the consequences, as the Tunisians do.

Foreign aid is sometimes an important factor in local survival, but the United States has reversed its priorities in Tunisia. It is substantially augmenting its military assistance, while economic assistance has been downgraded to a total of $12.8 million for FY 1984, not enough to do anything significant, and at one point was to be phased out completely by 1987. This decision apparently has been reversed, but the amounts being talked about—$3 million in economic support funds for FY 1985, are derisory. Military aid on the other hand, is programmed at $19.5 million in grants and $87 million in sales in 1984, and $16.7 million and $50 million respectively provided for 1985. While this will enhance Tunisia's minuscule military potential somewhat, it will not give it the ability to defend itself against Libya or Algeria, and, as noted in Chapter 4, it is alienating influential opinion makers in Tunisia who believe the expenditure is useless. Whether, on balance, this allocation of resources is the most sensible way of helping Tunisia is debatable. Increased emphasis on military aid under the Reagan administration is a phenomenon throughout Africa—a manifestation of the globalist approach, which often neglects the indigenous factors that actually determine how developing countries behave. Money that should be spent on education and social welfare is going for the military establishment, and people who need development will receive enhanced authoritarian control instead. The likelihood that arms will be misused for repression is less in Tunisia than it is in most African countries, but the risk that military capabilities will be seen as a shortcut to stability is real, nevertheless.

In any event, recent reports indicate that Bourguiba's powers are failing and that we are likely to witness a crisis in Tunisia within the next 12 months. No one knows how the scenario will unfold, but whoever the successor is, there will be a question as to whether he can manage the transition peacefully. And whoever he is, he will want the United States' blessing, while his opponents will either reject it or seek it for themselves, depending on whether they come from the left or the right. There will also be pressures from within Tunisia and from without, from friendly states such as Morocco and Egypt, for the United States to support one faction or another and to press some particular behavior on the Tunisian government.

Judging by past performance, the Tunisians themselves will be able to deal with the succession problem through a pragmatic political consensus, provided outsiders do not interfere too seriously. The great risk of interference will come from Libya, either in the form of extensive bribery of opposition elements, or an attempt at military or paramilitary intervention, or both—a new Gafsa raid coupled with military concentrations on the border and threats on the radio.

Either type of intervention would generate pressures for U.S. response, and the possibility that external military force will be required to restrain the Libyans is real, particularly given the likelihood that the military equipment to be supplied Tunisia by the United States will not be delivered and absorbed by the time Bourguiba departs the scene.

Policy Recommendations

While the gamut through which military actions in Tunisia might range is fairly wide, any act of U.S. military intervention would have serious political consequences in Africa as well as the rest of the Arab world. Nevertheless, the United States should consult now with the French, and perhaps the Algerians, on measures to be taken in the event Libya intervenes in Tunisia, and the United States should make clear that it is prepared either to intervene militarily or to support military interventions by others, as it did in Chad, to maintain order if that becomes necessary. It was the French who responded first with offers of help at the time of the Gafsa raid, and given their proximity and the extent of their interests, it is to be hoped that they would take the lead in responding to any similar incident in the future, but this cannot be assumed in the absence of consultation and some contingency planning. While the Algerians will object to any non-African military involvement in North Africa, they will perhaps understand the seriousness of the risk in Tunisia and appreciate the need for resolute action to block Libyan intervention there.

Assuming that there is a peaceful transition, and that Mzali or some other moderate is running Tunisia, the United States will still have to support the new government at least to the extent it supports the present one, and probably more. There is an alternative outcome, however, and that is a strictly internal uprising against the Westernizing policies of Bourguiba and/or his successor and a radical change in government as a result. The most likely time for this to occur would be within the period of a year or two after Bourguiba's successor assumes office, when social and economic strains could become unmanageable, particularly if the European economy continues to be in recession and this affects the Tunisian economy adversely. Although the likelihood of such an uprising does not seem great at this writing, there is enough going on beneath the deceptively calm surface of Tunisia to make it possible if certain factors—a disputed succession, increased unemployment and a depressed economy, continued dissention in the labor movement, a continuation of the Islamic revival, and a failure of the government to cope effectively—come together. Such a development could bring about the destruction of the U.S. position in Tunisia, not that this would entail any great material loss, but it would also put Tunisia in the ranks of the radical states, which would have important political and strategic implications throughout the region, increasing pressures on Morocco and reducing U.S. influence.

While it is doubtful that any amount of economic assistance the United States is likely to give Tunisia could prevent such an outcome, the risk of something like this occurring is one reason the United States will need to give substantial support to Bourguiba's successor. What this means in material terms is considerably more than $12.8 million in economic aid per year. It also means that the United States and France should consult on this danger as well as the risk of Libyan intervention and should agree on a coordinated policy to deal with it.

Libya

Libya poses the most serious immediate challenge to U.S. policy in the region, but Qadhdhafi's intrinsic importance as a factor for instability is probably not as great as U.S. policy would make it. He undoubtedly has destructive plans in the Sahel and the Sudan, as well as in North Africa, and he is in effective occupation of northern Chad today, but his capabilities are limited by his minuscule population base and the inexperience and immaturity of the Libyan elite. U.S. policies during the Reagan administration (discussed in Chapter 5) have been credited to three different but not mutually exclusive rationales:

1. U.S. actions (the clash over the Gulf of Sirte, the embargo on Libyan oil, the invalidation of U.S. passports for travel to Libya, and efforts to

organize and support opposition to Libya among the Europeans and Africans) have been taken in order to show the seriousness of U.S. disapproval of Qadhdhafi's support for terrorism and in the hope other Western powers will follow suit. If nothing else, the United States will at least know that its oil purchases are no longer funding Qadhdhafi's activities, and these measures may have some effect on his attitude.

2. The U.S. purpose is to make Qadhdhafi modify his behavior. To that end, there are other measures it will take if he does not moderate his actions.

3. The purpose is to hasten his downfall. It is unrealistic to expect meaningful behavioral modification from Qadhdhafi because he is incorrigible.

The United States' European partners have refused to follow it in this confrontation with Qadhdhafi because they have their own interests at stake and are not prepared to forfeit them for what they see as a U.S. obsession. None of them denies that Qadhdhafi is a destructive influence, but they all argue that it would be a mistake to close all the Western doors to him. Meanwhile, they are in a position to pick up some of the lucrative contracts that U.S. policies are denying to U.S. business. This is a familiar pattern— European willingness to let the United States do the unpopular tasks while profiting from the opportunities U.S. actions provide. This, if nothing else, highlights the need for closer consultation with the Europeans in an effort to involve them more directly.

Current attitudes on this subject within the U.S. government are reminiscent of those held about Gamal Abdul Nasser in the days of John Foster Dulles. There was little doubt in Washington then that Nasser was an evil, pro-Soviet dictator who should somehow be neutralized or eliminated. The United States supported plots against him, tried economic sanctions and propaganda operations, and tried to organize his fellow Arabs against him. In the end, it succeeded only in polarizing the area and in increasing Nasser's political stature, because he had withstood the United States successfully. Even the most unpopular leader has much to gain by defying the United States. Finally, it was the United States, and not Nasser who came around. The United States modified its behavior more than he did his. (In retrospect, it was probably impossible to do business with Nasser because he kept changing his position. As the late Malcolm Kerr remarked, it was like changing tires on a moving automobile.)[11]

Qadhdhafi is not Nasser, of course. He is not the leader of the central Arab state, Libya's small population has no role of cultural or intellectual leadership, and Qadhdhafi is not all that popular anywhere. He is much weaker politically than Nasser was, and although he has some following among radicals outside his country (the only North African leader who does), he is cordially disliked, not to say detested, by most of his Arab colleagues (as was Nasser, for that matter). Most importantly, the Arab world of the 1980s differs from that of the 1960s, and anti-U.S. postures do not have the automatic support they did then.

On the other hand, Qadhdhafi is much stronger economically than Nasser was. He is not dependent on foreign aid, he would be unaffected by an arms embargo, he is only marginally affected by the U.S. embargo on his oil, and he perhaps welcomes the relative austerity imposed by the oil glut, since he is known to think his people are being spoiled by affluence. It is most unlikely that he will modify his behavior, and short of landing the Marines, there is little likelihood any measure the United States can take will bring him down. If he does fall it will be because of internal dissent, not because the international community opposes him.

Policy Recommendations

No policymaker is allowed to start from *tabula rasa*. The United States is already too committed to its anti-Qadhdhafi posture, particularly after the events in Chad in the summer of 1983, to change it without serious loss of prestige unless and until Qadhdhafi himself changes. That is theoretically possible but unlikely to happen. It is furthermore dubious whether there is anything to be gained by a change in course at this point. There is almost no likelihood that, whatever it does, the United States will be able to do business with Qadhdhafi, and it should concentrate on limiting the inevitable damage that its present position entails.

The first resolve should be to avoid seeking and magnifying confrontation. This does not mean one must be sidestepped if it suddenly looms; it does mean the United States should not go out of its way to create and publicize one, as it did in the Gulf of Sirte in 1981. It is impossible for a great power to behave in that fashion, whatever the merits of the case, without projecting the image of a bully, which usually adds to the stature of the opponent if he survives.

The second resolve should be to avoid pushing Qadhdhafi into the arms of the Soviets. An eventual embrace between them may be inevitable, but the Americans should have no illusions that their behavior toward Qadhdhafi does not affect his attitude toward the Soviets, who are the alternative superpower. A display of U.S. airpower on the frontiers of Libya has to be visible if it is to have a deterrent effect, and if it is visible it is likely to impress on Qadhdhafi the need for powerful friends. It is probably no coincidence that Major Jallud, Qadhdhafi's senior associate, went to Moscow and discussed (apparently inconclusively) a friendship treaty, soon after the February 1983 U.S. display of airpower in connection with the Sudan crisis.

There are, of course, occasions when there is no alternative to resolute action, and intelligence sources in Washington maintain that the United States acted as it did in February 1983 because the Libyans were up to their necks in a plot to overthrow the regime in Khartoum, and also maintain that its actions were effective. It is difficult for the layman to evaluate these claims in the absence of confirming details, and even more difficult to evaluate the alternatives—the intelligence sources are as susceptible to group-think and self-justification as anyone else is. In this case, however, there is no intrinsic reason to doubt the story. Qadhdhafi has long been plotting against the Sudan, and his involvement there would be in conformity with an established pattern.

What must be borne in mind in judging the effectiveness of such displays of force is that they usually stimulate efforts at counteraction, because they are seen as threats. Even the leaders of the great powers sometimes imagine threats where none exist, and it is much more likely that the leader of a minor power will do the same. Qadhdhafi sees the United States as a threat to Libya. He can point to chapter and verse to support his contention, and we can expect him to take measures to protect himself. The most likely reaction is a turn to the Soviets, since he is not big enough to challenge the United States by himself. That this has not happened to date is an indication of the strength of Qadhdhafi's nationalism. It may also be due to lack of Soviet interest in involvement with such an unpredictable leader.

Given the confrontational nature of international politics in the current era, it is not surprising that the United States has tried to marshal African opposition to Qadhdhafi and has probably extended covert support to the Libyan opposition in exile. How effective either of these tactics will be is debatable; they are followed more for reasons of political machismo than because anyone has carefully plotted the consequences. To date their effect has been limited, but perhaps they will have more in the end. It should be remembered, however, that, unpopular though Qadhdhafi may be, he represents an authentic strain of Libyan nationalism, and his successor is likely to feel as he does about the superpowers. The United States should avoid putting itself on a collision course that makes it appear to be the enemy of the Libyan people. This does not mean it has to abandon its present posture; it does mean it should go no further unless there is serious provocation, that is, unless Qadhdhafi takes some step seriously threatening U.S. interests in the area, such as invading Tunisia, as he did Chad.

The Sahara

This problem is more important in its ultimate significance than the problem of Qadhdhafi, who, after all, is a transient figure. The Sahara is likely to be a permanent bone of contention, like Palestine, if it is not settled one way or another. Although the Chadian question alternates with the Sahara as the issue most likely to provoke the disolution of the OAU, the Sahara is the more complex of the two because it touches on the self-determination issue. The sudden eruption of serious fighting in July 1983, after almost two years of quiet, shows that the Sahara remains explosive, marking the fault line between the conservatives and radicals or, perhaps more accurately, the supporters of Morocco and those of Algeria. It involves sensitive political questions that are important to all African states, and it poses ideological and policy dilemmas for all powers seeking to be friendly with both Algeria and Morocco.

Policy Recommendations

Unfortunately, as noted in Chapter 7, there is not a great deal outside powers can do to promote a settlement before the parties are ready for it, and once they are ready there is no need of mediation by outside powers. The Hassan-Benjedid meeting and subsequent interchanges between the two states show that Algeria and Morocco are fully capable of getting together on their own when they wish, and it is far healthier that the impetus come from within than without.

Meanwhile, the United States should follow a two-track policy: (1) It should avoid giving the impression to the Moroccans or others that its support for Morocco implies a belief that Morocco's war is its war, or that it supports Morocco's claim to the territory in question; (2) at the same time it should look for opportunities to nudge the parties toward settlement, in spite of the limitations on its influence in this regard.

On track one, the United States should stop supplying cluster bombs and other controversial weapons to Morocco, it should reduce visits to the Sahara by its military personnel to those that are absolutely necessary for the administration of military aid programs, and it should avoid official pronouncements and gestures that can be taken as evidence of U.S. partiality. It should, furthermore, reaffirm publicly its position that the Sahara issue is still open and that it does not recognize Moroccan sovereignty there.

On track two, the United States should continue its support, and urge others to support, the OAU referendum proposal. Although Moroccan acceptance of that proposal may be disingenuous, the referendum has the virtue of being a clearcut proposal that both Morocco and Algeria are on record as accepting. Resolving the differences between them over the referendum is easier than starting from scratch with a new initiative. In the end, the referendum may not provide the basis for settlement, which may be reached through agreement on some plan of shared sovereignty, but it offers the most reasonable proposal to date, and it has the stamp of OAU legitimacy. Until it or some other proposal is implemented, the principal concern of the United States should be to stay out of the middle.

It has been suggested that the United States should use its aid programs and economic policies to move the parties toward settlement. The first problem with this is one of asymmetry—there is no U.S. aid to Algeria or the Polisario, and hence no leverage there. Nor, at this point, is there much leverage the United States can exert on Algeria through economic policies because, in the final analysis, the Algerians have other alternatives to the U.S. market, and U.S. economic interests would suffer as much as Algeria's by any attempt to impose penalties or embargoes.

In the case of Morocco, U.S. economic aid is too marginal to be influential, and economic relations are minimal. Past attempts to use military sales to move Hassan to a more moderate position have failed and, short of extremis, there is no likelihood of their working in the future, because the aid is not vital to Morocco. Even it it were, Hassan would still reject attempts to use it as an instrument of pressure because acceptance would derogate from his independence. He has said as much officially. In particular, given the likely domestic cost of his accepting a compromise settlement (witness the reaction against his proposal to the OAU for a referendum), there is no material inducement that would be enough to warrant a switch on his part. The hard reality is that aid programs almost never provide an effective instrument for political leverage, and this instance is no exception.

At the same time, continuation of U.S. military aid is the price of Moroccan friendship. Hassan has also made this explicit. If the United States wants and needs access to Moroccan bases, it will have to pay the price. Under the circumstances, there appears to be no workable alternative to continuation of military aid. The level should be determined by Morocco's legitimate defense needs, however, not by what it takes to conquer the Sahara.

Even if military and economic aid offer little leverage, the United States is not without resources. Its political support for Morocco, in the United Nations and elsewhere, is often of critical importance. Without attempting to use such support as a weapon, there are traditional diplomatic techniques for making use of it in ways that can have an effect. The lobbying and log rolling that go on at the United Nations are in the same category with that which goes on in Congress, often with similar results. There are also techniques in such matters as giving access to senior officials and supporting or countering diplomatic efforts of foreign governments in one's own country that both the Moroccans and Algerians have used effectively against the Americans in the past, and that they well understand when used against themselves. It is in the corridors of the United Nations, Foggy Bottom, and the Pentagon that the influence game can be played, not in aid programs.

Conclusion

Although none of the North African states except Libya is front-page news today, any one of them may well be tomorrow. This is an area in which circumstances change rapidly, and parts of this book will be out of date before it gets to the printer. All we can safely predict is that there will be change, that today's problems will eventually pass away and that others just as perplexing will take their place.

This is just as well, because there are no dramatic, ready-made solutions to any of the problems we have discussed. The most important single recommendation that can be made is that the policymaker approach the area cautiously and tactfully, respecting its unique character, realizing that things are seldom what they seem, that we rarely have all the answers, or even all the questions, and that we should avoid taking sides when we do not have to. While we should do all we can to help the states of the region maintain their independence, we should have no illusions about the effectiveness of aid, or about the stability of any arrangements that may be made with the states of the region. To a large extent the people of North Africa will solve their own problems, and they will do it in their own way. The last thing we should do is to take them, or their present condition, for granted.

Notes

[1] The classic study of this initial involvement, which has relevance for North Africa as well as the Middle East, is Bruce R. Kuniholm's *The Origins of the Cold War in the Near East* (Princeton: Princeton University Press, 1980).

[2] Originally the importance of the petroleum was indirect, that is, it was needed by Western Europe and NATO, not the United States. Providing it to those states was, however, perceived as a vital U.S. interest.

[3] For an informed discussion of globalist vs. regionalist approaches in Africa in general, see Helen Kitchen's *U.S. Interests in Africa*, Center for Strategic and International Studies, Georgetown University, 1983.

[4] Chapter 7.

[5] For a discussion of the value of the Moroccan access agreement, see the report from the Congressional Budget Office titled "The US-Moroccan Agreement and its Implications for US Rapid Deployment Forces—March 1983," which is an annex to the Hearings on Foreign Assistance Legislation of the House Sub-Committee on Africa, published in the summer of 1983. The burden of the report is that the Moroccan facilities "would provide increased flexibility and backup in case of an RDF deployment. This backup is important now because a new agreement . . . (with) . . . Portugal concerning the use of Lajes Field in the Azores has not yet been reached. . . . If an agreement on Lajes is negotiated and facilities (there) improved, however, then the importance of the Moroccan facilities to support Southwest Asia deployments would diminish." Although a new agreement on Lajes has since been negotiated, the Department of State maintains that the Moroccan facilities are still required to meet U.S. strategic needs.

[6] Joint commissions meet periodically in accordance with some overall agreement and discuss common concerns, such as cultural exchanges or economic or military aid. They tend to take on a life of their own and to breed staffs and papers, and their utility is debatable. In 1974 Secretary Kissinger offered one to Boumediene as an inducement to restore diplomatic relations, which had been broken during the 1967 June War. Boumediene responded that they were a waste of time and he didn't want one. Kissinger immediately agreed. He nevertheless proceeded to have them set up with Tunisia and Saudi Arabia, and U.S. bureaucrats have been involved in them ever since, to no great effect. Unfortunately, foreigners do not understand how lightheartedly the United States has entered into such arrangements, and have taken them more seriously than they should.

[7] See, for instance, William Quandt's *Decade of Decision* (Berkeley: University of California Press, 1977), pp. 37–71, for an insider's discussion of how U.S. policy on the Arab-Israel dispute was formed by Lyndon Johnson during the 1967 crisis.

[8]For a discussion of this point, see "Algerian Socialism and Its Critics," by John R. Nellis in *The Canadian Journal of Political Science* (September 1980).

[9]*Soviet and East European Aid to the Third World*, 1981, Department of State, 1983.

[10]This was spelled out in some detail by Colonel Slimane Hoffman, then chairman of the foreign policy commission of the National Liberation Front, in an interview reported by Pranay Gupte in the April 25, 1982, *New York Times*. He made a similar statement to the author in September 1982, and other Algerian officials have voiced the same sentiments in private discussions since then.

[11]"Coming to Terms with Nasser," *International Affairs* (January 1967), p. 67. It is interesting to note, in this context, that as with Nasser, our problems with Qadhdhafi are not over bilateral questions but over those affecting third countries. Qadhdhafi has been correct in his dealings with U.S. companies, and we have no territorial or other claims against him. Our complaints are about his actions against other states and peoples, such as, Egypt, Sudan, and Chad.

Bibliography

Morocco

Abu-Lughod, Janet. *Rabat, Urban Apartheid in Morocco*, Princeton, N.J.: Princeton University Press, 1980. A study of the social impact of town planning.

Bovill, E. W. *The Golden Trade of the Moors*, London: Oxford University Press, 1970. The history of Morocco's trade with Timbuctu and other centers in West Africa.

Burke, Edmund. *Prelude to Protectorate in Morocco: Pre-colonial Protest and Resistance—1860–1912*. Chicago: Chicago University Press, 1976.

Clarke, Bryan. *Berber Village*, London: Longmans, 1959. Story of an Oxford expedition to the High Atlas.

Dwyer, Daisy. *Images and Self-Images: Male and Female in Morocco*, New York: Columbia University Press, 1978.

Eickelman, Dale. *Moroccan Islam*, Austin: University of Texas Press, 1976. A study of a Moroccan pilgrimage center.

Fernea, Elizabeth Warnock. *A Street in Marrakech*, New York: Doubleday, 1975. A personal encounter with the lives of Moroccan women.

Geertz, Clifford, et al. *Meaning and Order in Moroccan Society: Three Essays in Cultural Analysis*, Cambridge: Cambridge University Press, 1979. A study of Sefrou, a Middle Atlas market town.

Harris, Walter B. *Morocco That Was*, London: Wm. Blackwood & Sons, 1921. Reprint. Westport, Conn.: Negro University Press, 1970. A classic account of Morocco and its court in the early twentieth century, by the resident correspondent of the *Times* of London.

Hassan bin Muhammad. *The Challenge: The Memoirs of King Hassan II of Morocco*, London: Macmillan, 1978.

Julien, Charles-André. *Le Maroc Face aux Imperialismes*, Paris: Les Editions J.A., 1978. A study of the French encroachment on Morocco, leading to the establishment of the protectorate.

Kramer, Jane. *Honor to the Bride*, New York: Farrar, Straus & Giroux, 1970. A fictionalized account of family life in Meknes, originally published in the *New Yorker*.

Lahbabi, Mohammed. *Les Fondements de l'Economie Marocaine*, Casablanca: Les Editions Maghrebines, 1977.

Laroui, Abdallah. *The Crisis of the Arab Intellectual*, Berkeley: University of California Press, 1976. A leading Moroccan intellectual discusses the problems of the Arab intellectual faced with the modern world.

Lazrak, Rachid. *Le Contentieux Territorial entre le Maroc et l'Espagne*, Casablanca: Dar al-Kitab, 1974. The Moroccan view of the territorial dispute with Spain.

Maxwell, Gavin. *Lords of the Atlas*, London: Longmans, Green, 1966. Reprint. London: Pan Books 1970. A popular account of the struggle between the pasha of Marrakech and the Alaouites.

Nelson, Harold D., ed. *Morocco A Country Study* (the Area Handbook), Washington, D.C.: Government Printing Office, 1978.

Parsons, Frederick. *The Origins of the Morocco Question 1880–1900*, London: Duckworth, 1976. A study of the designs of the powers on Morocco in the nineteenth century.

Rabinow, Paul. *Symbolic Domination: Cultural Form and Historical Change in Morocco*, Chicago: University of Chicago Press, 1975.

Rezette, Robert. *The Spanish Enclaves in Morocco*, Paris: Nouvelles Editions Latines, 1976.

Rijeheghem, Willy van, ed. *Employment Problems and Policies in Developing Countries: The Case of Morocco*, Rotterdam: Rotterdam University Press, 1976.

Selous, G. H. *Appointment to Fez*, London: The Richards Press, 1956. Morocco at the imposition of the French protectorate.

Spencer, William. *Historical Dictionary of Morocco*, Metuchen, N.J.: Scarecrow Press, 1980.

Waterbury, John. *The Commander of the Faithful*, New York: Columbia University Press, 1970. The best single description of the Moroccan political system.

Weisgerber, Dr. *Au Seuil du Maroc Moderne*, Rabat: Les Editions la Porte, 1947. Another description of Morocco on the eve of the protectorate, by a French doctor who traveled with the Sultan. As classic in its own way as the Harris book.

Algeria

Ageron, Charles. *L'Algérie Algérienne: de Napoleon III a de Gaulle*, Paris: Sinbad, 1980.

———· *Algérie Française 1942–1962*, Paris: Societe de production litteraire, 1980.

Balta, Paul, Claudine Rulleau, and Mireille Duteil. *L'Algérie des Algériens, Vingt Ans Apres*, Paris: Les Editions ouvrieres, 1981. A new survey of Algerian progress since the revolution.

Bourdieu, Pierre. *Algeria 1960: The Disenchantment of the World: the sense of honour: the Kabyle House or the world reversed: essays*, Cambridge: Cambridge University Press, 1979.

Churchill, Charles Henry. *La Vie d'Abd el-Kader*, Algiers: SNED, 1974. French translation of *The Life of Abdel Kader*, originally published in London in 1867. A stirring history of the principal leader of the Algerian resistance to the French in the 1830s.

Colonna, Fanny. *Instituteurs Algériens, 1883-1939*, Paris: Presse de la Foundation Nationale des Sciences Politiques, 1975.

Danziger, Raphael. *Abd al Qadir and the Algerians: Resistance to the French and Internal Consolidation*, New York: Holmes and Meier, 1977.

Dumas, Alexandre. *Adventures in Algeria*, Philadelphia: Chilton Company, 1959. Excerpts from the 1848-51 original. A classic travel book, with accounts of French treatment of the Algerians.

Harbi, Mohammed. *Le F.L.N.: Mirage et Réalité: des origines à la prise de pouvoir, 1945-1962*, Paris: Editions J.A., 1980.

Horne, Alistair. *A Savage War of Peace: Algeria 1954-1962*, London: MacMillan, 1977.

Hutchinson, Martha A. *Revolutionary Terrorism: The FLN in Algeria 1954-1962*, Stanford: Hoover Institution Press, 1978.

Jackson, Henry F. *The FLN in Algeria: Party Development in a Revolutionary Society*, Westport, Conn.: Greenwood Press, 1977.

Keenan, Jeremy. *The Tuareg: People of Ahaggar*, London: Allen Lane, 1977. The Tuareg are the veiled nomads of the deep Sahara.

Laffont, Pierre. *Histoire de la France en Algérie*, Paris: Plon, 1980.

Lazreg, Marnia. *The Emergence of Classes in Algeria: A Study of Colonialism and Socio-Political Change*, Boulder, Colo.: Westview Press, 1976.

Ottaway, David and Marina. *Algeria: The Politics of a Socialist Revolution*, Berkeley: University of California Press, 1970. Probably the best work in English on the early days of the Algerian Republic.

Peneff, Jean. *Industriels Algériens*, Paris: CNRS, 1981. A study of 220 private businessmen in Algiers in the period 1970-73.

Schliephake, Konrad. *Oil and Regional Development: Examples from Algeria and Tunisia*, New York: Praeger, 1977.

Shaler, William. *Sketches of Algiers*, Boston: Cummings Hilliard and Co., 1826. Description of Algiers on the eve of the French conquest by the then U.S. consul.

Spencer, William. *Algiers in the Age of the Corsairs*, Norman: University of Oklahoma Press, 1976.

Talbott, John E. *The War Without a Name: France in Algeria, 1954-1962*, New York: Knopf, 1980.

Temioni, Abdeljelil. *Le Beylik de Constantine et Hadj Ahmed Bey (1830-1837)*, Tunis: Publications de la Revue d'Histoire Maghrebine, 1978. The story of the leader of the Algerian resistance to the French in eastern Algeria.

Young, Ian. *The Private Life of Islam*, London: Allan Lane, 1974. A frank account of a British gynecologist's experience in the Kabyle region. Not for queasy stomachs.

Vatin, Jean-Claude. *L'Algérie Politique Histoire et Société*, 2^d edition, Paris: Presses de la Fondation Nationale des Science Politiques, 1983.

Tunisia

Allman, James. *Social Mobility, Education and Development in Tunisia*, Leiden, Netherlands: Brill, 1979.

Anthony, John. *About Tunisia*, London: Geoffrey Bles Ltd., 1961. A readable traveler's book.

Bennett, Norman R. *A Study Guide for Tunisia*, Boston: Boston University Press, 1968.

Boulares, Habib, and Duvignaud, Jean. *Nous Partons pour la Tunisie*, Paris: PUF, 1978.

Brown, Leon Carl. *The Tunisia of Ahmed Bey 1837-1855*, Princeton: Princeton University Press, 1974. A study of Tunisia's leading political modernizer and the reforms he instituted in the mid-nineteenth century.

Hawrylyshyn, Oli. *Planning for Economic Development: The Construction and Use of a Multi-sectional Model for Tunisia*, New York: Praeger, 1976.

Hermassi, el Baqi. *Leadership and National Development in North Africa*, Berkeley: University of California Press, 1975.

Micaud, Charles A., Leon Carl Brown, and Clement Henry Moore. *Tunisia: The Politics of Modernization*, New York: Praeger, 1964.

Nelson, Harold D., ed. *Tunisia, A Country Study* (Area Handbook), Washington, D.C.: Government Printing Office, 1979.

Perillifor, Louis. *La Conquete de l'Independance Tunisienne: Souvenirs et Temoignages*, Paris: R. Laffont, 1979.

Stone, Russell, and Simmons, J. *Change in Tunisia: Studies in the Social Sciences*, Albany: SUNY Press, 1976.

Libya

Allen, J. A. *Libya, The Experience of Oil*, Boulder, Colo.: Westview Press, 1981.

Bennke, Roy H. *The Herders of Cyrenaica: Ecology, Economy and Kinship Among the Bedouin of Eastern Libya*, Urbana: University of Illinois Press, 1980.

Cooley, John. *Libyan Sandstorm*, New York: Holt, Rinehardt and Winston, 1982. A journalistic account of Qadhdhafi's rise to power and current happenings in Libya.

Deeb, Marius and Mary Jane. *Libya Since the Revolution: Aspects of Social and Political Development*, New York: Praeger, 1982.

Evans Pritchard, E.E. *The Sanusi of Cyrenaica*, London: Oxford University Press, 1968

el-Fathaly, Omar. *Political Development and Bureaucracy in Libya*, Lexington, Mass.: Lexington Books, 1977.
el-Fathaly, Omar, and Palmer, Monte. *Political Development and Social Change in Libya*, Lexington, Mass.: Lexington Books, 1980.
Goldberg, Harvey E., ed. & trans. *The Book of Mordechai: A Study of the Jews of Libya*, Philadelphia: Institute for the Study of Human Issues, 1980.
Habib, Henri P. *Politics and Government of Revolutionary Libya*, Montreal: Cercle du Livre de France, 1975.
Waddams, Frank C. *The Libyan Oil Industry*, Baltimore: Johns Hopkins University Press, 1980.
Wright, John L. *Libya, A Modern History*, Baltimore: Johns Hopkins University Press, 1982.

North Africa—General

Abun-Nasr, Jamil M. *A History of the Maghreb*, London: Cambridge University Press, 1975.
Annuaire de l'Afrique du Nord, Editions de CNRS. An annual publication, in print for the past 17 years, containing articles on a wide range of North African subjects, a chronology, and a bibliography.
Berque, Jacques. *French North Africu*, London: Faber & Faber, 1967.
Brown, Leon Carl, ed. *State and Society in Independent North Africa*, Washington, D.C.: The Middle East Institute, 1966. Based on papers presented at the 1964 conference of the Middle East Institute by a group of leading scholars; a good, basic work.
Gellner, Ernest, and Jean-Claude Vatin, eds. *Islam et Politique au Maghreb*, Paris: CNRS, 1981. A collection of essays of uneven quality but of considerable interest to the serious student.
Julien, Charles-André. *History of North Africa*, London: Routledge, Kegan Paul, 1970. The classic history, well-translated.
Knapp, Wilfred. *North-West Africa: A Political and Economic Survey*, 3ᵈed., New York: Oxford University Press, 1977.
Moore, Clement Henry. *Politics in North Africa*, Boston: Little Brown, 1970. A paperback in the Little Brown series in comparative politics. Dated but basic.
Zartman, I. William, ed. *Political Elites in Arab North Africa*, New York: Longman, 1982. A series of essays on the political dynamics of North African states.

Islam

Arberry, A. J., trans. *The Koran Interpreted*, New York: Macmillan, 1955.
Craig, Kenneth, and Marston Speight. *Islam from Within: Anthology of a Religion*, Belmont, Calif.: Wadsworth, 1980. A useful selection of writings by Muslims.

Enayat, Hamid. *Modern Islamic Political Thought,* Austin: University of Texas Press, 1982.

Esposito, John, ed. *Islam and Development: Religion and Sociopolitical Change,* Syracuse: Syracuse University Press, 1980. Essays on the question of whether Islam is an obstacle to development.

Fernea, Elizabeth, and Basima Qatlan Bezirgan, eds. *Middle Eastern Women Speak,* Austin: University of Texas Press, 1977. A collection of historical and contemporary statements by and about Muslim women.

Guillaume, Alfred. *Islam,* Harmondsworth: Penguin Books, 1954. A basic description.

Lippman, Thomas W. *Understanding Islam,* New York: Times Mirror, 1982. A good layman's introduction.

McNeall, William H., and Marylin Robinson Waldman. *The Islamic World,* London: Oxford University Press, 1973. A collection of readable readings, historical and modern, on various aspects of the Muslim world.

Mitchell, Richard B. *The Society of the Muslim Brothers,* London: Oxford University Press, 1969. The authoritative account of the Muslim Brothers in Egypt.

Mortimer, Edward. *Faith and Power, The Politics of Islam,* New York: Random House, 1982. A readable and well-researched discussion of the nature of Islam and the Islamic revival.

Naipaul, V.S. *Among the Believers,* New York: Alfred Knopf, 1981. A readable, impressionistic and subjective account of a voyage, and encounters, among the Muslims of Iran, Pakistan, Malaysia, and Indonesia.

Qutb, Sayyid. *Islam and Universal Peace,* Indianapolis: American Trust Publications, 1977. Writings of one of the most influential fundamentalist preachers.

Rahman, Fazlur. *Islam,* Chicago: University of Chicago Press, 1979. An introduction.

—————·*Islam and Modernity,* Chicago: University of Chicago Press, 1982.

Said, Edward. *Covering Islam,* New York: Pantheon Books, 1981. An examination of Western treatment of Islam in the media and literature.

Stoddard, Philip H. et al. *Change and the Muslim World,* Syracuse: Syracuse University Press, 1981. An introductory overview of contemporary Islam.

Voll, John Obert. *Islam: Continuity and Change in the Modern World,* Boulder, Colo.: Westview Press, 1982. An excellent history of the evolution of Islamic culture.

Annex

Members of Discussion Group on North Africa, 1981–82

Stephen Stamas, *Chairman*
Jennifer Whitaker, *Group Director*
Ellen Laipson, *Rapporteur*

David L. Aaron
James E. Akins
Pauline H. Baker
Travers J. Bell, Jr.
Christine Bindert
Mark C. Bisnow
Leon Carl Brown
John C. Campbell
Robert A. Charpie
Roger J. Cochetti
Peter D. Constable
John P. Entelis
Richard E. Feinberg
Henry A. Grunwald
Ulric St. Clair Haynes, Jr.
Jean Herskovits

Benjamin L. Hooks
Charles Issawi
Henry F. Jackson
Miles Kahler
Lawrence C. McQuade
Charles William Maynes
Elaine L. Morton
Richard Parker
Lt. General John S. Pustay, USAF
Jane K. Rosen
Christopher Ross
William E. Schaufele, Jr.
David H. Swanson
Robert LeRoy West
R. Bayly Winder
I. William Zartman

Index

About the Author

Richard B. Parker is a former career Foreign Service officer who spent almost 30 years working in or on the Middle East and North Africa for the Department of State. During the 1970s he served as ambassador to Algeria, Lebanon, and Morocco, in that order. He is well known as a student of the Arab world, and on his retirement from the Foreign Service in 1980 spent two years teaching courses on the area as diplomat in residence at the University of Virginia, concurrently taking on the responsibilities of editor of the *Middle East Journal*.

Since 1982 Ambassador Parker has devoted himself to the *Middle East Journal* and to speaking and writing. This is his third book, his two other books being on Islamic architecture in Egypt and Morocco.